A STRANGER IN THE FAMILY

STEVEN NAIFEH and GREGORY WHITE SMITH

A STRANGER IN THE FAMILY

A True Story of
Murder, Madness, and
Unconditional Love

A DUTTON BOOK

AUTHORS' NOTE: *In the interest of protecting the privacy of individuals whose identities are not central to the true story told here, certain names and other descriptive details have been altered in several instances.*

DUTTON

Published by the Penguin Group
Penguin Books USA Inc., 375 Hudson Street, New York, New York 10014, U.S.A.
Penguin Books Ltd, 27 Wrights Lane, London W8 5TZ, England
Penguin Books Australia Ltd, Ringwood, Victoria, Australia
Penguin Books Canada Ltd, 10 Alcorn Avenue, Toronto, Ontario, Canada M4V 3B2
Penguin Books (N.Z.) Ltd, 182–190 Wairau Road, Auckland 10, New Zealand

Penguin Books Ltd, Registered Offices:
Harmondsworth, Middlesex, England

First published by Dutton, an imprint of Dutton Signet,
a division of Penguin Books USA Inc.
Distributed in Canada by McClelland & Stewart Inc.

First Printing, June, 1995
1   3   5   7   9   10   8   6   4   2

"Come from the Heart" by Richard Leigh and Susanna Clark © 1987 EMI April Music Inc.,
GSC Music and Lion-Hearted Music. All rights controlled and administered by
EMI April Music Inc. (ASCAP). All rights reserved. Used by permission.

Excerpt on page 187 reprinted courtesy of The Augusta Chronicle.

 REGISTERED TRADEMARK—MARCA REGISTRADA

LIBRARY OF CONGRESS CATALOGING-IN-PUBLICATION DATA:

Naifeh, Steven W.
A stranger in the family : a true story of murder, madness, and
unconditional love / Steven Naifeh and Gregory White Smith.
p.   cm.
ISBN 0-525-93973-3
1. Starrett, Danny.   2. Murderers—United States—Biography.
3. Rapists—United States—Biography.   4. Serial murders—United
States—Case studies.   5. Rape—United States—Case studies.
I. Smith, Gregory White.   II. Title.
HV6248.S6277N35   1995
364.1'523'09758635—dc20   94-48847
CIP

Printed in the United States of America
Set in Clearface
Designed by Steven Stathakis

This book is printed on acid-free paper. ∞

To
Tim Arwood
and Dan Ranger

for their bravery

Acknowledgments

This book could not have been written without the cooperation of the Starrett family. Gerry, Richard, their two daughters, and, of course, Danny, spent many, many hours with us over the course of more than three years. The interviews were often traumatic for them, forcing them to relive the most painful moments of their lives. The Starrett family agreed to cooperate in large part because they believed that a full account of their story might help prevent other, similar tragedies in other, similar families.

We are also grateful to both Augustus "Bud" Siemon, one of Danny's several defense attorneys, and Dr. Robert Storms, one of Danny's many doctors, for taking great chunks of uncompensated time out of their overburdened schedules to help us understand the legal and psychological aspects of this extraordinarily complex case. And to Bud Siemon for making available to us his voluminous Starrett files.

Among the many others whom we should both thank and absolve are Mike Adams, David Caldwell, Michael Eubanks, Katherine Evatt, Julian Jaynes, Henderson Johnson, Derek Jones, Everett Kugler, Martin Orne, Jack Swerling, Wanda Tarpley, and several people who requested to remain anonymous.

There are also debts to acknowledge "behind the scenes": to our typists, Suzie Riddle and Lynn Grady, for transcribing endless hours of interviews; to our editor, Matthew Carnicelli; to our publisher, Elaine Koster; and to our agent, Mel Berger, for his encouragement and persistence.

For a variety of reasons, the names of several of the principals in this book have been changed: in particular, Helen, Gail, Robert, and Sally Starrett; Conrad Frederickson; Arline Williams; Heather, Allison, and Flo Carpenter; Susannah, Julia, and Eric Hansen; Chrissy Loren, Alice, and Daryl Blake; Tammy Cranford; Tiffany Hart; Johnnie Corcoran and Sam McDowell; Joel Green; Andrea and Fred Porter; Agnes; and the Palmers.

Part One

1

JUNE 24, 1988. Julia Hansen tooted her horn a second time and waited for her daughter, Susie, to come out of the house. She rolled her eyes in mock exasperation. How could a twelve-year-old girl take so long to get dressed? At four in the afternoon? Julia had left the house almost an hour earlier to run some errands. "If you start getting ready now," she had joked with her daughter as she walked out the door, taking care to lock it behind her, "I'm sure I'll be back by the time you're finished." Now here she was, an hour later, and Susie still wasn't ready. She honked again. If this is what she is like at twelve, Julie wondered, what will she be like at sixteen?

She waited a few more minutes with the car running before deciding to make a show of her impatience. She cut off the engine, rustled deep in her purse for her house keys, then stalked to the door jangling the keys as loudly as she could and trying to shape her anger into just the right words.

The door was unlocked. Strange. She was sure she had locked it when she left. She called out, "Susannah," the full name that Julia loved but only used in a temper or, as now, in anxiety. No answer. She heard the television in the den—Phil Donahue's voice—and the radio from Susie's room upstairs. Susie always listened to the radio when she dressed. "Susannah!" She made a quick search, calling her daughter's name, but the house was empty.

She felt a twinge of some strange emotion, not fear yet, more like sadness. Twelve-year-old girls were always making spur-of-the-moment decisions, changing plans and not thinking about the consequences. All those hormones. Her best guess was that Susie's father, Eric, had gotten off work early, come by the house, and taken his daughter out for some shopping or to get a sandwich. Eric did that now and then, and Susie still loved it when he did—although that would probably change soon. To take her mind off the dark areas at the edges of her thoughts, Julia went to the laundry area and started sorting clothes.

Then she saw Susie's white Keds. Susie *always* wore her Keds. Later, Julia would say that seeing the Keds was the first thing that truly struck fear in her heart. She ran upstairs to Susie's closet to see what shoes she *had* put on for her father. But all her shoes were there. Every pair. None was missing. Could she have gone out in bare feet? Wouldn't Eric have insisted that she put on shoes? He wouldn't have taken her out without shoes.

Just then, Eric walked in.

"Where's Susie?" Julia demanded.

Eric understood immediately what the question meant, and it took his breath away. "You mean . . ."

"I thought she was with you," his wife answered.

"I just left work."

"Susie isn't here." Her words swelled with a stifled sob.

Eric bolted from room to room yelling his daughter's name, "Susie, Susie," while Julia followed, recounting the story of the last few hours. When they both paused, panting, in the living room, Julia put into words the fear that was screaming in her head. "Somebody has come and taken her."

Eric collapsed on the floor as the full horror of it crashed down on him, and the voice in his head wailed, "My baby! My baby! My baby is gone!"

On December 21, 1988, John and Carolyn McCrea came home to a note:

> *Mom and Dad,*
> *I'm going away for a few days.*
> *Jean*

It was definitely their daughter Jeannie's handwriting, on a standard white envelope, along with a list of library books she was planning to use for a paper on *The Great Gatsby*. The McCreas' maid had found the note when she came to clean earlier that day. She also found the back door wide open. Nothing else in the house was disturbed, except Jeannie's room, which was always a mess.

Carolyn McCrea had talked to her daughter on the phone at lunchtime. She was home then and seemed all right.

The police dismissed it as a "runaway situation." As soon as they found out that John McCrea had recently argued with his daughter and threatened to take away her car keys, they all but put away their pens. "All fifteen-year-old daughters argue with their fathers," John wanted to say. "But they don't all run away."

And why did she leave her driver's permit behind?

The police asked for a photograph, and Carolyn produced a recent school picture of a pretty, dark-haired girl wearing a button-up sweater and a beaming smile. The officer who took it whistled softly through his teeth in the universal sign of appreciation. Any other time, John McCrea would have taken it as a compliment. He knew he had a beautiful daughter and was proud of it, even if they fought from time to time. But now, that low, leering whistle filled him with dread.

Days went by. The police interviewed Jeannie's friends. Flyers and posters went up: "$1,000 REWARD. Jean Taylor McCrea." But under "status," with five options to choose from (Foul Play Suspected, Runaway, Lost, Parental Abduction, and Other), the police checked "Other."

Soon, she had been gone a week. And the only clothes she had taken were a coat, a scarf, and whatever she was wearing. No calls, no letters, no messages through friends. Reports of her whereabouts drifted in, proved to be false, and were filed away as the weeks bled into months. And, day by day, the horror crept in on John and Carolyn McCrea.

Daryl and Alice Blake came home from work about six-thirty on February 6, 1989, and found their daughter Chrissy's car parked in the usual spot, outside the back door. When they came in, they found her keys in the usual place, on the dryer, and almost all the lights in the trailer blazing—another sign that Chrissy, who had never paid a utility bill, was home.

But when Alice went to look for her, she couldn't find her daughter anywhere. She looked for a note but didn't worry when she couldn't find one. Chrissy was an independent seventeen-year-old. She had been known to take off with friends without a moment's warning. Alice hadn't seen her daughter since she left for school that morning. Against her better judgment, she had picked up Chrissy's room and made up her water bed, but she left the clothes on the floor where she found them. There was just so much the working mother of a high-school student should be required to do around the house.

Daryl Blake had spoken to his daughter later that day. She called to say a man wanted to come by the house and see her water bed, which the Blakes had advertised for sale. Daryl, a cautious man whose mobile-home dealership shared a view of the same small pond as his home, told Chrissy to ask the caller to come by sometime when Daryl could meet him. But when Alice phoned home again around five, no one answered. Apparently, Chrissy had taken off somewhere.

After dinner, when Chrissy still hadn't returned or called, Daryl and Alice began to worry. They started calling her friends. They drove to the local recreation center, where Chrissy had her Jazzercise classes, and asked around. No one there had seen her. When they returned to the trailer, they stopped to look at Chrissy's car. On the front seat, they saw her pocketbook and wallet. Daryl started to panic. Alice was the calm one. Hard though it was to believe, she reassured her husband, she had seen Chrissy leave her pocketbook and wallet in the car like that before. It probably didn't mean anything.

Just in case, Alice went back to Chrissy's room to see if she had missed something. When she saw the water bed, she let out a little, involuntary gasp. She had made it that morning. Sometime since then, the covers had been pulled down, which had to mean that Chrissy had shown the bed to a potential buyer. In a fit of denial, Alice went to remake the bed, as if whatever had happened could be un-done by this small act of reversal. But before she could begin, she saw something else that made her heart stop: the impression of a boot in the carpet next to the bed. It was a track that hadn't been there that morning.

She brought Daryl to see it.

"We'd better call the sheriff's department," said Daryl.

Through all the telephone calls and questions, Alice kept calm and collected. It wasn't until the police dive team arrived to drag the pond outside her home for her daughter's body that she lost her composure.

2

"I was *kidnapped!*" the girl screamed as Officer Mike Adams entered the house at 130 West Lynne Drive in Martinez, Georgia. "This man kidnapped me from our trailer! He came to the door. He said he was an insurance salesman and he was dressed in a suit so he looked safe and I let him in!" Her words ran together in a single, hyperventilating sentence. "I tried to run away, but he pulled a gun and told me he'd kill me!" She was young—no more than seventeen, Adams guessed—and, even in this state of frantic exhaustion, unmistakably pretty, with long chestnut hair, hazel eyes (bloodshot now), and doe skin. She said her name was Chrissy Blake.

"He held me captive in that house over there," she said, running to the window and pointing across the dark street to a neat, single-story brick house with white trim. "He's had me inside there since Monday. Whenever he went out, he put a chain around my leg, then chained me inside the closet, and then locked the door. . . ." Her face tightened into a grimace that choked off her story before exploding in sobs.

It was 2:00 A.M. on the morning of February 11, 1989, his shift was only half over, and already Mike Adams felt as if it was the longest night of his life. A mere three hours before, he had been at the sheriff's station in Evans, a little town near Augusta, Georgia, interviewing witnesses in a routine domestic homicide. Now here he was, face to face with what looked like the biggest case of his career.

Sheriffing in Columbia County hadn't always been like this. Back in the mid-seventies, when Adams was a teenager riding around with his buddies in the back of the county sheriff's only patrol car, whole weekends went by and *nothing* happened. In fact, *most* weekends, nothing happened. There just wasn't the population to support crime, not in Columbia County, anyway. Whatever crime there was—and there wasn't much—happened in neighboring Richmond County, especially in Augusta, the only real city within a hundred miles in this largely rural corner of Georgia.

In fact, there was so little crime that, for his first few years as a sheriff's deputy, Mike Adams thought he was bored. So he moved across the Savannah River and joined the highway patrol in South Carolina. By the time he returned, homesick, four and a half years later, things were different.

But until this night, he hadn't realized just *how* different.

The girl's story raced ahead. "When he got in the house, he asked about the water bed, the one we advertised for sale, so I went to call my dad. But when I picked up the phone, the man grabbed it. So I ran to the bedroom to get away from him, and that's when he told me, 'If you try to get away, I'll kill you.' "

She broke down again.

"Did he hurt you?" Adams asked as gently as possible. He had dealt with rape victims before, usually girls abused by their fathers, stepfathers, or other male relatives, but never anything like this, and he felt the usual pang of incompetence. Adams was a deft interviewer, but he was the first to admit that working a rape case made him feel all thumbs. Here he was, a burly, whiskered male, interviewing the victim, virtually always a female, about the awful, intimate things another male had just done to her. It always felt, in some ways, like a second rape.

If there had been time, he would have recruited one of the female dispatchers (the Columbia County Sheriff's Department had no female road officers) to interview the girl, but with a suspect still at large and a victim who seemed communicative enough to help in the search, qualms were a luxury he couldn't afford.

"Did he hurt you?" Adams repeated.

The girl looked away from him. "Well, he hurt me," she said softly, "but not the way you're thinking." She cast her eyes ever lower to avoid his look. "He made me pull up my top and . . . he made me . . . do things . . . and . . ."

"And what?" Adams prompted gently.

"He made *tapes!*" She looked up at him, her big eyes wide and filling with tears. "Don't tell my boyfriend, Todd!" she pleaded, sounding, for the first time, forlorn rather than frightened.

That was it, he decided. The intimate details would have to wait. She was unhurt. She was safe. Now he wanted the guy who had done it. "Is the man still in the house?" he asked.

"As far as I know," she said, relieved that the questions had stopped. "He fell asleep 'cause he was drinking. That's when I got up and ran. I started to take his car keys so I could drive off, but I was afraid he'd wake up. So I came here instead." She stopped, obviously struck by the story she had just told. "I can't believe I'm alive."

"Does he have any weapons?" Adams asked.

"Yes, a revolver, which I think he keeps in the bedroom."

Adams called the dispatcher, relayed the rough details of the girl's story, and requested backup. There was a drunken kidnapper and pervert, armed and dangerous, asleep on a couch 100 feet away.

He turned to the Thorntons, the couple who lived in the house and who had first called the sheriff's office. "Do you know this guy?" he asked, pointing at the dark house across the street.

"I spoke with him about three weeks ago," said Carl Thornton, a counselor for teenagers at a nearby clinic. "I found a license in my front yard which belonged to his wife. I returned it to him, and we had a little conversation."

"Are you sure it was his wife's?" Adams immediately had visions of other, previous victims—victims who hadn't been as lucky, perhaps.

"Well, they had a little girl," said Thornton, "about a year old, I'd say."

Adams flinched. A child?

Just then the dispatcher reported back that the house at 131 West Lynn Drive was occupied by a Richard Daniel Starrett.

"Starrett," repeated Thornton. "That was the name on the license."

So it *was* his wife, thought Adams, increasingly puzzled. And his child.

By now the backup had arrived. On his way out the door, Adams turned to the girl with one last look of comfort and one last question. "Did you leave the door unlocked?"

She smiled wanly. "As best I can remember."

The five other officers who had gathered outside the Thornton house followed Adams across the street. They took careful, measured steps, guns drawn. As they approached the little brick house, Adams noticed that the garage door was closed, the light on the front porch off, and the windows dark, all troubling signs. If the kidnapper had woken up and found his victim had escaped, he would have bolted without taking time to close doors and turn off lights.

Adams stepped lightly onto the porch and moved towards the door. He listened for any sounds from inside. There were none. He tested the cold knob. It was locked. He motioned to the others that he would have to kick the door in. In a house like this, recently built, that wasn't a problem, as long as his foot landed near the lock. Between the dead bolt and the handle was ideal, but force was more important than accuracy. He might not get a second chance.

3

The bleating of the telephone yanked Gerry Starrett from a deep, dream-filled sleep. Rising slowly through layers of consciousness, she heard her husband's voice in the bed next to her: "Yes. I'm the father."

Gerry barely had time to squint at the clock—2:45 in the morning—before she felt the rush of adrenaline. Where were her children? She saw them before her as if in a snapshot from the family album: Helen, with her husband, Conrad; Gail, with her husband, Pat; Robert, with his wife, Sally; Danny, and his wife, Heather, and daughter, Allison. That was all of them—all accounted for; all at home with their families, all in their beds at this hour.

"Could it wait until tomorrow morning?" she heard Richard ask, and then, after a pause, "All right." Clearly, it couldn't wait.

"That was the police," said Richard with a dazed look as he stretched to hang up the phone. "They want us to come down there." "There" was the police station.

"What for?" Gerry had faith in her inventory. Her kids may be grown and on their own, but she knew their orbits well. She was the astronomer of both her family and the sun.

"He said they'd explain when we got there," said Richard. "It has something to do with Danny."

"Danny?" Gerry's mind raced. "Has there been a car accident?" It was all she could think of, even though she knew Danny had no reason to be out on the roads at that hour.

Richard, who was already up and putting on his pants, dismissed her worst fears. "They don't call you for that."

"Unless he's dead," Gerry heard herself say. The strange news had tapped a well of anxiety she had forgotten existed.

Richard heard it in her voice and reacted impatiently. "If he was dead they wouldn't call—they'd come to the door."

Gerry couldn't help it. "Unless he's badly mangled and they need us to identify him," she said, startling herself.

After that, the trip to the police station—ten endless minutes— passed in silence. Richard, a man of few words, always preferred it that way.

4

With a sharp crack of splintering wood, the door flew open and Mike Adams rushed into the dark house, holding his gun out in front of him with both hands. The first thing he noticed as the light from the doorway fell across the living-room floor was a pair of shoes placed neatly at the foot of a couch. To Adams, it could mean only one thing: The man was still in the house.

He listened for movement in the darkness while his flashlight scanned the room. The coffee table in front of the couch was littered with empty Coors bottles, a nearly empty fifth of Bacardi rum, and the scattered entrails of a board game: Raunchy Trivia. On an end table were two more games: Tic Tac Strip and Pass Out. Across from the sofa he saw a weight bench. The images in his mind got darker and darker.

And there was still no sign of him. And no sound.

Adams led the others down a dark hall toward the back of the house. Door by door, room by room, they called out warnings, flung open doors, turned on lights, and searched the closets and corners. It wasn't a big house: a master bedroom on the right with a king-size box spring but no mattress, a bathroom, another bedroom with a crib and baby things, another bathroom. Surveying a white dresser top crowded with bottles of talcum powder and baby oil, cotton balls, and stacks of Pampers, Adams felt the same knot of puzzlement as before. The house of a kidnapper-rapist shouldn't smell like a baby's freshly powdered bottom.

After pausing and freezing, one last time, to listen for telltale sounds, Adams approached the last room in the house. He reached around the jamb and flicked the light switch. The sudden bright light revealed a small room filled with a huge mattress and a television. In the middle of the room, overlooking the mattress, stood a spindly tripod holding a video camera. Adams remembered what the girl had said about making tapes, but before he could finish the grim calculus, another officer turned on the VCR and a grainy image of the same girl he had just left flickered onto the screen. He recognized her immediately: the brown hair, the doe skin.

But there was a penis in her mouth.

In the instant before he saw that image, Adams thought maybe this had all been a mistake, a huge, awkward mistake. The wife and baby, the middle-class neighborhood, the sheer, melodramatic preposterousness of it all. Surely they had happened into some strange but harmless game.

"Turn it off," he snapped. When the other officers demanded to know why, Adams said he wanted to wait until the warrants arrived to do any searching. But the truth was simpler: He couldn't stand to watch.

Mike Adams always had a problem keeping his professional distance. Other cops always seemed better at it than he was. On road patrol in South Carolina, there were cops who could arrive at the scene of a bad accident, assess the damage, count the dead, load the injured, interview the hysterical survivors, file the reports, and *not blink once*. It didn't matter who was injured or how badly or how crazed the survivors: mothers whose babies had flown through the windowshield, kids whose parents had been beheaded by flying debris in the seat next to them, the corpses of schoolkids piled like cordwood after a bus accident. There were cops who treated these calamities the way nine-to-fivers might treat a run-in with a cranky boss: ho hum, another bad day at the office.

Not Mike Adams. For him, police work was a never ending battle with himself. He knew that if he came upon a wreck where somebody had been killed or badly injured and allowed himself to dwell on it, to take it personally, he would go slap crazy. "It's just part of the job," he would tell himself. "Look at it as evidence." That had become his mantra at times like this: "It's just evidence."

But, God, it was hard sometimes. Like the time he visited a little two-year-old boy in the hospital who had been sexually abused by his father. When Adams saw him for the first time in the ICU, the tot had a strip of tape right across his middle, from side to side, like a belt. "What's that for?" Adams asked a nurse. "The doctors had to cut him open," she said, "all the way open." It turned out that the father had shoved something up the little boy's rectum and ruptured his colon, and all the feces and bile had leaked into the body cavity, causing massive infection. When they operated, they had to cut him open all the way across, and the infection was so bad they didn't dare sew him up because they knew they would have to go back in. So they just taped him shut temporarily. He was just a little two-year-old. And they couldn't even sew him up.

Just evidence.

To shake loose from the memory, Adams busied himself by searching back through the house. On the nightstand beside the bed in the master bedroom, he found bottles of prescription drugs, several rolls of cash in large denominations tied in rubber bands, and, beside them, a wallet. Someone had left in a hurry. Inside the wallet, he found a driver's license with a picture of a good-looking young man with sandy hair and set jowls. The name on the license: Richard Daniel Starrett.

5

When Richard and Gerry Starrett arrived at the Columbia County sheriff's department, it was almost three in the morning and the parking lot was empty. A uniformed woman at the desk brusquely directed them to a back room where two men, Sheriff Otis Hensley and another officer, were waiting.

Gerry was the first to speak. "Is Danny under arrest?"

"No," said Hensley, a rangy man with a corkscrew accent. "A girl escaped from your son's house and ran to a neighbor's and called the police. Your son jumped in his car and left the scene. We need to find him. Do you know where he is?"

Gerry didn't even hear the question. "Danny didn't do it," she snapped.

Hensley tried patience. "Mrs. Starrett, we found videotapes and recordings and everything." And then again, more insistently, "Do you know where he is?"

Gerry, equally insistent, "What time did this happen?" She had talked to Danny that very night.

"About eleven or twelve, we think."

She had spoken to him much earlier than that, but it didn't matter. "Danny didn't do it," she repeated.

"No, you're mistaken," said Richard, who had finally caught his breath. "You talk about a girl being there. Our son is married. He has a daughter."

"Where are his wife and daughter now?"

"They're in California," said Gerry firmly. "They're visiting her folks. Danny couldn't go because of his work."

"He has a very good job out at the nuclear plant," Richard added.

Hensley was losing patience with this game. Every minute he wasted with them could be putting another mile between him and Danny Starrett. For all he knew, they were purposely delaying, giving their son the extra cushion of time that might make all the difference. "Listen," he barked. "We know he was there. We've got the girl. We just need to know where he is."

After an awkward silence, Richard motioned Hensley over to a corner of the room and whispered, out of Gerry's earshot, "Are you sure that this isn't just a thing where this girl went to my son's house and they had sex or something, and now she's crying rape?"

"No," said Hensley in a fierce whisper. "We've got videotapes."

Now it was Gerry's turn to lose patience. "Videotapes? Of what?"

"Is somebody trying to get money out of Danny?" Richard demanded with a wounded look at his wife. "Out of *us?*" He turned back to Hensley. "My son and I both work at SRS, but it's not like we've got a lot of money." SRS—the Savannah River Site—was the Department of Defense facility that produced most of the country's stock of tritium, a radioactive gas used to enhance the power of atomic weapons: to turn A-bombs into H-bombs.

Gerry would have none of their arguments. "I know my son Daniel," she insisted.

Hensley walked over to her and fixed her with an angry glare. "Do you want to see the videos?"

Gerry shook her head, and, for the first time, a crack appeared in her armor. "There's something wrong," she said to Richard plaintively, the quaver in her voice betraying the tears percolating behind the mask. "There has to be something wrong—the wrong house, the wrong person. *Something!*"

"Where would he go?" Hensley pressed.

"We don't know." In fact, they didn't.

"Well, if he calls home or comes back, you'll contact us immediately?"

"Of course," said Gerry.

"Of course," said Richard.

But they were both thinking the same thing: Danny wouldn't call and he wouldn't come back home. That wasn't Danny. If he had in fact done these terrible things, he would never bring that shame home.

In the car on the way back, Gerry tried one last time. "It has to be a mistake."

6

There would be no sleep for Mike Adams this night. By the time he finished making out search warrants at the Thorntons' kitchen table, the neighborhood was filled with so many police cars that neighbors, roused from their sleep by sirens and lights before dawn, thought a plane had crashed. About four o'clock, still hours before first light, Adams said good-bye to Chrissy Blake as a sheriff from Lexington, South Carolina, sixty miles away, arrived to take her back to her waiting parents.

At the house where Chrissy Blake had been held captive for five days, men in uniforms and dark suits stood in clutches, talking in low voices, while teams of investigators from SLED (South Carolina's State Law Enforcement Division), the FBI, the Georgia Bureau of Investigation, as well as the Columbia County Sheriff's Department, floated quietly around them through the small rooms. In every clutch, the conversation was the same: "Can you believe this guy had a wife and kid?" "Did you hear he was a nuclear engineer?"

By dawn, when Adams returned to the sheriff's station in Evans, the manhunt had begun in earnest. At first light, helicopters joined the bloodhounds that had been out for hours sniffing through the bare, brittle underbrush, first in the immediate neighborhood around West Lynne Drive, then in wider and wider circles extending deeper and deeper into the pine-covered countryside. During the day, as the search area expanded, planes joined the helicopters, cars searched the back roads, and roadblocks strangled traffic on the major highways. The order, plain and blunt, went out to more than 100 officers from seven agencies dragooned into the search: "We have got to get this man off the streets."

In nearby Evans, the huge manhunt soon burst the seams of the tiny sheriff's station, a space normally used only by a single dispatcher, road patrols changing shifts, and a deputy or two languidly making out reports. A thirty-three-foot motor home, seized in a drug bust the year before, was rushed into service as a temporary command post. Mike Adams, still sleepless, was among the deputies who manned the special SLED radio system that brought reports in directly from the search teams in the field and kept track of the leads they turned up—pathetically few in the first hours—on blackboards commandeered from the local school.

Meanwhile, in another room, other officers sat grimly around a video monitor, watching and rewatching the video of Chrissy Blake, searching desperately for clues that might help them find the man whose face never appeared on the screen.

7

Gerry Starrett inventoried the faces around the dinner table as she had every week for three decades. She knew she was lucky. Most mothers didn't get to see all their children every week once they began to have lives of their own. One by one the faces around the dinner table would grow up and disappear, leaving empty chairs as well as empty places in their mothers' lives. But not her children. They were all grown, all on their own, but they still came back every week to take their places at her table. Helen, the oldest, strongest, boldest, and most like her mother. From her ballerina days in junior high to her path-breaking days as one of the first female cadets at the Air Force Academy, no one ever mistook the petals of this magnolia blossom for anything other than steel. Next to her sat Gail, a shorter, curlier, less mercurial version of her older sister, who made life-and-death decisions every day from nine to five in her job as a medical administrator. And then, finally, sitting in fidgetless silence, Robert, unassuming almost to the point of vanishing, the youngest, the baby, still in school, but already married and father to Gerry's first grandchild.

There was one empty chair this day, however: Danny's.

"It just doesn't make any sense," said Helen, an attractive young woman who everybody said looked like her brother, only bigger-boned and more determined. "That's not my brother. If they told me, 'Helen, *you're* being arrested because *you've* done these things,' that's how surprised I feel. There's just no way."

Helen had said the same thing the day before when she returned her parents' first frantic phone call. She and her husband had been staying at a remote cabin in the pine wilds of southern Georgia—no ordinary vacations for Helen—when the caretaker pounded on the door and fetched her to his phone for an emergency call. After listening in stricken silence to her mother's report of what the police were saying—that Danny had kidnapped a girl and held her captive and then fled—Helen almost blacked out from the shock. It felt as though somebody had punched her in the gut, she said later. But as soon as she had collected herself, she moved quickly to stanch the flow of anxiety. "You're getting all bent out of shape over nothing," she told her mother firmly. "There's *no way*. Somebody is pulling your leg. Or it's a mistake. A colossal mistake."

Now, with everyone except Danny gathered around the dinner table, Helen again assumed the mantle of the eldest child, defender of the family, simultaneously indignant and reassuring. "Danny is the one we never have to worry about. We might have our fusses and fights, but Danny's the one you can always count on to stay calm. If you have a problem, Danny is the one who's going to help you. If he had a cookie and you wanted some of it, Danny would give you the whole thing, not just half. For heaven's sake, Danny's the Peace Corps candidate in this family."

Heads around the table nodded somberly in agreement.

"If it hadn't been for Danny," Gerry interjected, "we wouldn't all be here now." Indeed it was Danny who had pushed for these weekly family get-togethers, who did the planning and the phone calling to make them possible. They were still a family because of Danny.

"This person they're talking about," Helen continued, "the person who did these awful things, *that's not my brother.*" She folded her arms and fell back in her chair, just the way she had done for years.

Gerry and Richard Starrett had called their family together in extraordinary session, not just to tell them what had happened, but to meet with representatives of the FBI, SLED, and the other agencies hunting Danny. Yet when the entourage of men in uniforms and dark suits arrived and crowded into the small dining room, wedging their big, strange faces into places around her table, shuffling and displacing the familiar ones, Gerry Starrett felt the same tide of anger and indignation rising inside her that she had felt in the police station that night.

Harold Harrison of the FBI was the first to speak. "We understand this is a difficult time for you folks," he began, "but we're sure you understand the need to bring Richard into custody."

"His name is Daniel," Gerry interrupted. "Richard *Daniel* Starrett."

"Danny," Helen clarified.

"There are three good reasons for you to cooperate with us in finding your son," Harrison continued. He jabbed one finger into the air at a time. "One, to protect the public from any further harm—"

"Danny's not dangerous," Helen interrupted.

"Well, miss," Harrison corrected, "I'm afraid he has done some terrible things."

"What things?" Helen was uncowed.

"We'd rather not go into that right now," said Harrison, then continued emphatically: "Two, to protect Danny from himself—"

"Why would he need to be protected from himself?" Gerry wanted to know.

"We know he has a gun, Mrs. Starrett, and he told the girl who escaped that the only way it would end was if he ended it himself."

Gerry looked at him in utter bewilderment.

"That's nonsense!" Helen slumped back in her chair and folded her arms again.

"People from all kinds of families commit suicide," said Mike Adams, who still hadn't slept for two days. "Just as people from all different levels of society commit crimes." His sleep-deprived patience was slipping away, and he had seen too many families make the same excuses. He would catch a kid selling dope, and when he confronted the parents, they would shake their heads and insist, "Not my kid. My kid wouldn't do such a thing." And he would say, "Well, your kid just sold this crack to an undercover officer."

Helen followed the trail of his thoughts to their damning end. "There's nothing weird about *our* family," she exploded, sitting bolt upright in the chair. "There are no skeletons. We're about as boring as you can get, a middle-class American family. Our parents aren't divorced. We went to church. We went to school. We were in the Boy Scouts, Girl Scouts, Campfire Girls. You know, this kind of thing happens to other people, and you watch it on TV. This is *other* people. This isn't people like us."

Gerry then turned to Harrison. "You said there were three reasons. What is the third?"

"To get some help for Danny. He left home without his money, without his wallet, without his medication. All we know is that he has a gun. He's clearly sick and needs help."

"My son is not sick," Gerry insisted. "All we really know is that he's missing."

"Well, sick or not, he's never needed your help more than he needs it right now," said Harrison. "If you help us find him, I promise you that we will make sure he gets whatever help he needs."

Gerry knew they had to be wrong about Danny. She had thought about nothing else for two days. There had to be an explanation. She just hadn't figured it out yet—and neither had they. Everything would make sense eventually. But the sooner they found Danny, the sooner it would end. "All right," she finally said.

With that permission, Richard, who couldn't shake the belief that Danny had run for a reason, finally spoke up. "We all want to find out more, and the only way we can do that is to find Danny. So we will do whatever we can to help." Even as he uttered the words, he resented them. These people didn't want to help his son. They just wanted to catch him.

"Where do you think your son might have gone?" Harrison repeated.

"When he was little, anytime we made a move and he wasn't real pleased about it, he said he was going to run away and live with his grandma," said Gerry.

Harrison took the location and phone number of Gerry's mother, Arline Williams, who lived on a farm in Appling County in southern Georgia, and then asked, "Would he call you from there?"

Gerry could feel her blood rise. She had heard the same question before, several times, and given the same answer. "No. If Daniel has done what you say he's done, he won't want to involve us in it." She wondered why they would keep asking the same questions—unless they thought she was lying.

"Sooner or later, most people on the run contact their family," Harrison pressed. "Without his wallet, ma'am, he'll have to stop when he runs out of gas. That's when we expect him to contact you."

Gerry let the silence speak for her.

"Well, if he does," Harrison grumbled, "you'll let us know?" He solicited grudging nods from every family member at the table and then turned to Gerry. "Do you have a picture of Danny that we could use?"

That was it for Gerry. She looked at the faces around the table, the ones that didn't belong to her. Those people were all grown men. Most probably had children of their own. Surely they could see what this was doing to her and to her family. Surely there was no mistaking the shock, the numbness—the physical numbness—she felt. Just how insensitive could they be as they tore her family apart?

"No," she finally said. "I don't think we can do that." An awkward silence fell over the table. "We feel that Danny needs to be off the streets," she explained. "That part, there's really no question about. But a picture. No, I don't think so."

8

After two days of searching county by county through South Carolina and Georgia, tracking every lead and reported sighting, investigating every tip no matter how tenuous or improbable, Mike Adams's boss, Columbia County Sheriff Otis Hensley, admitted to being "unsure which direction the suspect has fled." There had been no confirmed sightings. None. When asked to comment on the progress of the search, Lexington County Sheriff James Metts could only express a strained hope that Starrett would surrender. "We think he's unaccustomed to the life of a criminal on the run," Metts offered lamely. "When he sees all the roadblocks we put up for him, as intelligent as he is, our hope is he will turn himself in and get some help for himself."

As for leads, they had only one: Starrett was driving a 1988 Chevrolet Camaro Z-28, Georgia license plate RSL-569.

On Saturday, February 11, the FBI issued a nationwide alert:

WANTED
ARMED AND DANGEROUS
Richard Daniel Starrett

9

Special Agent Ellen O'Toole, from the FBI office in San Francisco, drove to a tidy little house on Bellweather Lane in San Jose to interview Richard Daniel Starrett's wife, Heather. She began by asking Heather her level of education (high-school graduate) and her employment status (part-time cosmetologist at a beauty shop owned by her mother-in-law, Gerry Starrett). Heather introduced her daughter. "Allison's almost two," she said proudly.

O'Toole wanted to know why Heather Starrett was in San Jose instead of at home in Augusta, Georgia.

Heather, a slender, winsome young woman with wavy, processed blond hair, stared at the agent with wide, uncomprehending eyes. "Why, I'm visiting my parents," she said with a hint of indignation. "I try to get out here every six months or so. Once in the summer and then again at Christmas. I usually stay about three, three and a half weeks."

"How long were you here this past Christmas?"

Heather tapped her forehead as a sign of deep thought. "I came before Christmas and I returned to Georgia on February 4."

O'Toole hid her surprise. "February 4? That was only about a week ago."

"Yes." The blank look again.

"And you were here for more than five weeks?"

"Yes."

"And now you're back again?"

Heather, still uncomprehending, but beginning to be annoyed at the woman's prying skepticism: "Yes."

"Now, let me see if I understand this correctly," O'Toole recapped. "You spent five weeks here in California with your parents, then you flew back to your home in Georgia—stayed, what, four days with your husband—then turned around and flew back across country to be with your parents again?" She didn't bother hiding her puzzlement. "Do I have that right?"

Heather was unshakeable. "Yes."

"You'll excuse me for saying so, Mrs. Starrett, but doesn't that strike you as just a little bit strange?"

Heather began fidgeting with her cotton sweater, picking at invisible specks of lint. "Not necessarily," she said with a pout of defensiveness. "I'm very close to my parents. We're Latter Day Saints, you know, and family is very important to us."

"You and your husband are Mormons?" This information did not appear on O'Toole's briefing sheet.

"Not my husband, no," Heather corrected quickly. "I mean my parents are, and I was raised LDS."

O'Toole was losing patience. "Now, Mrs. Starrett, I don't care what church you were raised in, or how much you love your parents, it is unusual—not to say bizarre—behavior to fly across country, spend five weeks, return home, spend four days, then fly back. There must be some reason that you stayed in Georgia such a short time."

Heather tugged at her sweater for a long time before answering, eyes averted, in a faint voice. "It seemed strange to me, too. But Danny wanted it. He wanted me to leave."

"Your husband, Danny, wanted you to leave Georgia and come back here after only a few days?"

"He insisted on it. He said he needed to work out some personal problems. Alone."

O'Toole felt a wave of sympathy. Heather was pretty, all right, but did not seem especially acute. The fact that she was obviously easy to use didn't make it any less poignant that she had, indeed, been used. "When did you last see your husband?" O'Toole asked.

"Less than a week ago."

"Do you have any idea where your husband is now, Mrs. Starrett?"

"No." Her voice had dissolved to a whisper.

"What is your relationship with your husband like?"

"I don't know," Heather said. "I guess, like any couple, we've had our problems—recently, I mean."

"What kind of problems?"

Heather shrugged almost imperceptibly. "Just the usual marriage problems. Nothing serious."

"Has your husband ever been violent towards you or towards your daughter?"

Heather's eyes widened. "Oh, no," she said, batting her eyelids in astonishment. "Never."

Agent O'Toole retreated to a litany of routine questions: other residences, safe-deposit boxes, storage facilities, bank accounts, credit cards. "Danny has both a Visa like mine and an American Express gold card," Heather said in answer to the last. "He's very proud of that gold card."

"Who would you say your husband is closest to—"

"His parents," Heather interrupted. "Danny is very close with his parents."

"Anybody else who you think might—"

"You know," Heather interrupted again, changing the subject, "Danny is quite ambitious politically. At one time, he told me he wants to be president of the United States. And he has a schedule for it. By the year 2004, he wants to hold some sort of local political office." It was clear from her tone that she considered this a critical piece of the puzzle. "He's strictly a Republican, of course."

O'Toole dutifully made a note and then asked, "Is there anything else you want to tell me?"

"There is one thing," Heather confided, leaning closer and lowering her voice. "If Danny gets upset and has to be talked out of doing anything, you know, foolish because of what's happened, tell him to think about his wife and daughter."

O'Toole was surprised. "Not his parents?"

"Oh, no," said Heather. "It would only upset him if you mentioned his parents or anybody else from the family. He'd be embarrassed for them to know what he's done."

10

As Gerry Starrett walked into a convenience store not far from her house, she noticed right away that something was different. A knot of customers had formed near the door, an unusual place, crowding around a bulletin board that usually held nothing more interesting than photocopied notices of choir rehearsals, houses to let, and garage sales.

She saw the picture first. Not a picture, really, but a crude drawing of a clean-shaven, round-faced male with regular features and neat, close-cropped hair. Amateurish as it was, it clearly conveyed the impression of an attractive young man.

In the next instant, Gerry registered the words above the picture:

WANTED
KIDNAPPING/CRIMINAL SEXUAL CONDUCT
Richard Daniel Starrett

Her eyes went back to the drawing. Suddenly it looked hideous, now that she knew who it was supposed to be. The blank eyes, the cross-hatched cheeks, the crooked, pursed lips: This was a drawing of a monster, not a human being. And certainly not Danny. "That's not my son," she said out loud.

It wasn't until she turned to leave that she realized the truth: They had used that awful drawing only because she had refused to give them a picture.

In fact, that awful drawing was everywhere in Augusta: in stores and restaurants, in schools and public buildings, in the paper. Everywhere she looked, it seemed, she saw those blank eyes staring out from under the name "Richard Daniel Starrett." The police had made a specific plea to the media. "The Starrett case is one in which the media can help or hurt law enforcement," proclaimed Bob Ford, Lexington Sheriff's Department information officer, "but in particular can help by running photos of the fugitive. The more eyes we have, the better."

Except that it wasn't a photo. It was this hideous cartoon.

And the image of Danny they painted with words wasn't any better. Every time Gerry tuned into a TV or radio show, she could hear her son described. "Federal officials say Starrett fits the profile of a serial sex offender and killer—smart, tough to catch, and prolific," intoned the anchor of the six o'clock local news show. "Starrett is typical for a serial rapist," concluded another station's expert. "They look really normal, 71 percent are married, and some of them have kids." Had this expert ever met her son? She turned on the news one night—soon after it happened, when she was still watching TV—and saw a reporter standing in front of the house on West Lynne Drive that Chrissy Blake had fled to. He was saying that the owner of the house, Carl Thornton, refused to be interviewed. Why? *Because he feared possible retaliation against his family by the fugitive, Richard Daniel Starrett.*

She saw the inevitable interviews with Danny's neighbors, standing self-consciously in their yards, saying the inevitable: "He was kind of quiet." "He kept to himself." "I guess he just snapped." A few, startled into honesty, said nice things. "He took great care of his convertible," said Mike Weber, who lived across the street from Danny. "He was very particular of that car." Judy Saunders, another neighbor on West Lynne, told a newspaper reporter that Danny "was a very nice and very loving father." When Gerry read that, she almost cried. But others saw a chance to air old grievances. "I never saw him outside," complained a neighbor who also didn't want to give his name for fear of reprisal. "He never cut his grass." As if Danny would come back and kill someone for criticizing his lawn care.

In interviews, spokespeople for the sheriff's department, FBI,

SLED, and all the others described a Danny Starrett as ugly and alien to Gerry as the drawing on the bulletin board. Sheriff Metts told the world that Danny "had problems at work and at home and had developed a drinking problem." Starrett "cannot survive on the run," Metts predicted. "But if he continues to run, the chance of a violent encounter is greater. The only safe place for Richard Starrett is under police custody." The sheriff of a neighboring county claimed that evidence linked Starrett to a bizarre incident in which an unidentified man had taken "suggestive pictures" of an eight-year-old girl on the steps of a county school by posing her "in such a way that you could see up her dress."

As the search dragged on, official descriptions grew darker and more sinister. "Starrett is a master of disguise," Sheriff Metts gamely informed the press. "He has been known to use the names Mike Reed and Rex Stanet and may have residences in several areas." To Gerry he was just making excuses for the fact that the biggest manhunt in Columbia County history, maybe in Georgia history, had so far produced nothing—not even a sighting.

And the longer her son eluded them, the more shrill and bizarre their excuses became. Soon they were saying that Danny was "connected to a Satanic network that dealt in drugs and violence." A South Carolina newspaper reported that the police had "uncovered evidence of the occult in Starrett's home"—a report that Sheriff Metts confirmed with an almost imperceptible reservation: "Evidence was found that indicates Starrett *may* have dabbled in satanism or the occult." Four days after Danny disappeared, Gerry picked up a newspaper and read "unconfirmed reports" that her son had kept his victim Chrissy Blake alive "because he intended to sell her to the makers of pornographic 'snuff' films in which young women are killed on camera."

This was her son they were talking about.

It was inevitable that the same media would find their way to the Starretts' door. At first, at Gerry's insistence, family members merely hung up the phone and refused to answer the doorbell. Richard was the first to weaken. A lifetime of empty philosophical chatter and locker-room bonhomie had left him utterly fearless and guileless in the face of the media's glibness—and therefore utterly defenseless. When he read reports in the paper that Danny had experienced problems at work, he buttonholed the next reporter who called. "I want you to know that my son has received four substantial raises since he was hired by Bechtel in January 1987," he fumed. "Four raises! Every single one of his job evaluations has been excellent. Are you writing this down?"

Unfortunately, he was. A day after the story with Richard's protest appeared, Bechtel announced that Richard Daniel Starrett's employment was formally terminated. A company spokesman said the action was taken because Starrett "had exceeded the maximum number of days of work that could be missed without an excuse."

In the same article, Richard bragged about Danny's involvement in local politics, more specifically, Republican politics: how he had served his time in the trenches working for the party's candidates in the 1988 election. The next day, the Republican party chairman reluctantly admitted seeing Daniel Starrett at GOP headquarters on the night of George Bush's election but hastened to add that Danny "was not an officeholder or major contributor to candidates," and had no ongoing connection to the Republican party. Message: We don't know him.

11

On February 14, Trooper Kevin Kennedy of the Texas Department of Public Safety was working stationary radar on U.S. 10 westbound, at the Thompson overpass thirty miles east of Houston. At about eleven P.M., a car flashed by, and Kennedy checked its speed: eighty-six m.p.h. He turned on his red-and-blue lights and chased the speeder to a rest area at the 788-mile marker. After writing the ticket, he decided to check out the rest area. The highway department had been having trouble lately with transients using the rest rooms, water fountains, and picnic tables as make-do motels, and this was about the time when they began to settle in for the night.

But this night the only car in the area was a red Chevrolet Camaro convertible. Kennedy, who considered himself something of a car buff, made an appreciative noise as he passed the car and noticed its Georgia plates. Probably some tourist who bit off more highway than he could chew in a day, thought Kennedy, or a salesman saving a night's motel bill.

Reflexively, on the off chance that the car was stolen, Kennedy wrote down the license number, RSL-569, and radioed it back to the dispatcher in Houston. Then he continued on his way, cruising the length of the rest area.

When he finished his pass, there was still no response on the Georgia license. The registration must have come back clean and they just hadn't bothered to tell him. He began to leave the rest area, heading west, when suddenly his radio crackled to life. "Georgia license RSL-569 is registered to a Richard Daniel Starrett," said the dispatcher excitedly, a tone of voice Kennedy had rarely heard on the radio. "Vehicle and driver are wanted out of Georgia. Driver is considered armed and dangerous. Sheriff's Department, Columbia County, Georgia, requests you place a hold on this subject and on the vehicle. They hold felony warrants on the subject for aggravated sodomy and false imprisonment. They will extradite this subject."

Kennedy did what he always did when he heard the words "armed and dangerous"—he called for backup. Unit 2148 responded with troopers Johnnie Corcoran and Sam McDowell on board. Five minutes later, their car pulled quietly in behind Kennedy's. Both cars were blacked out.

Kennedy approached the driver's side of the red Camaro with his service shotgun in both hands, pointed straight ahead, and his finger on the trigger. The other two troopers approached the passenger's side, one carrying a service shotgun, the other a revolver.

Kennedy inched as close to the car as he dared, close enough to get a look in the driver's window. Inside, he saw a white male reclining in the driver's seat, apparently asleep. He looked exactly like the kind of person Kennedy expected would drive a car like this: young, professional, attractive, well dressed. The word that came immediately to mind was *yuppie;* not your normal "armed and dangerous" type.

Kennedy was beginning to have doubts about this arrest. Still, the man did fit the description of the wanted subject that had been radioed to him: Twenty-nine-year-old white male, brown hair, collar length, blue eyes, five feet eleven inches tall, 170 pounds, no facial hair."

So Kennedy played it by the book. After shining his flashlight at the driver's hands to make sure he wasn't holding any weapons, he motioned the other troopers into positions around the car where they could see any quick movements.

Then he pounded on the window. "State police!" he shouted. "Keep your hands where I can see them!"

The man's eyes blinked open. He squinted fiercely and quickly drew his hands up over his eyes to shield them from the glare of the flashlights.

The sudden movement startled Kennedy. *"Don't move,* Mr. Starrett!" he shouted. "Just get out of the car with your hands up."

The man inside seemed to hesitate for a moment and then reached for the door.

"Slowly!" Kennedy warned.

As the man emerged from the car, barefoot and blinking, Kennedy passed his shotgun to one of the other officers, grabbed the suspect by one arm, turned him against the car, and patted him down. "Are you Richard Daniel Starrett?" he demanded.

"Yes, I am," said the man in a thin, reedy voice. He didn't sound like a criminal, either, thought Kennedy. He was growing more and more doubtful about this bust. "I'm on my way to California to see my wife and baby," said the man.

Before he could say anything else, Trooper McDowell read him his rights, handcuffed him, sat him on the curb out of the way, and stood guard over him while Kennedy and Corcoran searched the red Camaro. On the console they found an ID card from the Bechtel Corporation. The picture on the card was of the suspect. The name: "Richard Daniel Starrett."

There was no mistake. As unlikely as it seemed, this was their man.

When Effie Lou Skinner, the booking officer at the Harris County Jail, looked up and saw the young man with sandy blond hair, she thought he was probably lost and looking for directions. He looked dazed—as though he wanted to be anywhere in the world other than where he was—or was that just exhaustion?

Then she found out who he was.

"Do you have suicidal tendencies?" She began the litany of questions in her most practiced, bureaucratic tone.

"No."

"Are you homosexual or bisexual?"

"No."

"You have been charged with kidnapping and assaulting a young woman in Georgia. Are you aware of that?"

"That's not true," the man said. "I have a good job—I'm making $38,000 a year—and I have a loving wife, a kind and gentle woman." Then again, with more conviction, "It's just not true."

12

For a while, Gerry Starrett thought the only thing she wanted in the world was for her son to be found safe—until she heard on TV that he had been captured in Texas. Instead of the expected relief, she felt a fresh wave of anxiety: What would they do to him? Her first instinct was to do what she always did when he was in trouble, what she had always done since Danny was an infant crying in his crib: Go to him. "Let's fly to Texas," she said to Richard the instant she heard the news from Houston. "Let's go right now."

Richard, too, reacted as he always did. "What good is that going to do?" he asked. "We can't do anything for him."

"You don't know that," Gerry flared. "Let's go and see. Surely we can do *something*. We can't just sit here."

But Richard was adamant, in the way he reserved exclusively for his wife. "No, it will not do any good. Why don't you just call a lawyer?"

Gerry fumed and fretted for hours—in the way she reserved exclusively for him—but did take the advice about a lawyer. After several frantic phone calls, she finally reached Henderson Johnson, a lawyer who had his own small firm in Aiken, a town on the other side of the Savannah River in South Carolina, about halfway between Augusta and Columbia. She outlined the case for him in breathless, abbreviated strokes. She was especially concerned about the latest reports of the arrest in the newspaper alleging that Danny had had a gun in his car, which made him sound sinister and dangerous, of all things.

Johnson, who had been following the case in the local papers, listened calmly and then finally said in his most soothing, good-ole-boy baritone, "Why don't y'all come in and talk to me?"

"We need help right now!" Gerry exploded. "We're in the middle of something that can't wait! What we need is someone to pick up the phone and call Texas to find a lawyer for him. Or get on a plane and head out there to see him."

Johnson promised to call the Houston jail and talk to Daniel or, failing that, to leave a message for him to call Johnson collect. That seemed to calm Gerry for the moment.

But fifteen minutes later, she called Johnson back. "Did you talk to him?" she demanded.

"I left word," said Johnson, "but he hasn't returned my call."

"I thought so," Gerry fumed. "That's not like Danny. I'm sure they're not giving him the messages. Isn't that against the law?"

"If they're preventing him from talking to a lawyer, yes, ma'am," said Johnson. He wanted to say that if the police in Houston were keeping Danny away from his lawyer, it would be the best break he could get. But he promised to keep trying.

Gerry and Richard also kept trying. They placed a half dozen more calls to the Harris County Jail. Gerry longed to hear the sound of her son's voice. She knew it was the only thing that would let her rest—something she hadn't done in days.

But they never did get through, and Danny never called back.

That same night, Gerry, Richard, and Helen Starrett drove the twenty miles to Aiken and met with Henderson Johnson. The lawyer had tried to make the meeting for the next day, but Gerry couldn't wait that long.

Henderson Johnson was a courtly, grizzled teddy bear of a man, a "simple country lawyer," he called himself, with a salt-and-pepper beard, piercing blue eyes, and a voluptuous low-Carolina accent.

"Let me explain to you what I call the stairsteps of the criminal prosecution," he began in his best country-store style, one that had charmed countless jurors over his thirty years of practicing law. "The ground floor is the crime, of course. Now, do we know exactly what your son will be charged with?"

Gerry and Richard looked at each other, as if daring the other to utter the words. Neither could. After an excruciating silence, it was Helen who answered. "Kidnapping and sexual assault."

"But Danny didn't commit any crime," Gerry added quickly, as if to erase the words. "I know he didn't." The pent-up frustrations of the last two days suddenly poured out. "This is our *child* they're talking about, our *son*. He couldn't have done these things. It's impossible. We know him. He's our boy. There's just no way he did these . . . things . . ." She still could not bring herself to say the words ". . . these horrible things."

Johnson affected his most reassuring tone. "Unfortunately, Mrs. Starrett, the criminal process is the same whether the accused is ultimately proven innocent or guilty. For our purposes at the moment, the accusation is all that matters."

After her outburst, Gerry withdrew into sullen silence, but not before muttering, "That doesn't seem right."

Johnson went on to describe the warrant process, the arrest, and the arraignment. "Then the next step is to get a bond and get him out of jail."

Gerry came to life. "Can Danny get a bond? Can we get him out?"

Johnson shook his head. "I don't know what the law is in Texas, Mrs. Starrett, but I doubt it's possible. Besides, they'll probably have him back here before we can get anything arranged."

Gerry asked about a bond in South Carolina or Georgia. "Can we keep him out of jail here until the trial?"

Johnson scratched his white whiskers. "I kinda doubt it. Not in a case where the defendant is facing a life sentence."

"A life sentence . . ." Gerry's face turned ashen. "You mean, Danny could spend the rest of his life in prison?" She hadn't permitted herself to think about such things before now. She had been so concerned about seeing him alive again and safe. "But Danny didn't do anything."

Johnson spoke slowly, evenly, as if instructing a child. "When a magistrate sets bond, he doesn't know that, Mrs. Starrett. His criteria are, number one, what kind of crime is it? Is it a crime against a person or a crime against property? Number two, what is the past criminal record of the person?"

"Danny doesn't even have a speeding ticket," Gerry interjected.

"Number three, is he married? Does he have a family and roots in the community?"

"Danny's married. He has roots. *We're* his roots."

"Four, does he constitute a threat to society if he is released?"

"Danny isn't a threat to anybody."

"You may know that, but the judge will be listening to Chrissy Blake."

"She could be lying, you know," Gerry muttered. "Or it could just be a case of mistaken identity." She realized her protests had lost force since the meeting began. She was trying to maintain a fire in the middle of an onrushing flood.

Johnson went on to summarize the last steps of the criminal process: the preliminary hearing, the grand jury, the pleading, the trial, and if there was a conviction—he paused to allow Gerry to object—the "ever endless appeals."

Gerry listened distractedly to Johnson's long-winded descriptions and when he was finally finished, remained conspicuously silent while Richard asked about money. Johnson told them that his customary fee for a criminal defense of this kind was $25,000 to $50,000. He wouldn't be able to give them a firm figure until he knew more about the case, but for a serious offense like kidnapping, the fee would probably fall at the upper end of that range.

While Richard struggled with that figure—they would have to sell everything they had in the world and borrow still more to come up with that kind of money—Gerry finally broke her silence.

"Mr. Johnson," she said very gravely, very conclusively. "What are our chances?"

Johnson thought it curious that she said "our chances," not "his chances." "I would love to paint a rosy picture for you, Mrs. Starrett," he said. "I wish I could tell you that we will prevail and your son will go free, that I can play enough Perry Mason tricks in the courtroom to make all the evidence go away. The problem is, if I do paint that rosy picture for you, sooner or later that rose will fade and then you'll look at me and say, 'Well, you dumb sonofabitch, you didn't even tell us what was going to happen.'"

Gerry leveled her gaze at Johnson, steady and unblinking. "What is going to happen?"

"It's impossible to say for sure, especially this early."

Undeterred. "Your best guess then."

"Well, the police have apparently found some evidence of criminal activity in your son's house. Then there is the girl who escaped. There appears to be more than just circumstantial evidence of a crime being committed."

Undeterred. "So, what is going to happen?"

"Plus he appears to have fled the police. So it would be reasonable to assume there is some guilt there. I know you're his parents, but I have to be honest and upfront with you."

Undeterred. "What is going to happen?"

Johnson screwed up his courage. "He'll probably get a life sentence for kidnapping."

"But that's not fair," Gerry wailed, in a sudden burst of frustration that surprised even her. *"It's not right."*

Having been pushed this far, however, Johnson refused to retreat. "I'm afraid it's not a case of fair or just, Mrs. Starrett. The system is set up to do certain things, and that's what it does and it does them well. It's not like on TV. After watching TV, you probably think the cops lose ninety out of a hundred cases. In fact, they win about ninety-nine out of a hundred cases, and the one that gets away is the one that's got money. The system is built to win, and it wins."

Gerry stood up and, with only a quick, vague promise to "be back in touch," left the room. Richard and Helen followed on her heels.

13

Mike Adams grabbed his cap against the whirlwind of the helicopter blades just as the chopper hit the ground, bending trees and flattening a big circle of grass in the field beside the sheriff's substation in Evans. It was a perfect metaphor for Adams's life ever since his late-night visit to the little house on West Lynne Drive. For four days, he had been buffeted in the whirlwind of the biggest case of his career. He had only recently begun to catch up on his sleep, and with Starrett still on the loose, what rest he got was brief and fitful.

Now, with Starrett captured, his life had been churned up again. Carroll Campbell, the governor of South Carolina, had lent his private jet to the Lexington County sheriff to fly to Houston immediately and retrieve Starrett rather than schedule his return on a commercial airliner, the usual procedure. Adams had been chosen to represent the Columbia County Sheriff's Department on the flight, and a helicopter had arrived to whisk him to the airport in South Carolina where the governor's jet awaited. Law enforcement in Columbia County had definitely changed.

After a refueling stop in Meridian, Mississippi, the ten-passenger turboprop jet arrived in Houston with Lexington County Sheriff James Metts and his chief investigator on the case, Detective Bill Galardi; two agents from the South Carolina Law Enforcement Division, David Caldwell and Jim Springs; prosecutor Knox McMahon; two FBI agents; and Adams aboard. When the group arrived at the Harris County Jail, they had to split up: one group to interview Starrett, the other to inventory the car that had been impounded and search it for evidence. Adams knew which group he wanted to go with. He had been obsessed with Richard Daniel Starrett for four days, sitting at the table in the makeshift command post, working the phones and the blackboard, trying to piece together the puzzle of this man. Now he wanted to meet him, talk with him, see, finally, how those strange pieces fit together, if they did.

But investigators Galardi and Caldwell went alone to the "psych" ward, where Starrett had been segregated from the other prisoners "for his own protection," while Adams followed Sheriff Metts to the impound building to search the car. Adams didn't see the prisoner until the next day at the extradition hearing, and then only briefly. Starrett, with a muttered "I'll just go," agreed not to fight extradition and waived the hearing. Within a few hours, the papers were signed, and the Harris County sheriff delivered his prize to the door of the waiting jet—and to Mike Adams.

Adams directed Starrett, shuffling awkwardly in handcuffs and leg irons, to one of the inward-facing seats at the front of the cabin and took the forward-facing seat beside him. Only then, as the plane taxied towards the runway, did Trooper Adams take his first long look at the man he had been hunting.

He looked younger than twenty-nine, the age given on the wanted notice, and nothing at all like the police drawing. He was smaller, slighter than Adams had pictured him, his features more refined. When Adams put his big hand around Starrett's arm to help him into the plane, he felt like only bone. Now, as he sat inspecting Starrett's sagging profile, Adams found himself confronting something that all his sleepless hours in the command post hadn't prepared him for. The smooth cheeks, the tousled, sandy blond hair, the thin lips and delicate nose, the hairless backs of his hands: This wasn't a man, thought Adams; this was a boy. And he felt something he hadn't expected to feel and wasn't prepared to feel: sympathy.

14

When Gerry Starrett heard that her son had returned home, she felt a rush of relief and elation, the first buoyant feelings she had felt in days of leaden ordeal. "We have to go see him," she told Richard, "right now."

For once Richard didn't disagree. In the five days since his son disappeared, his usual complacence had melted into a burning indignation. Ever since that evening around the dinner table, he had suspected that the police and FBI were just using him, that all the talk about "helping Danny" was a lie. He had found this business offensive—conspiring against his own blood—but had gone along with it anyway.

Now, with Danny's capture, his worst fears had been realized. Already doors were shutting. Moments after hearing the news from Texas, he had called Harrison, the FBI agent in charge. "Do you remember the conversation where we said we'd help you get Danny off the street and then you said you'd help us because you knew he was sick and needed help?"

"Yes," said Harrison.

"Well, he's off the street and we need that help now."

"I'm sorry, Mr. Starrett," said Harrison in his best officialese. "That's not my department. My job is catching them, and then it goes to somebody else."

Richard felt a flush of bitterness and anger. "In other words, everything y'all said at the dinner table at my house that night was just so much hot air?"

"Well, I wouldn't say that," was all Harrison could say.

When Gerry called Danny's doctor at the Humana Hospital in Augusta, the physician wouldn't talk either. The FBI had told her not to.

"I'm Daniel Starrett's mother," Gerry said.

"I have nothing to say to you," the doctor recited coldly. "I cannot talk to you." And she hung up. Just like that.

This was a battle the family would have to fight alone.

Immediately Gerry gathered that family around her. "We have to go see Danny," she told them all on the phone. And they all came: Helen, Gail, Robert, even Robert's wife, Sally. Only hours after the governor's plane touched down at the airport in Columbia, the Starrett family was speeding toward the Lexington County Jail to reconnect with their missing link.

They arrived at the new jail a little after 10:30 in the morning. Gerry led them through the doors, feeling, for the first time in all this mess, empowered. She and her family came as messengers of hope to show Danny, by their numbers and their spirit, that his cause was not lost; that the world may have turned against him, but his family never would; that he was, despite everything, still loved. The thought of being there for her son made Gerry almost giddy.

They were met at the desk by Captain Adrian Bost, a big, broad-shouldered, ex-football player in a deep-blue uniform. Gerry had spoken to him on the phone before leaving Augusta to make sure they would be permitted to see Danny if they came. Bost had assured her they would.

Without expression, Bost handed Richard a piece of paper. Gerry instantly recognized her son's handwriting:

I don't wish to have any visits at this time.
I will get in touch with any visitors at a later date.

The note was signed "Richard D. Starrett" and witnessed by Captain Bost and the two investigators, David Caldwell and Bill Galardi.

"I don't believe it," said Richard. These people—Bost and the others—were the same people who had prevented his son from contacting a lawyer in Texas. For all he knew, they had deprived Danny of food and water and sleep as well as legal advice in their determination to extract a confession. And once they got what they wanted, once they broke him, it wouldn't matter who saw him.

Gerry recognized the anger building in her husband's eyes and moved to defuse it. They had come here on a mission, and venting their rage at Captain Bost would only complicate matters. Besides, she understood the note. It was Danny, all right. She should have foreseen it. Of course he didn't want to see his family—or more exactly, he didn't want his family to see him. Not like this.

Gerry had a better idea. She suggested that everyone write a letter to Danny "telling him how we feel, how much we love and support him, and how much we want to see him." Out of somewhere, she produced paper and pens. "I'm sure Captain Bost will deliver them to Danny." She looked at Bost with a pleading, coquettish expression. "I'm sure he understands how we feel."

"Tell you the truth, ma'am," said Bost with a nearly impenetrable

STEVEN NAIFEH AND GREGORY WHITE SMITH

drawl, "I feel real bad for the victims' families. I always feel sympathy for them. . . . But not for the guy who did it." He pointed back towards the cells where the prisoners were kept, where Danny was.

The anger flashed in Richard's eyes again.

Gerry felt more embarrassment than anger. "Well, we are Daniel's family," she reminded Bost.

"He knows who we are," Richard fumed. This was so typical of the police he had met in the last five days, Richard thought. They all treated his son as an untouchable, as trash. They would sit around drinking their coffee and talking about his son as though he were some kind of animal, as though he had no family, or his family didn't care about him. They were all like Bost.

Richard had heard as much of it as he could tolerate. So he put his face in Bost's bigger face and spilled out all the anger of the last few days. "I suppose if you're gonna take people and lock them away, maybe for the rest of their lives, you've gotta believe that it's okay to do it, or you couldn't live with yourself. I suppose you've gotta believe that you're protecting society by getting these people off the streets. You can't let yourself imagine what it would be like to see *your* son locked up in a cell, maybe for the rest of his life. You couldn't do that and still go home and sleep at night, could you? So you have to believe that all the bad guys are really bad. That they're all scum. And they're all that way because they chose to be that way. They asked for it, and they deserve every lousy, degrading thing you can do to them and their families."

When the notes were finished, Gerry collected them and handed them to Captain Bost. "Now, you'll take these to Danny, won't you? And tell him we're here for him." She patted Bost's big elbow to speed him on his way—and to apologize for her husband's outburst.

After ten minutes, which seemed like an hour of utter silence, Bost returned without the notes. "He says he'll see you," he announced grudgingly.

Bost led Gerry, followed by her family, down a long hallway, past several guarded doors. The building looked new from the outside but smelled prematurely old on the inside, as if the years lost by its inmates had been somehow subtracted from its own life-span. The floors and walls were dirty beyond their years, the windows dark beyond their years, the air heavy and foul as a nursing home, suggesting more and even stranger arithmetics of the soul. With each step, Gerry's heart sank deeper and deeper, and the tears welled up higher and higher.

The hallway led to a row of visiting stalls, each a phone-booth-sized niche with a window of dirty glass where a phone should have been. In the middle of the window was a small hole. It had been designed to allow voices to pass back and forth, but because the glass around it was so dirty and the room so dimly lighted, it also served as a peephole—the only way to get a clear view of the world on the other side of the window.

Gerry stepped up to the hole first. There was no chair in the booth and barely enough room for one or two visitors at a time. The rest of the family waited their turns at an awkward distance. Gerry looked through the hole and saw on the other side a large space, like a dayroom, lined with exercise equipment. At first she couldn't see anybody, but she could tell by the noise that there were prisoners somewhere in the room, and her mother's radar told her that Danny was nearby.

"Danny?" she called out softly.

Suddenly, from out of nowhere, he appeared in the little circle.

Her heart leapt. She leaned forward, pressing her forehead on the filthy glass, straining in the darkness to fill her vision with the full sight of him. After all this, she couldn't stand not to see all of him.

The first things she noticed were the bags under his eyes; then the sunken, unshaven cheeks, the ashen skin, and the matted hair. He looked terrible, awful, devastated, as if he didn't want to be alive. He looked *dead*. She pushed back from the little opening so he wouldn't see her cry. Not right now. No tears, she told herself sternly over and over, her throat tightened against the rising tide. He needs me to be strong.

She leaned back into the hole and struggled with a smile. Danny's face registered nothing. The black shadows of his eyes were unchanging. She waved her hand in front of the hole. "Danny," she called faintly. "Danny? Do you know me? This is Mom." She waited for a response, a look, a light. Nothing. She tried again. "This is Mom, Danny." She felt the tears strangling her words again and drew back from the window to hide her weakness.

Even if he isn't talking, Gerry told herself, it's important to be here, to remind him of where he came from and who he is. Even if he isn't listening to our words, he sees reflected in our eyes honestly what we know he is.

"Danny, I know your father wants to talk to you." She motioned to Richard.

Richard, too, was unprepared for what he saw. Only a week before, Danny had been sitting in his usual place at the family dinner table, holding forth on local politics and business trends, making his brother and sisters laugh. Father and son had talked about their plans to go into the real-estate business together: how Danny would get his broker's license, and they would buy fixer-uppers, increase their value, and then sell them. Richard, in fact, had already bought their first property, and the two of them were splitting the mortgage payments until they could find a renter. Danny was convinced they were going to make a fortune. He had a way of making even the loftiest dreams sound real and just over the horizon.

This was the image of Danny in Richard's mind when he stepped into the little booth in the Lexington County Jail and peered through the dirty, tinted glass at the stooped, shadowy figure of his son. Danny was dressed in a baggy, wrinkled prison smock more humiliating than any hospital gown and looked, as Richard later told a friend, "as if his life had ended": gaunt and vacant and connected to the feeling world by only the thinnest of threads.

What have they done to my son? Starved him? Beaten him? The questions throbbed in Richard's head. Clearly, the police were doing everything they could to make him talk. That was why Richard hadn't been able to reach him in the crucial hours after his arrest in Texas, why the FBI had hung up when Richard called, why Danny hadn't returned any of Henderson Johnson's messages.

"Don't you worry, Danny," he heard himself say. "We'll get you out of here."

He talked a little while longer—about their real-estate partnership—"just the two of us, Starrett and Starrett, father and son"—about foreclosure sales and rental rates and big profits, as if by reprising the dinner table conversation of the week before, by reliving their former life, he could roll back the whole ugly intervening week and reclaim his son. Even as Richard talked, though, he thought about how much had been lost, probably forever, in a week. He thought about how quickly life can change. One day you're sitting down to dinner with your family just as you have for thirty years; a week later, you're looking at your broken child through dirty glass. This must be how the parents of accident victims feel, Richard thought. Or parents whose kids are hit by cancer or AIDS or one of the thousand other scourges out there.

Only this was worse. There was something about this, something different, something that separated him from all those other suffering parents; but he didn't want to think about it, not yet anyway. It was a terrible thing to think, but it was true, and later he would say it out loud: Cancer would have been easier.

Richard finally stepped back and, one by one, Helen, Gail, and Robert spent their time at the window, mumbling words of support and encouragement, biting back tears. By the time their half hour of visiting time was up, everybody was crying—everybody except Gerry. And Danny still hadn't said a word.

As they gathered themselves to leave, Richard sidled into the booth for a last word. "Danny, we've got to go now, son. They won't let us stay any longer. But I promise we'll visit every time they let us, for as long as they let us stay. If they open the doors, we'll be here. I guarantee it, son." And then, to save Danny from the sight of still more tears, he ducked out the door.

Gerry, too, had a last word. Alone and dry-eyed, she leaned close to the little hole. "I love you, Danny," she whispered. "Everything's going to be okay. Please believe that. We're going to help you." She turned to walk away but quickly turned back with one more thought. "We're praying for you."

That night the Starrett family did indeed pray for Danny. They gathered in the living room of Gerry's impeccable house on Marty Drive, joined hands, and asked God to watch over their loved one in his time of need.

They prayed for God to give them the strength they needed to "weather the storm." When her turn came, Gerry prayed for God to bring her family safely through this, their "darkest hour."

"And remember," she added when the prayer was finished, "the darkest hour is always just before the dawn."

15

Sitting around the makeshift "command trailer" in the parking lot in Evans, surrounded by empty bags of fast food and boxes of Krispy-Kreme doughnuts, Mike Adams slowly built the case against Richard Daniel Starrett.

The search of Starrett's house on West Lynne Drive had turned up an RCA video camera; a blue canvas bag full of videotapes, including the one that Adams had already seen; a pair of brown cloth gloves; stained sheets and towels; newspapers in which classified advertisements had been circled; a pair of Smith & Wesson handcuffs; a starter pistol; a revolver; plus a pile of notebooks and maps; gasoline, motel, and car-rental receipts, all of which could be important pieces of the puzzle. There was even a receipt hinting that Starrett had rented a storage unit somewhere under another name.

And the search of Starrett's red Camaro in Houston had turned up another handgun—the same one, Adams bet, that he put to Chrissy Blake's head.

When Heather Starrett, accompanied by her mother, returned from California to retrieve some things from the house on West Lynne Drive, Mike Adams met her there.

"I never guessed he would do anything like this," Heather wailed even before Adams began his questioning. "I still can't believe it." In particular, she couldn't believe what she saw at the house she had shared with Richard Daniel Starrett for a year. It certainly wasn't the same house in which she had raised her two-year-old baby. The windows were boarded up, and the interior rooms had dead-bolt locks on the doors between them. The king-size bed—the bed she had shared with Danny—had been split apart: the mattress in one room, under the leer of the video camera; the box springs left in the master bedroom. The house had been stripped of all their family pictures, all the pictures of Danny's family, of Heather, and even of little Allison. This was not her house, and she sifted through the debris left by waves of crime-lab technicians as if through a pile of someone else's soiled clothing.

Adams started by explaining to her what her husband was accused of doing.

"How could he have done those things?" she wailed again.

"We were hoping that you could help us answer that question," said Adams. He had been chosen to interview Heather Starrett not just because he knew so much about the case. He also had the two qualities indispensable to a good interrogator but rarely found in the same person: a warm, disarming manner and a deeply suspicious nature—good cop and bad cop in the same person. Anybody else would have looked at the pretty, vacant-eyed woman across the table and just assumed she was a dizzy California blonde who had stepped off the edge of her little lifeboat of a world and was floundering to find her way back. Adams, however, couldn't get it out of his head that her trip away from home had been so conveniently timed.

"It's pretty weird for a wife to be gone that long—almost a month. Especially after you'd already been gone for Christmas only the month before."

"The second trip, Danny told me to go," she insisted. "He said I needed to go. It wasn't a planned thing."

"But you had no indication that he was setting up anything"—he searched for the word—"*special* while you were gone?"

"No."

"Nothing like this?"

"Absolutely not."

"Why do you suppose he was so eager for you to go?"

"I don't know."

"Has anything been different between you and your husband lately?"

"Well, after I had the baby, things changed."

"What changed?"

"You know, personal things."

"Ma'am, you'll have to be more specific. What kind of personal things?"

"Well, before that we had a normal sex life."

"You mean you stopped having sex?"

"We stopped having normal sex."

"He wanted you to do different things?"

"Yeah. He wanted me to do . . . things." She waited, hoping he would pass on.

He didn't. "What kind of things?" Adams pressed.

"You know." Her eyes hugged the floor. "Oral things." Long, awkward silence. "And he wanted me to do it for the longest time. Then . . ."

"Then what?" Adams coaxed.

"He wanted . . . we tried videotaping."

Adams thought of the videos of Chrissy Blake. "And that was a change?"

"Oh, yes. That was a complete change. And I didn't like it at all."

"When was the last time you had sex with your husband?" Adams heard himself ask.

"When I came back from California last time, after Christmas, we tried, but . . ."

"But what?"

"It didn't really work out."

"Why not?"

"He couldn't keep it, you know, hard." A deep blush swept over her face, which she tried to hide behind her hand. "But don't most men have that problem?" she added quickly. "I mean, every once in a while?"

Adams decided to change the subject. "What kind of reading materials does your husband keep around the house?"

Heather was so relieved at the change, she answered almost cheerfully, *"Playboy* and *Forum,* that kind of thing. Like most men."

"So he liked pictures of nude women?"

"Yeah, I guess so." Suddenly she was on the defensive again. "Like all men. But his regular reading was psychology and history and that kind of stuff."

"Any pornography?"

"Excuse me?" The indignation again.

"Did he keep any hard-core pornography around the house?" Adams let his exasperation show. "The X-rated kind?"

"I don't recall seeing any."

Adams returned to the subject Heather seemed most awkward with. "Other than the sex thing, how was your marriage?"

"Well, recently we've been having some trouble," she said, hedging. "With his headaches and not working, it's kind of put stress on the family. Nothing specific." Adams sensed something very specific indeed.

"Had you talked about getting a divorce?" he asked.

"Oh, no." The defensiveness again. "I couldn't talk about that. Danny would have flipped out."

"Were you *thinking* about a divorce?"

She paused for too long. "No," she finally said without conviction.

"How did he feel about your going off to California with your child?"

"He didn't like being separated from Allison, but he wanted me gone."

"Mrs. Starrett, did your husband have any secrets from you?"

"None that I know of. Danny wasn't the kind to keep secrets. He was an open book."

"Were there any rooms in your house that were off limits to you?"

"No."

"Did you know your husband had rented a storage locker?"

"No," said Heather with a look of genuine surprise. "What was in it?"

Adams didn't have the heart to tell her.

16

They had found Danny's storage unit.

Mike Adams was there when a posse of FBI agents and sheriff's deputies cut the combination lock on rental locker 132 at Van Guard

Self Storage in Martinez, Georgia, just down the road from the Starrett house, and squeezed into the dimly lit space piled to the ceiling with cardboard boxes. At first glance, he saw little that looked like it might be useful to the investigation: just piles of junk, some in bags, some in buckets, some just scattered about loose, and lots of cardboard boxes.

It wasn't until Adams and others began dragging the locker's contents out into the gray light of a February morning that he realized what they had stumbled on. In a green-and-white canvas bag stuffed inside a white plastic pail they found a pair of handcuffs; a Taser gun, the kind used by police to immobilize suspects; a wooden-handled whip; a dog leash with a metal chain; lengths of leather cord; rolls of duct tape; and an orange rubber ball. Another bag held a police badge, a badge holder marked "Special Officer," a starter pistol, a box of ammunition, a police call radio, and a blue light like the ones used by police in unmarked cars. In still another bag they found wigs, mustaches, glasses, and a metal box containing letters addressed to Rick Stanet and Rick Stonet at different post office boxes in Augusta. Inside the letters were photographs of women bound and gagged at gunpoint.

"It's like King Tut's tomb," cracked one cop as he held up a hunting knife in one hand and a pair of bolt cutters in the other.

And that was before they looked in the boxes.

The first one Adams opened was filled with books, mostly paperbacks. Big deal, he thought, the guy's a reader. Then he looked at the titles: *Slave Girl, Slave Market, Raped Daughters, Degraded Raped Daughter, Captive Princess, Bondage Wife, Kingdom of Pain, Women in Cages*. He burrowed deeper into the box—there must have been fifty books in it: *Kidnapped for Sex, Captured Women, Rope Tricks— Bondage Annual, Women in Tit Torture, Fetish Bizarre, Bound to Tease, Bound and Spanked*.

He opened another box: *Encyclopedia of Modern Torture, Torture Interrogation and Execution, Autopsy*. Someone else, searching another box, held up a book *How to Build Your Own Underground Prison*.

Soon it became a game, the kind of black game, thought Adams, in which cops take such grim, professional glee. Sitting in a circle on the cold pavement, each with a box of yellowed books and foxed magazines, they dug into their boxes, searching for the topper, and then when they found it, shouted like bidders at an auction, holding up their prize for all to see:

"Science Against Crime"
"Burglary Made Simple"
"The Illustrated Art of Lock Picking"
"Methods of Disguise"
"Criminal Investigations"
"Crime Stoppers"

The game was interrupted briefly when another officer pulled from the locker a sheaf of posters. With the others looking on, he unfurled them one by one: "Die Master Die," "Night of the Blood Monster," "New York Ripper," "Sadismo," "World of Horror." Out of the corner of his eye, Adams saw someone walk by with a plastic pail filled with video-tapes. He saw only two titles: *The Texas Chainsaw Massacre* and *Slumber Party Massacre.*

Gradually, almost ashamed, the bidding resumed.

"The Art of the Nude"
"How to Say No to a Rapist and Survive"
"Diary of a Rapist"
"The Want-Ad Killer"

The last one put an end to the game.

Later, on more thorough inspection, they would find two books on the serial killer Ted Bundy, *The Stranger Beside Me* and *The Killer Next Door,* as well as a box of newspaper clippings on Bundy's execution in Florida three weeks before for the murder of a twelve-year-old girl—only one of more than twenty women Bundy claimed to have killed.

Adams returned to the locker and staggered out with a box packed solid with magazines. He riffled through their titles: *Submissive Prostitutes, Blood Root, Blood Bath, Sex Crimes, Mass Murder, Missing Persons.* Another box was brought out filled with issues of *Monster Time.* Another with more than 100 copies of *Inside Detective Magazine.* Another with *Official Detective Magazine.* Another box with *Master Detective Magazine.* And another with *True Detective Magazine.*

And still more boxes were brought out: box after box, filled with the same magazines.

The final count took days to complete: 18 calendars "depicting nudity and/or violence," according to the official inventory; 71 fliers on "erotic and violent videos"; 116 posters "depicting bondage or violence and sex"; 935 books depicting nudity, horror, and sexual violence"; and 1,197 magazines "containing sex, horror, violence, and bondage."

But to Mike Adams the most intriguing find in this "cesspool of perversion," as one official labeled it, was a stack of maps. Ever since Chrissy Blake's escape, the media—*that* cesspool of perversion," Adams called it—had been filled with stories, breathlessly told, of similar crimes still unsolved. Everybody wanted to jump on the Starrett bandwagon, a surefire ratings and circulation booster. Adams had seen it before: A criminal gets his name in the paper, and suddenly he's linked to everything from the Kennedy assassination to Mrs. Appleworthy's treed cat. When a South Carolina paper speculated that Starrett was the man who had been seen harassing grade-school girls the day after Chrissy Blake escaped, Adams figured the coverage had hit bottom. (The man responsible was later arrested.)

But there were two cases that Adams couldn't get out of his head. Both involved young girls who had been assaulted by strangers who had come to the door in response to classified ads. In both cases, the men had forced the girls at gunpoint to "do things" and recorded the acts with a video camera. One girl lived near Columbia, South Carolina, and the other in Charleston. Maps of both cities were found in Starrett's locker.

Adams took pictures of some of the items recovered in the searches of Starrett's house and storage unit and drove to Columbia to show them to one of the victims, Tiffany Hart. The boots in the picture, she said, looked "roughly like" those her assailant had worn, and Starrett's notebooks "looked familiar," but she couldn't positively identify the gloves, the camera bag, or the gun in the pictures.

It wasn't much, but Adams refused to give up. He promised to return with photographs of Starrett as soon as he had them. Meanwhile, sheriff's offices all across Georgia and South Carolina continued to comb their files of unsolved cases.

17

Bringing books and magazines to Danny in jail made Gerry feel so useful. The first time she did it, they had to turn her back at the door because she had too many. They allowed him to keep only two books and three magazines at a time, and she could visit just twice a week. A maximum of four books and six magazines a week! "That is nothing to Danny," she scolded them when they stopped her. "He *devours* books and magazines. That's an afternoon's reading to him!"

He had been that way since he was a little boy: always wanting to know more, hungry for new knowledge. At nine or ten years old, he was reading almost a book a day. On weekdays, he would run into the kitchen when Gerry came home from work, climb up on the counter while she made dinner, and tell her all about his latest book. "Did you know, Mommy . . ." he would say before beginning, and then, when he was finished, breathless with excitement, "Isn't that interesting?" On weekends, he might disappear into his room and read for two days straight, coming out only for meals.

As for all she had seen in the papers and on TV about Danny reading pornography and detective magazines, she knew it wasn't true. In all his growing up, he *never* read pornography, and he certainly never had crime magazines, or whatever they wanted to call them, in his room. If anyone would have known about them, she would have. Danny couldn't keep secrets from her; she was his mother. She cleaned that room.

Danny looked unusually pale as they ushered him into place behind the glass partition. He had been transferred to the "psych" ward of the Columbia jail, and although the visiting facilities were better than at the Lexington jail, Gerry knew that the world behind the glass was considerably worse. Gone was the big day room filled with noise and camaraderie. Danny was now being kept in a tiny, windowless cell with only a bed and a light that never went out. Somehow—Gerry had no idea how—the authorities had gotten the idea that her son might be suicidal, so they left the light on twenty-four hours a day "for his own safety." Without a window, he had no way of knowing if it was day or night except by the schedule of his meals. That was the only thing that broke up his day—his week—except for his mother's visits.

"I brought you some books," she said brightly. "The Nixon biography you asked for and"—she held up *Presumed Innocent*— "I thought you might enjoy this."

Danny leaned toward the glass to look. His nose turned up. "I really don't want anything that's fiction," he said. "I really, at this time, I just want to know what's happening in the world."

Suddenly, the image of a world out there and Danny in here, alone, under a light that never went out, caught Gerry by the throat. She choked back tears with a rush of words. "Danny, I don't know how you're doing it. I just don't know how you're doing it with no one to talk to. Because I have a lot of friends. I am fortunate to have a lot of friends. I love people, I really do. So for me to be in a place . . . I think the light being on all the time wouldn't bother me nearly as much as not being able to have people to talk to. That would be the most cruel punishment they could give me. How do you do it?"

"But, Mom," said Danny, "you forget. I get a lot of visitors. I get some of the greatest visitors in the world in here."

Gerry felt a cold wave of dread. She knew he was alone in his cell, segregated from the other prisoners. She knew that his only visitors were his family. What was he talking about? Had the days of loneliness and confinement driven him crazy? "What?" she stammered. "What are you talking about?"

"You don't get it, Mom. I sit down with Plato and Socrates. I get to talk with them. I have great visitors here with me all the time." Slowly the dread began to drain away. He was talking about the books she had brought the previous week, a book of quotations and an anthology of western philosophy. (She was always in awe of his erudition.) He was making a joke. Wasn't it just like Danny to make a joke to lift her spirits, to help *her* deal with what he was going through?

But that's the way he always was. Whenever she had a problem, Danny was always the first to help. The time she had been thinking about changing jobs, Danny was the one who listened. Not Richard. Danny listened to her complaints, gave her as much time as it took, never looked at his watch—brainstorming and planning until everything was figured out and she felt better. Even after he went off to California and married Heather and had a family of his own, Danny was still the one who cared.

When she had gained all that weight, Danny was the one who helped her lose it. If he saw her cheating with a bowl of ice cream or a bag of potato chips, he would wag his finger lovingly and remind her of all the terrible things that bad nutrition would do to her. He discouraged her from having wine with her meals. "You don't want to develop a need for it," he warned softly. And when business worries had her wound up, he was the one who encouraged her to take long walks to relieve the stress. He would even come over and walk with her, urging her gently to go farther when she was ready to quit.

He treated his brother and sisters the same way, always trying to help them with their problems. Gerry thought of something her daughter Helen had said on the way back from the first visit: "Danny's always been the hero of our family."

Gerry looked through the tinted glass at her son. Never in his life had he ever given her a single reason not to love him: never in trouble at school, never on drugs, never without a job, never without a kind word or a generous act or an eagerness to help.

He's still the same Danny, she thought. Still the same hero he's always been. What else could she do but love him?

18

"That's him, that's him right there," cried Tiffany Hart pointing at Photograph No. 3 of the five photos Mike Adams had laid out on the table in front of her.

Photograph No. 3 was of Danny Starrett.

As she signed her name, the date, and the time below Photograph No. 3, her eyes were drawn to the face in the picture: the sandy blond hair, the blue eyes, the very fair skin. The last time she had seen that face was in June 1988, seven months before, when the man had appeared at her door in response to an ad: "Dining set for sale, $150." He looked only three or four years older than she. She was twenty-one. He wore cowboy boots with inch-and-a-half heels, and a long-sleeved, shiny polyester shirt buttoned at the cuffs.

He walked in carrying a nylon camera bag. "It has a lot of equipment in it," he explained. "I don't want to leave it in the parking lot." She didn't think anything of it at the time.

He looked at the wicker dining set. "I really like it," he said, "but I'll need someone to help me carry it to my truck. Is there anyone around?"

"My husband will be home in a few hours," Tiffany answered.

He asked to use the phone. She said okay. When he came back a few seconds later, he was pointing a gun at her, a gray revolver with a wooden handle. "This is a stickup," he said. "I want your money."

"I don't have any," she said.

To her surprise, that didn't seem to bother him. He ordered her into the bedroom and told her to sit on the edge of the bed. He produced a set of handcuffs and cuffed her hands behind her back. He seemed to know what he was doing.

"Get down on your knees," he ordered, pointing at a spot next to the bed. "I want a blow job."

When Tiffany refused, the man stuck the gun in her face and said, "You'll do what I say if you don't want to get hurt."

She knelt down where he said. The man removed her glasses and set them on the dresser. He pulled her shirt up, exposing her breasts. She wasn't wearing a bra. He fondled her breasts.

The man then took a video camera from the canvas bag and set it on the dresser. He moved her stuffed tiger and amplifier to make room for it. Then he took a white sheet, neatly folded, and set it on the corner of the bed opposite her. He put the gun next to it while he adjusted the angle of the camera.

Tiffany jumped up and lunged for the gun. He saw her. For a second, they both had their hands on it. Then he pushed her away. "Don't ever do that again," he yelled. "If you try that again, I'll hurt you."

He sat on the edge of the bed, unzipped his pants, pulled out his flaccid penis, and forced her down between his legs. It was small, circumcised, and soft. "I want a quick blow job," was all he said. "Then I'll go."

Tiffany started to get hysterical. "Please don't hurt me," she cried. "Please don't rape me."

"All I want is a blow job," he said.

"Why don't you go jerk off in a car?" she said.

That got him angry. He pushed the gun into her face again. "If you don't want to get hurt, you'll just do what I want. Do you understand?"

She did.

"More tongue," he ordered. "Use more tongue."

When it was hard, he stood up and pushed down on her head, forcing her to take it deeper. She began to choke. He pulled out and went to check the camera angle. Then he returned and forced it on her again. "Don't spit it out," he warned, "or I'll have to hurt you."

But it was no use. As soon as he started to come, she started to choke. "Swallow it," he ordered. "Swallow it!"

The last time she had seen the man in Photograph No. 3, she was looking up from the floor of her closet, hog-tied and weeping, and he was standing over her. His last words: "Now, isn't that better, now that we're all done?"

19

"That's him! That's the man!" Tammy Cranford screamed as she ran to her father with the newspaper clutched in her hand. She threw it down on the table in front of him and pointed with her delicate hand at the picture of Richard Daniel Starrett on the front page. "That's the man, Daddy! That's the man that did it!"

"It" had happened more than a year before, around Christmastime 1987, when Tammy Cranford was a blooming fourteen-year-old. A man had come to the door and asked to see the couch that her father had advertised for sale.

Tammy thought he seemed like a nice man: young and handsome and well dressed. His cologne smelled good. Only the mirrored sunglasses bothered her—she couldn't see his eyes.

"I've come to see the couch," he said. He had a boy's voice.

"Go around to the garage," Tammy told him. "I'll meet you there."

She opened the garage door and let him in.

"Can I use your phone?" the man asked.

Tammy hesitated.

"If you don't let me in the house, I'll hurt you," he said.

As soon as he was inside, he took the phone off the hook. Then he told her, "Come upstairs with me."

They went to her bedroom, where the man pulled down his pants and forced his penis into her mouth. "Suck it," he instructed. "Suck it. And when something comes out, swallow it." Tammy didn't know what he meant, but she tried to do what he wanted. She didn't want him to hurt her.

When he was done, he told her, "Stay in your bedroom and don't tell anyone about this or I'll come back and hurt someone."

When Tammy's parents came home, she told them. They rushed her to the emergency room. The police dusted for prints and searched the neighborhood but found nothing. In the year since, Tammy had managed to put the experience behind her, like a bad dream, expecting—hoping—never to see that face again.

That face!

20

"Yes, ma'am, that's the man."

"Are you sure, Susie?"

Susannah Hansen focused her eyes on the pictures spread out in front of her and studied them with all the intensity of a thirteen-year-old girl. "Yes, ma'am, I'm sure," she said, pointing her tiny finger at the picture of Richard Daniel Starrett. "That's the man."

To Susie, it seemed forever since the man in the picture had come to her house in Irmo, South Carolina, and asked to see the freezer that her mother was selling. In fact, it had been only six months. Susie had been twelve at the time.

Now that Susie identified the man in the picture, the nice policewoman wanted to know all about that day in June 1988 when Susie had first seen him.

"What did he say when he came to the door?"

"He said he wanted to buy the freezer," said Susie, a pretty girl with long, blond hair.

"So what did you do?"

"I guess I showed him where it was."

"Then what happened?"

"He wanted to know if he could go to the bathroom. So he went to the bathroom, and when he came back, he goes, 'Well, let me just give you my card,' and when he reached to get his card, he pulled out a gun, and then he asked me if I had any jewelry. I said no, and then he grabbed me by the arm and he goes, 'If you try to scream, I'm going to shoot you.'"

"You went outside with him?"

"Uh-huh, he had me by my wrist."

"What happened after he took you outside?"

"Then he took me to his car, and he pushed me inside, and he told me to get on the floorboard, and then he put a sheet over my head, and then he drove me for I don't know how long, two hours or so, I guess. Then he took me out after we got somewhere and handcuffed me."

"What did he do after he got you out of the car?"

"He brought me into the house, and he locked me in the closet."

"And when he brought you out of the closet, what did you see?"

"Just the mattress. And, uh, he had a camera."

"And what did he do then?"

"He pushed me on the mattress, and I was screaming and every-thing, so then he put a little ball in my mouth."

"Did you still have your clothes on?"

"Uh-huh, and so, uh"—she looked away, down at her shoes, black patent pumps, Sunday shoes, and began to stutter—"and I, uh, I . . ."

"Would it help if I asked you some questions?"

Softly, "Uh-huh."

"Okay." She gently put her hands on the girl's knees. "Did he kiss you?"

Down at her shoes. "Uh-uh."

"Did he take your clothes off?"

More softly. "Uh-huh."

"Did you say yes?"

The reply was barely audible. "Yeah."

"Did he have to un-handcuff you to take your clothes off?"

"Yeah, he took the handcuffs off, and then he put them back on."

The policewoman thought she saw an opening. "Did he take your shirt off before he took your pants off?"

As if her head were on a string and someone had yanked it from be-low, Susie's eyes fell to her shoes again and her voice collapsed to a whisper. "Uh-huh."

"Did he take off any other clothing other than your shirt and pants?"

In a tiny voice: "My bra."

"Did he leave your panties on?"

No discernible response, just a low, involuntary, "Mmmmm."

"Is that a yes or a no, Susie?"

Tinier still. "Yes, ma'am."

"Can you tell me what happened after that?"

No response.

"Did he ever remove your panties?"

No response.

"Did he put his hand in your underwear?"

No response.

"Did he kiss you after that?"

No response.

"Did he touch you at all?"

After a long pause, from some distant place, "Uh-huh."

"Where did he touch you?"

No response.

"Did he touch your breasts?"

From the distant place again, "Uh-huh."

The policewoman retreated. "Did he take any photographs?"

Susie attacked the new subject with a flash of enthusiasm and relief. "Just one," she announced proudly, "and then he said he was fed up."

"Why was he fed up?"

Proudly, "Because I fought him."

"Did you fight him hard?"

"Yeah, I was screaming and everything. Whenever he was in the room, I was screaming. He put his knees on my arms, and I screamed because it hurt, and he goes, 'Well, you're just going to have to do what I say.' And he got mad, and whenever I would scream louder, he would push the pillow in my face."

"Until finally he said he was fed up?"

"Yeah, he was too tired and he gave up."

"So what did he do after he gave up?"

"He put me back in the closet. He put the sheet back on me, and I was still handcuffed, too. And then, after about an hour, I guess, he took me out and took me to the car again, and he put me back down on the floorboard."

"Okay, Susie. Did anything unusual happen in the car?"

Suddenly, without warning, the door slammed shut again. Susie put her head down and lowered her voice to a tiny, frail whisper. "Uh-huh."

"Do you want to tell me what that was?"

No response. She didn't.

"While he was driving, did he try to touch you?"

No response.

"Can you tell me what happened?"

No response.

"Did he ask you to do something," the policewoman gently persisted, "or tell you to do something to him?"

Her prodding coaxed a whisper out of hiding. "Uh-huh," said Susie. "Yes."

"Was it anything sexual?"

After a long silence, "Yes, I guess."

"Tell me what was it that he told you to do."

No response.

"Did he unzip his pants?"

"Uh-huh."

"Did he expose his"—the policewoman gestured between her legs—"genital area?"

Susie understood. "Uh-huh."

"Did he have you touch his penis?"

"Uh-huh."

"He did?"

"Yes."

"How?"

No response.

"With your hand?"

"No."

"With your mouth?"

"Yes."

"Was he real forceful? Did he pull your head down, or did he just tell you to do it?"

"He told me—" Susie began, but then reconsidered. "He pushed my head down."

"Did he say anything while he was doing this?"

"He goes, 'Well, if you don't do it, I'm going to take you back.' " She raised her voice for the first time, reliving the moment. "He was going to take me back to his house. He was real angry when he said it."

"Did he at any time grab you and force you over to put your mouth on him?"

"He grabbed my head, pushed it over."

"Did you put your mouth on his penis?"

Susie, withdrawing, said, "I told him I wouldn't do it and so, you know . . . but he made me."

"This is probably going to be a real difficult question for you to answer. Was this man . . . when he unzipped his pants, was he aroused? I mean, did he have an erection? Do you understand what I mean by that? Did he have an erection?"

Withdrawing. "I don't know."

"You don't know if he had an erection?"

"No."

"If you don't, I'll explain it."

No response.

The policewoman tried to bring her back. "What I mean by an erection . . . was his penis, uh, hard, kind of stiff-looking?" But the vacant look on Susie's face stopped her short. "Is this making any sense to you?" she asked.

Susie looked down at her shoes and shook her head. "Uh-uh, no, ma'am," she said.

21

After local TV stations began flashing pictures of Daniel Starrett on the screen, Mike Adams couldn't keep up with the calls. Every day another call, another lead to follow up, another distraught or hysterical girl on the phone pouring out her story of torment and escape. Some—like the sixty-five-year-old lady in Aiken who claimed that the man on the TV had kidnapped her dog when he tried and failed to nab her—could be safely ignored. Others couldn't.

Like the eighteen-year-old girl from Augusta who said she had received a call in late December, only two months before, from a man who wanted to see some tables her mother was advertising for sale. "He wanted to know if my parents were home, and I said, 'They're busy.' And he said, 'Are you sure you're not alone?' And he kept on asking, 'Are you sure you're not alone?' " Then he hung up, and ten minutes later he was at her front door. She opened the wooden door but kept the storm door locked. She told him to come back when her parents were home, but he kept begging, "Can't you just let me in? I came all this way. Please let me in." But she said no and closed the door. It took him five minutes to leave.

She described the man who came to her door as "a short white guy," about five seven or five eight. Not heavy. He looked "kind of wimpy." Late twenties or early thirties, with a "red-looking complexion, kind of like a sunburn." His hair was brown with a touch of blond; he had brown eyes and weighed about 175 pounds. His hands were chubby but little, and he wore glasses with brown plastic rims.

The description matched Starrett. Adams wished all witnesses had such photographic memories.

The girl had been watching the local news at her grandmother's house when a story aired about the kidnapping of Chrissy Blake. "The minute the picture came on," she told Adams, "I kind of froze for a while, and then started crying, and then started screaming, and kind of went into hysterics because I recognized the picture as being the same man that came to my house."

To Adams, the girl's story rang true for another reason: The man had come to the door in response to a for-sale ad in *The Carolina Trader*. This was the "signature" element, common to all the assaults, that the police had tried, unsuccessfully, in the end—to keep out of the media coverage, to filter out crank calls.

This was no crank call.

And there were similar calls coming into law-enforcement offices all across Georgia and the Carolinas. In Charleston, police wanted to question Starrett about two unsolved sexual-assault cases in their area in the previous year, especially one in which a man had handcuffed a young woman and videotaped the event. In North Carolina, police were looking into the possibility that Starrett was linked to the rape of a Brunswick County woman south of Wilmington. And in Georgia, the bizarre facts surrounding two unsolved sexual assaults in the Atlanta area had, to Mike Adams, a suspicious familiarity about them. In one a man had tied a teenage girl up and forced her to give him oral sex. In the other, a man had tried to do the same thing but abandoned the assault when the victim exploded in a wailing siren of screams and sobs.

Within a week after Starrett's capture, Adams's department was telling the media that the Chrissy Blake case appeared to be "just the tip of the iceberg." "We definitely think we have a serial kidnapper and sexual assaulter on our hands," said one official. "Once this case unfolds, we think it will get a lot deeper than what it is now."

The search for more victims quickly spread to other states: Alabama and Texas, because Starrett had passed through them on his flight from arrest; California, because Starrett had once lived there; Tennessee and Florida, for no better reason than that they still had on their books several unsolved cases involving similar crimes against similar victims.

But the case that Mike Adams and every other law-enforcement officer in a 100-mile radius most wanted to crack was that of Jeannie McCrea.

Jean Taylor McCrea was the fifteen-year-old Columbia girl who had disappeared from her house in December 1988, the one who left the note:

> Mom and Dad,
> > I'm going away for a few days.
> > > Jean

Examining the note, police at first passed it off as another runaway, nothing more. Friends described her as "rebellious," "bad-tempered," and "depressed," a girl who "was mad at her folks a lot," according to one of them. From the parents' side came dark tales of "bad friends." To the police it was a familiar story: Teenager fights with parents over school, boyfriends, drugs, whatever; parents crack down; kid bolts. Sad but familiar.

That was more than two months ago. Not one of her friends had seen or heard from her since. She had missed a trip to New York City with the school chorus in January. "She was ecstatic about that trip," a distraught friend told a reporter. "That's all she could talk about." Despite leaving home without clothes, without money, and without her driver's license, she hadn't called her family. A nationwide bulletin featuring a school picture of Jeannie, smiling and pretty, and offering a thousand-dollar reward hadn't produced a single lead. That was *not* part of the runaway pattern. More and more, as the weeks went by without any break in the case and no word from Jeannie, police began to fear the worst. Amid the flood of reports, both confirmed and unconfirmed, from victims both real and imagined, undammed by the arrest of Daniel Starrett, an official in Irmo reminded the press, "We've got to keep in mind we've still got a lady missing. We don't know if it's connected to Starrett."

To find out if it was, an investigator from the Charleston police department traveled to the Lexington County Jail to speak with Daniel Starrett. He wasted no time with formalities. After introducing himself, he asked, "Where is Jeannie McCrea?"

Starrett didn't blink. "I don't know any Jeannie McCrea," he replied.

22

Behind the perfectly spherical bushes of the neat, brick ranch house at 207 Marty Drive, Gerry Starrett assembled her family for another meeting and prayer. They all had seen the articles in the *Augusta Chronicle*, daily front-page articles detailing the horror: the latest victim to come forward with her story about their Danny; the latest condemnation from some law-enforcement official; the latest analysis of their son's "disease" by some psychiatrist or expert who had never met him; the latest rumor about distant, ever more unspeakable crimes.

"It's like a nightmare that you never wake up from," Richard was saying. "Every morning you wake up knowing that it's going to be the same as it was yesterday, that nothing has changed, that it's always going to be like this. You're in hell, and you're always going to be there."

Gerry paced the floor of her immaculate living room, tastefully decorated in blue and white, as she listened to her husband's angry voice. He had never been one to show any emotion other than anger, and that only rarely. Now, it seemed, hardly a day passed without an outburst like this one. Every once in a while she stopped at the cabinet containing her most prized possession, a collection of unicorns—"an animal that never existed but should have," she explained to visitors—and adjusted one of the little porcelain figures.

Gerry didn't think it was fair that so many people—the police, the media, the public—were already judging Danny. "They're coming to lots of conclusions and making predictions without really knowing anything about Danny," she said, "and nobody knows what really happened!" She was his mother, and even she didn't know what really happened. "We don't know the whys and the wherefores," she told her family, gathered on the sofa and chairs around the coffee table with the Living Bible, Chinese figurine, and arrangement of dried flowers on it. "And we've known Danny all these years."

"Why doesn't anyone wait for the facts?" Helen complained.

"No one wants to hear the facts," Gerry answered, struggling not to feel anger. "Probably because the whole thing frightens them. It frightens people to hear that you could be leading such a normal life and have such a bright future and then have your life explode in your face. Or have it happen to someone you love. That is frightening to anyone. If they believe what his family is telling them about Danny as we know him, they have to face the possibility that this could happen to *them*. And that is just too unnerving."

Finally, Gerry knew there was only one way to quell the anger. They would pray. At her unspoken signal, the family formed a circle, bent down on their knees, and joined hands.

"Dear Lord," Gerry began, "help us to judge people by who they are and what they do, not by what other people say about them. We have all had the experience of being warned about somebody in a negative way.

The people who say these things mean well. They are not malicious. They may be telling us these things because they are trying to protect us or enlighten us. So we should not blame them for trying to warn us. It means they care about us.

"But we also should not believe them blindly. We should not be willing to accept someone else's stories or ideas about another person. Help us to expect the best from people, not the worst. Because then we will get the best from them."

After addressing the media, Gerry had a few closing words for the police. "We pray that there are people out there who are truly interested in knowing the whys and wherefores as much as we are. And we pray that a few of those people are in positions somewhere that they can find out what really happened. We ask this not just for *our* peace of mind, but for all those who have suffered through similar trials, all those who have been trapped by ugly rumors and vicious lies and are struggling to understand why this is happening to them and their loved ones. For all of them, as well as for us, so that we might prevent this from happening to someone else somewhere else, please, God, help us to understand the truth."

23

"You want the truth?" said Danny Starrett. "I'll give you the truth."

He was talking to Detective Bill Galardi of the Lexington County Sheriff's Department and SLED agent David Caldwell. In fact, Starrett had been talking to the same two investigators almost from the moment of his arrest in Texas.

It was all they could do to keep him from talking before Galardi read him his rights. They laid a yellow legal pad in front of him listing the names and phone numbers of attorneys and told him that at any time he could stop the questioning and call any of the listed lawyers— or any other lawyer. But he never did. The closest he ever came was when he said, "At some point I might want to talk to an attorney," but then added whimsically, "I don't think I want one just yet."

"Let us know when you do," a puzzled Galardi advised him.

A few days later, at the jail in Lexington County, Starrett finally did agree to see Henderson Johnson. "Mr. Starrett," Johnson told him, "whether or not you hire me to get into this case, you really need to keep mum. You don't have to talk to anybody, and nothing is going to happen to you if you refuse to talk."

But Starrett didn't seem to hear him. "No," he said blankly, "I want to tell them everything."

And that's exactly what he did—in a little room downstairs in the sheriff's offices next to the jail—starting with Chrissy Blake.

"I wanted to be nice to her," he began in a distant, disembodied voice that floated above their questions rather than responding to them. "I even bought her two kinds of ice cream. I respected her because she was a good person—also because I respected her virginity. I was concerned about her because she was sick and kept throwing up. I tried to get her to eat, but I think she may have caught a virus of some kind. So I gave her fresh fruit, an orange, and vitamins."

"How much oral sex was involved with Chrissy?" Galardi demanded.

"I don't know," Danny responded from the haze. "Even once was bad enough. I feel terrible, I mean, I keep thinking what I would feel like if someone did something like this to my daughter." Then he asked a strange question: "Can you stop people like me?"

Losing patience, Galardi answered in the hardest tone he could muster, "If we have the evidence."

For a moment, the cloud around Starrett seemed to lift. "You already have all the evidence you need," he said. "You don't need anything more."

It took Galardi and Caldwell a minute to realize he was talking about the videotapes.

"You have it all," Danny repeated, lost again. "I'm dead."

"Well, just for the record," Galardi pressed, "why don't you tell us your version of how it happened? How did you pick Chrissy Blake?"

Starrett obliged them in a tone that left no doubt as to who was doing whom a favor. "I got the want ads from the *Carolina Trader* and made calls from pay phones. I was looking for someone who sounded like a young woman in her teens or early twenties. I always looked for items for sale that would give me an excuse to get inside the house. When I got to Chrissy's, she just let me walk in. I could not believe that, in this day and time, people would just let me right in, but I was always dressed respectably. I knew appearances counted.

"Chrissy attempted to make a phone call. She said she had to call somebody, but I took the phone away and pulled out my gun and told her that it was a stickup. The gun was not loaded. I never kept it loaded, but I kept the bullets in my pocket. If someone came, I guess I would have run away. Sometimes I thought that by having the bullets I could commit suicide if I was caught. But I don't believe I could ever kill myself.

"I told Chrissy that this was a kidnapping for ransom and that if she did as I told her she would not get hurt. I told her to lay in the backseat and cover her face with a blanket. I told her a ridiculous story about working for an insurance company and knowing about ransom. I can't believe that anyone would believe a story like that. This was the same M.O. I had used other times."

"Other times?" The sudden turn caught Galardi and Caldwell off guard. "How many 'other times'?"

"There have been a total of five," Starrett obliged, "but only three abductions."

The detectives quickly turned to fresh pages in their notebooks and began scribbling as Danny continued his account without prompting: "Everything began in 1987, during the Christmas holidays," he explained. "The first girl was the one from the north Columbia area who was returned to her home, then the girl in north Atlanta, then the one in Charleston, then the one in south Atlanta, and finally Chrissy Blake."

The breadth of the admission temporarily took the detectives' breath away. Teams of investigators from a half-dozen agencies, state and federal, were working around the clock to connect Starrett to these (and other) crimes. Now Starrett had blithely beaten them all to the punch. Galardi and Caldwell didn't know where to begin.

So Danny began for them. "The girl in Charleston didn't want to do anything," he said, with a strange, even touching, melancholy in his voice. "I don't know her name."

"Did you know how old the Hansen girl was?" Galardi asked, pointedly providing the name.

Starrett didn't flinch. "I'd guess about fifteen," he said distractedly. "She was a fair-size girl." Both detectives knew she had been, in fact, twelve at the time of the assault, but they refrained from correcting him. "I made only three calls to get in touch with her. I normally made at least a hundred calls before I found one that sounded right. I told her to do what I said and she would not get hurt."

"Was there any oral sex?" Caldwell pressed.

"I tried to talk her into oral sex, but she wouldn't do it." The sense of rejection again. "When we were in the car, I tried to make her do it, but she wouldn't do anything. At one point I did pull off her shirt and told her I wanted her to do something, but she just kept crying."

"So what did you do with her?"

"I took her to the house. She was the first one I ever took back to my house. I put a ball in her mouth to quiet her, and then I locked her in the closet."

"How long was she at your house?"

"About an hour, maybe an hour and a half. I also tried to do oral sex in the car on the way back to her house, but she wouldn't do it. I dropped her off near where she lived. No harm done." He smiled at the detectives—a mirthless grin, like a reflex. If it had been crooked, lopsided even a little bit, it would have seemed grotesque. But it was perfectly even and symmetrical and unremarkable and chilling.

"Why did you choose the Lexington County area?" Galardi wanted to know.

"Because it was in another state, another town, far enough away but easy to reach on the interstate."

"Did you check out places before you made contact with the victims?"

"It varied. Sometimes I would just go right in."

"How did you explain being away from work during the times when you committed the crimes?"

Starrett shrugged. "I'd call in sick."

"What about your wife?"

"I sent my wife and child to California." His eyes glazed over again. "I have a loving wife—a kind and gentle woman—and a good job. I'm making $38,000 a year." The two detectives noted his use of the present tense. "Of course, we got caught up in the credit-card syndrome, like a lot of other young couples." Of all the acts he had confessed, his tone suggested he thought this was the most damnable.

Galardi asked if Starrett had made videotapes of any victims other than Chrissy Blake.

"Yes," Starrett teased. "But all those other tapes were destroyed."

Galardi was skeptical. "What do you mean, 'destroyed'?"

Starrett equivocated. "Well, I presume destroyed. I threw them in a Dumpster off I-20 in Alabama when I headed west."

"So the other victims, like Hansen, were also on tape?"

Starrett clearly didn't like hearing names. "I don't remember who-all was on the tapes."

"How many tapes and pictures were there?" Caldwell asked.

Starrett began to fidget. The questions were beginning to bother him. "A few," he said dismissively.

"Where did you keep them?"

"At a rental warehouse in Martinez." A few days earlier this would have been a revelation, but no longer. Police had already discovered and emptied out the storage locker.

By now Galardi was fed up with Starrett's attitude and convinced that behind his drifting attention he was hiding something. "Where did you take the girls from Columbia and Charleston?" he pressed, hoping to rile him.

"I didn't take them anywhere," Starrett snapped. "Everything was done there, at the house."

Galardi pressed his advantage. "Where did you take the Hansen girl?" The name again.

Starrett snapped again, "I've already talked about that."

Galardi snapped back, "Where is Jeannie McCrea?"

Starrett opened his mouth too quickly, but caught himself. "I don't know any Jeannie McCrea," he said with dead calm.

Galardi's patience had run out. *"Where is Jeannie McCrea?"* he demanded.

"She's gone," said Starrett.

The suddenness of the reversal startled Galardi. "Gone where?"

"I don't want to discuss it," said Starrett as his face screwed up in a prelude to a sob. "I never meant to hurt her. You know, it's funny, but I fell in love with her. I think she fell in love with me, too. But I'm not sure I know what love means anymore."

"You took her from her house! You held her captive!" Galardi couldn't hide his indignation.

The sobs were out in the open now. "For a few days, but then she wanted to stay," said Starrett. "Don't you see, she fell in love with me. We drank and played games. We partied. She smoked cigarettes. We went to the beach together. We fell in love!"

"Where is she?" Galardi roared.

But Starrett wasn't listening. "You know, I've always been an analytical, hardheaded kind of person. I mean, I have trouble believing in fate and karma and ESP and all that kind of stuff. But one night we were sitting around the fireplace and talking, and Jeannie said that she had always known that we were going to meet someday."

"Where is she?"

"You have to understand, Jeannie was kind of a loner. She didn't go with the crowd in high school. She didn't have a boyfriend."

"Where is she?"

Starrett looked them in the eye for the first time. "She's with God."

"You mean she's dead?"

Another sob. "I never meant for anyone to get hurt. After Jeannie was gone, I missed her so much. I wanted Jeannie back—I thought I could find another Jeannie, even though I knew it had to end sooner or later. I got the want ads and made calls looking for someone who sounded like Jeannie. Chrissy sounded like Jeannie, but she wasn't Jeannie."

"Where is she?"

"Chrissy wasn't Jeannie."

"Where is she?"

"In a safe place."

"Can you tell us where she is?"

"No. But I could take you there."

On the way to the car, Galardi and Caldwell could hear Starrett mumbling to himself, repeating over and over, "I loved Jeannie. I loved Jeannie. Chrissy wasn't Jeannie."

How many girls would he have gone through, Galardi wondered, looking for another Jeannie?

Starrett pointed to a break in the woods beside Mayer Road, just off Highway 176. Galardi realized that they weren't far from Stillman Drive in Irmo, the street where the McCreas lived. "She's down there," Starrett said. "There's a creek down that road. Her body is near the creek. It's a place where I thought she'd be happy. It's close to her home. You know, I've ridden by here several times since I left her here. I would have buried her, but some cars came by, and I had to leave."

The detectives searched along the streambed in the area Starrett had pointed to. Galardi was the first to see it: a large, shiny, shapeless object. As he approached, he realized it was a garbage bag. He tore a hole in it and saw a green blanket. Before going any further, he returned to the car and asked Starrett, "What was Jeannie wrapped in when you left her?"

"Garbage bags and a green blanket," he said.

An autopsy was performed on the body of Jeannie McCrea, and two bullets were removed from her chest. Oral and vaginal smears showed positive for semen. A ballistics test confirmed that the two bullets had been fired from the revolver found in Starrett's car after his arrest in Texas. On February 17, 1989, Columbia County Sheriff Otis Hensley announced that Daniel Richard Starrett would be charged with murder.

24

Gerry Starrett couldn't cry. The newspapers and television bristled with banner headlines and lead stories: "Lawmen Seek Man in Kidnapping," "Starrett Arrested Near Houston," "Starrett Faces Murder Count," "Lawmen Connect Starrett to Three More Sexual Assaults," "Starrett Charges Mount Up." And Gerry couldn't cry. They were calling her son, her Danny, a "serial kidnapper," a "brutal murderer," a "remorseless killer." But still she couldn't cry.

She couldn't eat, either. Every time she tried, she would lift the food halfway to her mouth and then . . . it just wouldn't go any farther. She couldn't make it. She couldn't make her hand bring the food any closer, no matter how long it had been since her last bite.

Again and again, she watched the videotapes of various family gatherings, videotapes of Christmases and birthdays and anniversaries. There was Danny opening presents, Danny blowing out candles on a cake, Danny hitting a badminton birdie. Danny with the energy just oozing out of him, Danny laughing and moving, making people feel good just to be around him. And she would want to laugh, but couldn't. Then want to cry, but couldn't. Then want to eat, but couldn't.

She went to Richard. "We have to talk," she said.

Without a word, Richard turned away, walked to his room, closed the door, and refused to come out.

She couldn't cry, she couldn't eat, she couldn't talk, and she didn't want to think.

All she could do was sit in the den, surrounded by her collection of self-help and self-improvement books, and watch ghostly images on the videotape flicker, again and again, through their pantomime of family life.

Finally a friend, a psychologist, came to visit. "The reason you can't eat is the same reason you can't cry," the friend told her. "You have all these emotions built up inside"—she made a fist against her stomach—"and you need to let them out. You need an emotional release." She went to the kitchen and mixed a glass of warm salt water. "Go into the bathroom and drink this," she told Gerry. (She wanted Richard to do the same so they could hold each other afterward, but Richard refused to come out of his room.)

Gerry did as she was told: drank the warm liquid, threw up violently, and, even before she could wipe herself off, erupted in sobs.

But within an hour she was back in front of the TV, watching the familiar images yet one more time, looking into her son's face every time it flickered onto the screen, looking, looking for something—she wasn't sure what—searching not just the face, but her "mother's memory" of that face and all the faces at all the ages that preceded it—for some sign, some clue, some hint of the horror to come.

Part Two

25

Was there something about his birth? Gerry Starrett strained to re-member. Danny had been full-term. A normal pregnancy. Except . . . There was that time, two weeks before he was due, when her water broke and she rushed to the hospital. The doctor feared she was in labor and kept her there all night before dismissing it as a false alarm and sending her home.

And Danny hadn't left her willingly; they had to tweeze him out with a big pair of forceps. Gerry could still remember her shock when she saw him for the first time: his head all black and purple with bruises from the nose up. Her first baby, Helen, had been premature but *perfect*. No bruises. Small, but perfectly formed: a beautiful, picture-perfect baby. Not Danny. But surely there were lots of forceps babies in the world, and they all didn't grow up and . . .

Had Danny been different from other babies? He certainly had been more difficult than any of her other children. Of course, Helen had spoiled her. Helen was such an easy baby; all she did was eat, sleep, and dirty her diapers. She practically took care of herself. Not Danny. Seemed as if he cried all the time, all day and all night. And went to the doctor. Gerry was constantly toting him in for checkups, especially for diarrhea. He never did get over that diarrhea. Drove his father crazy. But what could that mean?

And what about the time she had to rush him to the doctor in the middle of the night because he refused to drink anything? Danny be-came so dehydrated, the doctor wanted to check him into the hospital immediately. But Richard said no. They didn't have any medical insur-ance. They couldn't afford it. The doctor told her to force-feed Danny fluids—a mixture of orange juice and sugar water. She could remember mixing it, frantically, in the middle of the night: the orange liquid, the eyedropper, his resilient little lips and locked gums.

But how was she supposed to know that inadequate medical care might lead to something like *this?* There were lots of people who couldn't afford to take their babies to the hospital in every emergency—and all those babies didn't grow up and . . .

Was it the way she treated him? True, she had used baby-sitters more often than she would have liked. Richard was a student at Georgia Tech at the time, and she had to work to support him, so Danny was left with baby-sitters a lot. When he was only a week old, she had to turn him over to a twelve-year-old from across the street, Andrea Herter. And, yes, Danny did begin to act differently after that. Gerry's straining memory began to yield up vague, half-formed images: a stranger at her door, a distant neighbor in the apartment building where they lived. "Your baby was crying all day yesterday," the stranger was saying. "What are you doing to it?"

Gerry, guilty, apologetic, defensive. "I'm not home during the day. We have a baby-sitter."

Soon she herself began to notice that something was wrong. Danny developed a fierce diaper rash. And then the gradually dawning truth: The baby-sitter wasn't changing him. That was why he was crying all day. But now, almost thirty years later, other, darker possibilities grew in the cracks of those dim memories: Had Danny been abused?

What about Andrea's older brother, Fred? He baby-sat Danny, too. What about the maid, Agnes? She was often alone with Danny. And what about the neighbors, the Palmers? They were religious people, fanatics, really. They were always coming over to convert and save him. At the time, they seemed harmless enough, but . . . How could she think such a thing?

Besides, if Danny had been molested at an early age, wouldn't she have found out about it sooner? If not at the time, then later, when he was five, or six, or ten, or fifteen? If his problems really went back that far, wouldn't they have shown up before now? How could he have grown up the model child he was?

She never had to discipline him. He disciplined himself. Of her four children, he was the only one who kept his room neat. The others would drop things all over their bedrooms and never picked up after themselves. But not Danny. Danny had to have things neat. *More* than neat. If you opened a drawer, all his pencils would be in a box, all pointed in the same direction, all sharpened to the same length, and all the pens would be pointed in the other direction. It was the same way with everything: books, socks, underclothes, toys, shoes, you name it. Everything had its place, and if anyone moved anything, he would get terribly upset.

He was the same way about his appearance. Other boys ran around and played in the dirt and had to be dragged into the tub. But not Danny. He had to be immaculate all the time. He would go in and take four or five showers a day, so that when any of the other kids tried to take one, Gerry would hear screams from the bathroom: "There's no hot water!" Later, after Danny went off to Georgia Tech, she always knew when he was visiting. If she turned on the hot-water faucet and cold came out, she said to herself, "Danny's home."

She remembered the time when Danny was ten or eleven, and Richard sprayed him with a water hose. It was just a joke, poking fun at Danny's showering habits. But Danny wasn't amused. Furious, he packed himself a lunch and headed off, vowing never to come back. He got only as far as his tree fort down the road, where he spent the afternoon feeling sorry for himself—until he got hungry and came home. The memory of his anger made Gerry smile. "It's amazing how quickly your principles fly away," he had told her later, "when your stomach starts to growl."

Of course, he never drank or smoked or overate, and he had no patience for those who did. "Anyone can control their negative impulses," he would say. He didn't even have dressing on his salad. And he was punctual. You could count on Danny. If he said he'd be there at nine o'clock to pick you up, he was there. And Danny always answered you. He always looked you in the eye. That's why people trusted him.

26

Soon after his arrest, Richard Daniel Starrett was transferred from the Lexington County Jail to Columbia Correctional Institute, a grim prison dating from the dark age of penal design. At CCI, confined to the death-row cell block "for his own security," Danny sat down with a state-appointed psychiatrist and talked about his past. Later, he put some of his observations and memories into an "autobiographical sketch."

I am extremely obsessive-compulsive about order and neatness. Someone told me that if you've got all this chaos going on inside, it's much more important to have orderliness and control around you. I guess that makes sense. But I always had obsessive-compulsive tendencies. I would count things. I would count the squares in the panels in the windows, the tiles on the floor, all kinds of things.

I also "jumped over" things, mentally, with my eyes. I can remember when I was a child, sitting on the school bus, and I would become mesmerized by jumping over each shadow falling across the road, each shadow of a lamp post or a tree. I would go into a hypnotic trance as I stepped over each one in my mind. I'd do it all the way to school and all the way back home. I was a zombie. Later, when I learned to drive, I can remember "jumping over" tar-filled cracks in the road with my eyes as I drove. I would do these things without even thinking about them or being aware that I was doing them. As the habit intensified, it began to wear on my nerves.

It seemed to grow stronger over the years. At Georgia Tech, there was a main sidewalk going from the student building to the math or the science building. I'd find myself walking down that sidewalk, and I would try to step over the cracks in it. You've heard the old saying: Step on a crack, break your mother's back. That wasn't going through my mind, but I wanted to step over each step—and step perfectly in the center of each step.

That kind of thing has come and gone since I was a child. I knew it was obsessive-compulsive, and it irritated me. I didn't want to get caught up in it, but I had to do it.

27

Danny was a hyper child. Of course, when she was raising her brood, she realized, she didn't know what the word *hyperactive* meant. Kids were simply "unruly" or "discipline problems" or, in the most extreme cases, "holy terrors." Danny had been, at various times, all those things. He simply could not stay still. He was constantly moving: running, jumping, climbing, falling. She couldn't get him to sleep at night; she couldn't get him to stay quiet during the day. She had a memory of him at eight or nine, running through the house, covered with sweat, humming with nervous energy. Even in those few moments between explosions when he would sit down, his little foot never stopped twitching.

He had problems at school. Classes bored him. The teachers went at one pace and he went at another. He couldn't ask the questions he wanted to when he wanted to. That was why he never did particularly well in school. He was smart enough—smarter than almost everybody else in his class—but unchallenged. And bored. Gerry remembered one teacher's comment: "Danny could do better if he would just settle down and apply himself." But settling down was the last thing Danny Starrett could do. They didn't understand: He was *hyperactive.*

It was hard on Danny's siblings, too. He just couldn't leave them alone. He could not walk into a room with them without making a scene. He would tickle them, or "zap" them, or pick at them, taunt them, challenge them—anything to get their attention, anything to annoy them. And annoy them he did. If Gerry heard the kids fussing or screaming at one another, she could be sure Danny was at the center of the storm. He had to be refereed so often it became a family joke: Danny's pick-and-tease routine had landed him in trouble again.

But he was never mean. He never hit anyone. There was never any violence—any real violence. That's why the other kids never held his picking and teasing against him. Most of it was aimed at getting them to go outside and *do* something rather than sit around the house watching TV. First he'd ask, then he'd try to persuade, and only then would he start harassing them. And even then, Gerry remembered, the teasing was always in fun. He was never vicious the way some kids can be. In all his years of squabbling with Helen, for example, he never teased her about her weight.

That was so typically Danny, she thought; not a mean bone in his body.

28

My overly active sex drive seemed to go hand in hand with my overly active metabolism. I could never sit still, and according to my parents, it was much more than the normally exuberant energy of youth. I ran circles around other children, they said. I found most things boring, and nothing could hold my attention for very long. I was in constant need of action and stimulation, and as a result, I was forever getting into trouble and mischief. I would explode out of my room in a burst of uncontrollable energy, and until it was expended, I could not be stilled.

My mother claims that from what she has since learned about childhood behavioral problems, I must have suffered from hyperactivity. In fact, she asserts that I never grew out of it. Most of my family, friends, and coworkers would readily agree with her. Many of them characterize me as being "hyper" and are forever telling me to "slow down." I never like people telling me that. Although I've always been aware that I seem to have more energy than most, I feel it is simply the result of a naturally higher metabolism.

I've always had a passion for danger. As far back as I can remember, I loved to take risks—or, more accurately, I needed to take risks. I felt almost driven to it. In a world which I found frequently boring and terribly understimulat-

ing, I craved the feelings of exhilaration these acts gave me. Looking back, many of them strike me as having been foolishly risky. I could have easily ended up dead on numerous occasions. But then, I've had more than one person accuse me of having a "death wish."

As a child, one of my favorite pastimes was tree climbing, a common enough boyhood diversion. But in my case, merely climbing wasn't enough. I enjoyed going as high as I possibly could, finding limbs of barely sufficient size, and then leaping from one to another in death-defying style. If my mother had ever seen me doing this, I'm sure she would have passed out on the spot. I also enjoyed rock climbing, or rather, cliff climbing, whenever I was lucky enough to find an old rock quarry or such. I can't begin to count the number of times that I would find myself climbing by my fingertips to an extremely precarious position where one slip would have meant sudden death on the rocks far below.

I was always doing crazy stunts on my bike. I liked to jump my bike across ramps, farther and farther until eventually I crashed. I would ride my bike to the top of a hill; then I'd stand up on the seat, lift up one leg, and let go with one arm, and I'd go flying down the hill on one foot and one hand. Crazy stunts like that.

I recall another incident when a friend and I were out in a field playing with bows and arrows. I came up with another exciting idea. I began shooting the arrows straight up in the air and then dodging them as they came hurtling back down. My idea of a darts game was for two people to throw darts back and forth at each other while standing far apart. I found this much preferable to throwing them at stationary targets. I was forever trying to coax someone into going out into the yard and trying to hit another person with darts. I thought that was the greatest thing ever. My friends fled in terror.

Yet I could never seem to get enough of the feelings

these acts gave me. It sounds crazy, but it was almost as if I were addicted to my own adrenaline.

When I was old enough, I acquired a car and my risk taking quite naturally extended to that. I loved fast cars and fast driving. I guess, in this respect, I was no different than most boys, but merely driving fast and occasionally drag racing didn't exhaust all the possibilities for me. I also enjoyed lying, sitting, standing, and climbing all over the exterior of the car as someone drove it at high speed down the road.

One time, driving back from spring break in Daytona Beach to Georgia Tech, I told my friend who was driving that I needed to step outside for some fresh air. He said, "Go ahead, but I'm not stopping." I said, "Fine, no problem." So I rolled down the window, climbed out of the car, hooked one leg over the door and hung the rest of my body outside. I was drinking a beer and waving at people and we were flying down Interstate 75. If I'd taken one little bump, one little slip, I would have been bouncing down the highway at 70 mph. Just crazy things like that.

It was also while I was at Tech that I took up skydiving.

When I moved to California, I bought my first motorcycle. I had it for only a few months when I suffered my first accident, slamming into the side of a car that had pulled out onto the road after failing to see me. I flipped over the top and landed on the other side. My motorcycle was totaled, but somehow I escaped with only bumps and bruises. With the insurance money from the settlement, I purchased a much more powerful bike. It was a Honda Saber 700, shaft-driven and liquid-cooled. It had a top-end speed of 145 mph. I can't begin to describe the sensations that would flood through my mind as I went streaking down a deserted highway on a weekend morning at 145 mph. Sadly, I was forced to sell it to cover moving expenses when I went back to Georgia.

I remember as a child reading The Lord of the Flies. *It fascinated and intrigued me no end. Man, or rather, boy in a*

*state of nature. It reminded me of the summers I spent run-
ning wild and free. Sometimes I would lose track of time and
place and of myself. It was a feeling that both exhilarated and
terrified me. But then, those emotions are the story of my life.*

29

And then, Gerry remembered, something very strange happened. After
years of tearing through the house, unable to stay still even for a
minute, Danny disappeared into his room and began reading. *Reading,*
of all things!

Danny had been the only one of her kids who always had problems
with school. She could still remember that embarrassing moment when
his first-grade teacher called. "We can't promote Danny to the second
grade," she told Gerry. "He can't read well enough." And if that wasn't
bad enough, she went on to say, "I think it might be a good idea to take
your son to a psychologist." Imagine! Danny needing a psychologist.

But she took him. And after watching Danny play in a room full of
toys and giving him some intelligence tests, the psychologist concluded
that Danny was "a very, very bright boy. I can't see any good reason why
he shouldn't be able to read. Except . . . ."

"Except what?" Gerry demanded.

"How long has your son been stuttering?"

In fact, Gerry had first noticed Danny's stutter when he was three or
four. For a while, she just regarded it as another manifestation of his in-
ability to stand still. "If you'd just slow down when you talk," she would
tell him, "you could say what you want to say." Then one day he came
racing into the house while she was cleaning and began pouring out an
excited account of his latest adventure—and Gerry couldn't understand
a word he was saying. Irritated, she scolded him for babbling and sternly
instructed him to "just spit it out." Danny burst into tears. "Mommy," he
sobbed in frustration, "don't you know what I'm thinking?"

After that, Gerry realized that Danny really did have a problem; that it wasn't merely the result of a fast mind tripping over a slow tongue. Every time one of his sentences came flying down the track and jumped the rails, and his words started piling up like unhinged boxcars, she would grab him by the shoulders and say in the most comforting, nonaccusatory voice she could summon, "Just slow down."

The psychologist didn't think it was that simple. He suggested that Danny's reading problem might be related to his stuttering. He thought Danny was dyslexic—that he was reversing letters and numbers—and that was why he had trouble reading. Worse, he wanted Danny to wear a patch over one eye to correct the problem.

That was the last time Gerry and Danny saw a psychologist.

For the next few years, Danny did all right in school. As best Gerry could recall, the teacher promoted him to the second grade, and afterwards he made mostly Bs and Cs with an occasional A. Every time the report cards came out, he would get upset. His grades were always the worst in the family, and he felt they should be the best. So did Gerry. After all, he was her brightest. But she also knew that he could have made all As if he'd just applied himself.

When he was ten or eleven, Danny discovered books. He started disappearing into his room for whole days, even whole weekends, coming out only for meals, fighting with his mother when she wanted him to turn the light off at night. He read "like a crazy person," Gerry remembered. His shelves were crammed with books, his drawers filled with books, his floor covered with books. None of her other kids—no other kid that Gerry knew—had nearly as many books as Danny. And he was very possessive about them. When he was finished with a book, he wanted to keep it. He didn't like to loan his books to friends or family, and he didn't like anybody browsing through his library when he wasn't around. That's how much he loved books.

At first, he preferred stories about horses and dogs: *Misty, Sea Bright, The Black Stallion, Irish Red, The Call of the Wild.* His favorite authors were Jim Kjelgaard and Jack London. Then, like a lot of adolescent boys, his interests shifted to science fiction and fantasy, then to nonfiction science—the space program, astronomy—then to nonfiction in general. Gerry couldn't think of a topic that wasn't represented in Danny's library. In high school, he attacked the Bible with ferocity, reading it carefully, page by page, making notes, asking himself questions, and looking everywhere for answers. He loved magazines, too. He was constantly begging her for subscriptions to all kinds of magazines for Christmas and birthday presents—*Time, Newsweek, Omni, Reader's Digest, Life, Business Week*—everything he could get his hands on.

Well, not everything. Gerry had read in the newspapers about Danny's supposed appetite for pornography and detective magazines, and she didn't believe it. Danny had too much taste for that kind of thing. He referred to anything that wasn't up to his standard as "mind dribble." That was why he didn't watch much TV, and when he did, it was always PBS or *60 Minutes* or *20/20,* those kinds of shows. Never sitcoms or dramas. He liked news and debates, current events and politics. Those were the only things that really interested him.

30

When I was ten, I think, I made a very important discovery. I was riding my bike one morning when I came across an abandoned building and, being obsessively inquisitive, I went in to take a look around. In the corner of one room, I found a box full of adult magazines. Some of them were typical girlie magazines with which I was now familiar, but most were of an entirely new type which I had never seen before. They contained pictures of girls in various stages of undress and tied up in all sorts of imaginative ways. I really couldn't understand the point of all the ropes, chains, and tape, but in association with the nude and seminude girls, I found it all terribly exciting.

After spending the rest of the day looking through them, I took the box and hid it in a closet in another room. In the following months, I spent every free moment in that old building, looking at my secret treasure of magazines. The guilt I felt was tremendous, but it was no match for the strange and wonderful feelings which overwhelmed my innocent mind.

Shortly thereafter, I was at a friend's house and we were playing war with dart guns. I hid behind the bed in his parents' bedroom hoping to ambush him when he came by. As I lay there waiting, I noticed two books under the bed. Out of curiosity, I looked at them. One was called The Midnight Rapist. *I didn't even know what the word meant. The front cover showed a picture of a man in a ski mask climbing through a window. I can't recall the title of the other book, but on the cover was a picture of a girl and a dog. Because they were hidden under the bed, I figured they had to be naughty books and so later on that day, I slipped them out of the house to read, intending to put them back after I finished.*

I began with the one showing the girl and dog on the front cover. I loved stories about horses and dogs, and I couldn't possibly see how anyone might write a naughty book about dogs. I soon found out, however, after reading only a small portion and became sickened and threw it away in disgust. The second book proved to be almost, but not quite, as shocking as the first. It was about a young man who became infatuated with a girl living down the street. He tried to ask her out on several occasions, but she continually rebuffed him. One night, he put on a ski mask, crept down to her house, entered through an open window, and raped her.

The rest of the book recounted his further exploits as he began to engage in these midnight forays on a regular basis. I was overwhelmed by conflicting emotions of excitement, fear, and guilt as I read this book. It was similar to the feelings I experienced when looking at the bondage magazines earlier, the Playboys *a few years before that, and the times I played doctor with neighborhood girls.*

Later, when I moved into my first apartment, I bought a VCR. That was a big mistake.

31

Was Danny different? Gerry Starrett asked herself the same question again and again, and the answer kept coming back the same: Yes, but in a good way.

Like the way he could draw.

Danny started drawing early. As early as three, he was drawing animals that she could recognize. None of the other kids in their neighborhood could do that. She remembered him coming to her at three, all blond hair and dirty hands, tugging at her skirt and begging her, "Draw something, Mommy. Draw a pig." And when she did, he'd tell her that it didn't look like a pig and beg her, "Draw something else, Mommy. Draw a cow. Please, Mommy." And then, when she did that, he'd complain in a puzzled voice, not only that the cow didn't look like a cow, but that the cow and the pig looked alike. "Everything you draw looks the same, Mommy," he would whine. And, of course, it was true. She didn't know how to draw.

But Danny did. For a while, crayons and pencils were his favorite toys. He started off drawing houses and spaceships, trees and animals, clowns and Santa Claus; then moved on to more adolescent male subject matter: castles, tanks, and jet fighters. Gerry knew almost immediately that he had real talent. She saw what the other kids in the neighborhood, older kids, were doing, and nothing was as good as what her son was doing. To encourage him, she bought him a tin of watercolors. If he was so good at drawing, she thought, just imagine how good he might be with paints. There wasn't anybody to show him what to do. Neither she nor Richard nor anyone else in their families had ever painted. For heaven's sake, they were all *farmers*. She just handed him the box of paints and hoped for the best.

Sure enough, almost immediately, he started mixing paints as though he knew what he was doing, stirring little drops of water onto his pallet of colors until he had just the right tint at just the right consistency. Before long, he was painting whole scenes. The things he did were wonderful—or at least Gerry thought so. She showed them to everyone who came to the house. This was something to be proud of, and she knew it. No other child his age could mix colors and paint pictures the way Danny could.

Gerry remembered one in particular, a scene of what Danny described as an "Easter Egg Factory." It was a cutaway view of a vast underground city, like an ant farm, containing many chambers where multicolored eggs, jellybeans, candy eggs, and all the other traditional Easter basket goodies were manufactured and then transported up to ground level, where the Easter Bunny could pick them up and deliver them on Easter morning. When Danny came running to her with this picture in his hand, Gerry was amazed. It was so inventive, so panoramic, so colorful and charming.

Yes, Danny was different: wonderfully different.

32

I had been doing a lot of childish drawings. I remember one in particular of Easter bunnies and an underground city where all the stuff for the Easter baskets was made. It had underground vaults and conveyor belts and escalators and all that kind of thing.

But there were some other drawings that I had completely forgotten about until I sat down to record the events of my life, and it troubled me so much to recall them I almost didn't even put them down. In fact, they are so terribly bizarre that I hesitate to even mention them now.

I recall that for a brief period of time, a few months per-

haps, when I was seven or eight, I became obsessed with drawing pictures depicting devices for trapping girls, who would then be killed, chopped up, packaged, and sold as meat. Every single phase of this "process" was rendered in detail on paper. These were the same kind of factories as my Easter bunny drawings, with underground vaults, conveyor belts, escalators, and the most important thing about these drawings, like the Easter egg factory, was that it actually worked, chopping up girls and making them into dog food. Not humans in general, only girls.

I can't explain it. I don't know where it came from. It was so completely out of keeping with my character and my fantasy life both in childhood and as I got older. It was completely alien to me, a piece of the puzzle that doesn't fit. It's so sadistic, it's almost beyond words. Especially when you picture a seven-year-old boy drawing this stuff. If you were to tell that to a psychologist, he would say "classical sadistic tendencies," but some of the other classical sadistic tendencies in a child, like tormenting animals, are just the opposite of me. I love animals.

Where such a warped idea came from at such a young innocent age, I do not know. But it troubles me greatly to realize that I did have it. What does it mean? Is it possible that God would allow the soul of a child to become so distorted or possessed? Or was I perhaps born this way? Was I doomed from the very beginning?

33

Poor Danny, thought Gerry. His whole life seemed hexed. For all his brightness and energy, bad luck had dogged him since the day he was born. She remembered that awful day in 1962 or '63, when Danny was only two or three. Richard had to go to the store, and Danny begged to go with him. He was so proud to be riding in the front seat of that 1957 Ford Fairlane next to his father, so excited about the ice-cream cone his dad would buy him when they got there.

He never did get that ice-cream cone. Halfway to the store, the passenger's side door flew open on a turn, and Danny tumbled out, head first, onto the street. Richard stopped the car, picked Danny up, and rushed him home, sobbing. Gerry would never forget the sight of her husband standing in the doorway of their little student apartment with Danny in his arms, a big, ugly knot already rising on the boy's forehead. She didn't know what to do. This was the first time one of her children had been seriously hurt. Her first instinct was to rush him to the hospital. But Richard said no. "He looks sleepy," he said, "and it's nap time. Let's just put him to bed."

Gerry protested as much as she dared, but Richard was firm. "Just let him go to sleep," he said. "He'll be fine when he wakes up." When Gerry still resisted, Richard gave her one of his lectures. "People go to doctors too much," he pronounced. "Back in Wyoming, when I was a boy, the only time you went to the doctor was when your arm was in two pieces. If you got thrown off a horse or something and got all banged up, you just went home and went to bed. You just lived through it."

Miserable and fearful, she went along and put Danny to bed. She didn't sleep at all that night. But every time she checked on him, he seemed to be sleeping soundly. The next morning, however, when she went to his room, she couldn't wake him up. Oh God, she could still feel the panic in her throat as she shook his little body and begged him to wake up. Finally, he opened his eyes and Gerry burst into tears. But the rest of the day, he was groggy and disoriented, and he kept going over to the sofa to lie down, or just curling up on the floor wherever he was and falling asleep. By the next day the entire top of his head, from the nose up, had turned into one big, ugly, multicolored bruise that didn't go away for weeks.

The memory of it filled Gerry with remorse and guilt. She should have taken him to the hospital as soon as Richard showed up at the door. She knew it then and she was only surer of it all these years later. She should have put her foot down.

Was that it? she wondered. Was it as simple as that? If she had rushed Danny to the hospital twenty-five years ago, could she have avoided everything that had happened? But how could she have known?

She didn't make the same mistake the next time, though.

It was only a few years later. They had moved to a brand-new apartment building with all electric appliances—so new that the construction crews were still working when the Starretts arrived. The memory brought back an image of Danny at six, pulling his little four-wheeled wagon. Somehow he persuaded her to make lots of sandwiches, cookies, iced tea, and Kool-Aid, all of which he loaded into his wagon and took to sell to the construction workers at lunchtime. After he reimbursed her for the supplies, he made a nice little profit for himself. He was always such an enterprising soul.

Once again, she wasn't there when it happened. Once again, Richard came rushing back to the apartment with Danny in his arms, unconscious this time. He had been playing on the slide, Richard explained, hanging upside down by his ankles from the top, when he fell, head first onto the asphalt nine feet below. It wasn't enough for Danny just to get to the top and slide down like the other kids, thought Gerry. Oh, no. He had to climb around and hang like a monkey. That's the way it always was with Danny.

This time Gerry didn't wait for an argument from Richard before rushing Danny to the hospital. She stayed at his bedside the rest of the day and night as Danny lapsed in and out of consciousness. The doctors performed some tests and observed him for a few days before determining that there was no serious damage. "Kids are resilient," was the line Gerry remembered hearing when they released him.

Oh, God, were they wrong!

Less than a year later, Danny started falling down a lot. Gerry didn't think anything of it at first. It just seemed like his own fault. He was always running places; he never just walked, like a normal kid. All of this falling down just looked like one more way to irritate her, one more way to get attention. Besides, the doctors had pronounced him okay, right? So she just fussed at him and told him to *slow down*.

Then one day she and Danny went to the mall together, and suddenly, in the middle of a crowd, Danny collapsed in front of her. One leg slipped out from under him and he fell flat on his face. It happened so abruptly she almost tripped over him. Everybody stopped and stared. Now she wasn't just irritated—she was mad. She grabbed his arm and jerked him up and started scolding him. "I'm just not going to allow this anymore!" she yelled. "I'm going to spank you real good if you don't stop this!"

Danny burst into tears. "I can't help it!" he cried over and over. "First my head hurts, and I get dizzy, and then my leg falls down!"

That was the beginning of the nightmare. Over the next few years, they took him from doctor to doctor for test after test. They discovered that his left foot wasn't growing at the same rate as his right one, and one leg was already shorter than the other. Danny started favoring one leg when he climbed stairs, and they had to buy a different size shoe for each foot. And the headaches and dizziness continued.

Then a doctor in West Virginia scared Gerry to death. "Danny needs to be admitted to the hospital immediately," he told her. "I think what's going on is very serious, and we need to look at it right away. I think we're dealing with a brain tumor."

The tests they did were more like torture: sticking needles in his head and shooting air into his spine. She spent many nights in tears thinking about the pain Danny was enduring. And when she saw the X rays, huge needles sticking in the base of his little skull, into his very brain, she felt a knot in her stomach that made her nauseous. He was only seven! He barely understood what was happening to him. And what did they learn from all that pain? Almost nothing. They did discover that Danny exhibited something called the Babinski reflex, which, as far as Gerry could tell, meant that his toes curled the wrong way when the doctor drew a stick across the bottom of his foot. The doctor told them that a patient with the Babinski reflex had "a high probability of a malignant tumor in the head."

They couldn't find it, though. Even after that hellish battery of tests, they couldn't find anything. They couldn't explain why he was having headaches or falling down. "It's probably a result of the concussion," they said, "but we don't see a tumor. That's not to say it isn't there. We just can't find it."

"Is it going to get worse?" Gerry asked.

"We can't really say. There's really nothing to do but watch him."

Gerry did just that. As Danny grew up, she watched the bad leg grow stronger and stronger, until the tendency to collapse disappeared. The bad leg didn't grow as fast as the other one and the difference in size was still obvious, but in time Gerry and the rest of the family got used to the limp. Even Danny got used to it and somehow trained the weaker leg not to buckle underneath him.

The headaches, however, didn't go away. In fact, they got worse, as did the spells of dizziness that accompanied them. Danny became unusually sensitive to light. If Gerry went into his room and turned on the lamp, he would bolt awake, no matter how careful she was not to make any noise. With the slightest light he couldn't go back to sleep. She also noticed that his eyes were often red, and that just wasn't the case with the other kids.

He tried various medicines, but nothing seemed to work. It was just something they all learned to live with. From time to time, the dizziness would get so bad he would black out for short periods. Sometimes the headaches would be terrible every day for two weeks and then, inexplicably, go away for several months. And then, when it seemed like Danny had stopped complaining about the headaches, they would start again. During the worst bouts, she tried to get him to see a neurologist, but as soon as he decided to go, the pain would disappear along with his resolve.

If only she had pushed harder, Gerry thought. If only she hadn't gotten used to it—used to the headaches, used to the dizziness, used to the lameness.

If only Danny hadn't been so brave, so uncomplaining. She had known all along that something was wrong, definitely wrong. It didn't take a doctor to see that. But what should she have done? What *could* she have done?

People told her not to blame herself. Danny could have looked out for himself, they said, especially later when the headaches persisted. But she was the mother. *She* was the one in the family who was supposed to worry about such things. Richard often accused her of being a worrywart, imagining terrible things that could never possibly happen. If only she had been *more* of a worrywart for Danny, done *more* imagining, maybe she could have foreseen . . . maybe she could have prevented . . .
If only . . .

34

I've suffered from headaches since I was a child. Ever since I was eight or nine, I would get these dizzy spells and headaches. Sometimes they were strong. Sometimes I had to lie down. Sometimes I fell down. I could go for months without an attack, but then they would hit me every day for a week or more. I took different medicines for them, but nothing did much good. In general, I just learned to live with them.

But there came a point when they weren't just head-aches anymore. I remember it happened in a physics lecture at Georgia Tech. I was sitting there listening to the instructor giving his lecture. I noticed this girl sitting in front of me. She was kind of sitting back and her blouse was kind of puffed up so that it gave me a view. I glanced away from her because I needed to pay attention to this lecture—there was a test coming up—but my eyes kept being drawn back. I was starting to get frustrated with myself, and I was starting to get tense. I started to feel one of my headaches coming on.

I was trying to pay attention to the lecture when, all of a sudden, I thought I heard somebody whispering behind me. Here I am trying to listen to the lecture, and here's this girl sitting there, and now, on top of that, there's somebody whispering behind me and I can't understand a word that's being said and my headache is getting really bad. I'm getting more and more frustrated and more and more tense, and I keep hearing whispering behind me. So finally I turn around to give whoever's whispering a dirty look and there's nobody there—three, four rows back, there's absolutely nobody there!

My head is pounding now. I feel as if I'm having a heart attack, because I know I heard somebody whispering behind me. I just couldn't make out what they were saying. I kind of freaked. I grabbed my books, jumped up, and left the class.

In the following weeks, again and again I felt the head-

aches and heard the whispering. But eventually I realized it wasn't coming from outside but from inside. I realized the whispers were thoughts. My first idea was that this was just some Freudian mumbo jumbo going on inside me, and all I had to do was get a grip on myself and stay calm. Don't panic, I told myself. Think your thoughts correctly and everything will just settle down. It will go away.

But it didn't. The headache spells began to increase in both frequency and intensity. The thoughts became more pronounced and more independent. You have to understand, they came of their own accord. I'd be sitting there trying to read a book, trying to study, trying to watch TV, whatever, and they would just come out of nowhere. It started with broken words and parts of sentences, and half the time I couldn't understand what the hell they were saying. It was very frightening, but I kept telling myself: This is just the subconscious playing tricks on you somehow. Just stay cool and it'll go away.

But it didn't. I wasn't able to study. I started missing classes. When I went to class, I couldn't concentrate. The episodes varied in intensity. The headaches and voices would fade for a few weeks, and I'd start to feel better, but then they would come back again. As time passed, I found myself avoiding people more and more. I dated less. I was afraid to be around girls, even those I knew well. I felt out of control. I had always been a bit of a romantic. I thought I would find my true love, sweep her off her feet onto my waiting stallion, and then gallop away to live happily ever after. But life was turning out to be a lot more complicated than I had anticipated.

Some mornings I was just afraid to get out of bed. I didn't even want to go outside. I just wanted to stay in my room. So I withdrew further and further. It was just a spiral: The more frightened I got, the more confused I got, the less I could concentrate, the less I went to class, the less I went anywhere, the less I talked to anyone.

At that time, I didn't know if I was going crazy. I actually entertained the thought that I was possessed by demons. When I was a child, I was very religious. So I began seeking out some of the various religious groups on campus: a Bible study group in my dorm, a campus Christian ministry, a South Korean evangelist. Sometimes I was almost close to tears I was so frustrated. I just couldn't get anything out of any of them. I was on a spiritual quest, and I couldn't find God.

I soon learned that there were certain visual stimuli that triggered these attacks, triggered them in an automatic kind of way, almost against my will. The first time I remember it happening, I was shopping at the 7-Eleven. I had a jug of milk in one hand and a few other things. I was walking down an aisle with refrigerators on one side and a magazine rack on the other. And there was a whole display of detective magazines.

The detective magazines back in the early '80s were more violent and had more violent and sexual themes juxtaposed than they do today. And very graphic pictures. The sexually violent images were very graphically depicted. Back then, the covers always featured staged photos of scantily clad girls being threatened in various ways by men with endless assortments of weapons, a perfect combination of sex and violence. There was something about them that seemed to trigger something in me, almost against my will. First, I would feel a headache coming on, giving me warning, but then, boom, it just came out.

Anyway, I began to collect these books and magazines. And it seemed the whole point was just to have them. With the detective magazines, I would just start flipping through them, I would read a couple paragraphs, and then I would close them up. I would buy true-crime books, fiction crime books, detective magazines, all that kind of stuff.

So I'm walking down this aisle in the 7-Eleven, and I see these detective magazines. I start to feel a dull headache. I feel this sense of panic, and I know it's coming. I'm losing control. I'm standing there trying to hold on to this milk and whatever, wanting to walk on by, feeling it coming over me. To make a long story short, I buy the magazine. I don't want the magazine, I don't want anything to do with the magazine, but it gets bought.

I tried to fight it. I tried to avoid magazine racks. But it was a losing battle. Triggers were everywhere: in books, in movies and on TV, in the news. Any time an attractive girl appeared on the screen, I felt in danger.

It was dangerous for me to watch movies. Most modern ones seem to be filled with themes of sex and violence. Especially horror movies. I can remember, as a child and teenager, being absolutely fascinated by horror films. I liked the chills and thrills they gave me. But I never thought of them in terms of a sex and violence "fix," at least not on a conscious level. I suppose that I've probably seen just about every horror movie made during the last thirty years. The number has to be well in excess of five hundred.

I can remember briefly dating a girl from Agnes Scott College during this time. One night, we decided to see a movie. She wanted to see The Exorcist. *I tried to convince her to pick something else, but she was adamant. I was terrified. Especially then, with thoughts of insanity and even possession running through my mind, the last movie in the world I wanted to see was* The Exorcist. *I kept my eyes cast down during most of it. What little bit I did watch was, as I expected, sickening and highly sacrilegious. It upset me terribly. I wish I'd never seen it.*

I didn't know what to do or who to turn to. I thought about going to see the school psychologist-counselor, but I was terribly afraid, and, I guess it may seem strange, embarrassed and ashamed as well. I felt like there was something wrong with me. I was an up-and-coming young man. I was going to make it big in the world. I had big dreams. My sights were set on going somewhere. I couldn't be caught going into some shrink's office and telling him I thought I was going nuts. Besides, if I didn't go to a counselor, then nothing serious was going on. I could handle it, and eventually it would go away.

I began taking Valium and other prescription painkillers for the headaches. I acquired these medications from my mother's bathroom cabinet, which usually had a supply. Eventually, I went to see a doctor to get my own prescriptions. I kept all of this from my family, as I always had, because they would only worry, and I didn't want anyone to know anyway.

As long as people were acting as if everything was normal, as long as everything was kept hidden, as long as appearances were maintained and no one looked at me out of the corner of their eyes, I was all right. I could continue to pretend that everything was normal and not do anything about it, not seek any help, not go see a neurologist or a psychiatrist, not tell anyone. I lived life on the surface when it came to interacting with other people. It's the way I'd always been; showing a smiling face to the world, while just behind it stood a solid black wall that no one could get past, not even me. I just wanted to stay calm: Don't get excited, don't panic, make sure that no one notices anything, and everything will be okay.

It didn't work out that way.

35

Danny never had a problem with girls—at least not that his mother could see. Gerry had watched with interest and bemusement as the fairer sex discovered her Danny. Like most males, he had his schoolboy crushes. The first one she could remember was Annette, a girl in Danny's fourth-grade class. Gerry recalled one incident in particular that seemed to sum up Danny's attitude towards girls. The family was living in Atlanta—not long after Richard's student days at Georgia Tech—and Danny had accompanied Gerry to a little store where she did her grocery shopping. While they were there, Danny found a display of birthstone rings and insisted on buying the appropriate one for Annette. Gerry knew right then that her Danny wasn't a little boy anymore.

Then there was the little Hispanic girl in Panama, where Richard had gotten a job with the Army Corps of Engineers. Gerry couldn't remember her name. She was so pretty and Danny was so shy. They were both so young. They considered themselves dating, but when you're that age and you don't have a car, dating consists of holding hands in the hallway, writing notes, and maybe eating lunch together. Occasionally Gerry would take them to the roller-skating rink for a "big date." They were so cute together: little blond Danny and this little dark-haired Spanish girl.

Before long, though, Danny had found someone else: a blonde this time. Susan was her name, and she was a knockout, with long golden hair, brown eyes, and a beguiling smile. Danny fell for her—hard. Gerry could remember him swooning around the house declaring himself "madly in love." He was all of thirteen or fourteen, and he was crazy about her. If it's possible for two people to be in love at such a young age, Danny and Susan were. They spent every free minute together, it seemed to Gerry, including long, romantic walks by the lake as well as long, unchaperoned evenings at Susan's house when her parents were away—Danny thought his mother didn't know, but she did. And when the two lovebirds weren't together, they talked interminably on the phone, to the dismay of the families at both ends of the line.

Then it all came crashing down. Almost overnight, Susan's father was transferred back to the States, and Susan was whisked out of Danny's life. At the ripe old age of fifteen, his heart was utterly broken. Or at least that was what he claimed. Gerry tried to assure him that he would soon find somebody else and the pain would go away, but Danny insisted that there would never be another Susan. "I never imagined that a human being could hurt this much inside," he told his mother with tears in his eyes. "My heart is crushed. Life has cheated me." For a while, Danny and Susan continued their ardent courtship by letter, but soon Richard was transferred to New Jersey, the family moved, and Susan's letters stopped coming.

It took Danny almost two years to recover from Susan, Gerry recalled. The whole time they were in New Jersey, he hardly dated at all. He seemed to withdraw into himself more, which was not like Danny at all, and he spent more and more time alone in his room, reading. Still, Gerry felt certain that his crushed heart would eventually mend.

And she was right. Soon after the family moved to Augusta, Georgia, Danny began dating again. His senior year in high school, he enrolled in Augusta College and suddenly found himself a man of the world, out on his own, away from home. Before long, he had a new girlfriend named Teddy. They went out dancing a lot, Gerry remembered, to all the discos in Augusta. Danny had always been a good dancer. Back in New Jersey, his father had taught him and his sister how to jitterbug. By the time they reached Augusta, they were winning dance contests and teaching disco dancing at the officers' club at Fort Gordon, the local army base.

Teddy was a smart girl. A good dancer and very pretty, with long brown hair, she was also the first woman Danny brought home. Late on weekend nights, after the dance clubs were closed, Gerry suspected that they were doing some "exploring" of a more intimate nature. Danny was the right age, after all. Teddy looked like a willing co-explorer. The times had changed. Gerry remembered the trauma that Helen had gone through at fifteen, when her first boyfriend asked her to hold hands and she broke up with him because it "violated her Christian values."

But it was different with a boy. Gerry had once summoned up her courage and asked Danny what he thought love between a man and woman meant. He told her that his fantasy of the ideal relationship was of a knight in shining armor. "I want girls to like me, to love me," he said. "I like to impress girls, but I want them to like me for who I am. I like intimacy, companionship, communication, sharing and caring."

Not a bad start, she thought. There would be plenty of time for him to learn about the rest.

36

I like to think that I had a relatively healthy attitude towards sex. I can remember being interested in girls at a very early age—and I don't mean curious, I mean interested. I believe I was about nine or ten when these thoughts became a daily part of my life. However, even before then, I can vaguely recall incidents of playing doctor with various neighborhood girls. I remember one occasion in particular when I had a girl do a kind of striptease for me. I was about seven at the time.

I can remember it exactly. It was in Mineral Wells, West Virginia. There was a little field out behind the house and the grass was growing real tall. We were sitting out there—she was a little girl, about my age—and she just did a striptease, took all her clothes off. Another time, I got into a refrigerator box with a girl and played doctor. It was just the typical childhood kind of thing, a normal part of growing up.

I didn't begin to feel a sense that something was wrong until I got up to ten, eleven, twelve. Somehow, even at that age, I knew that thinking about girls was bad and naughty. My parents were loving but typical middle American in their attitude about sex. They weren't prudish. They showed affection for each other openly in front of us kids, but sex was still something secret, not to be talked about. And I kept many thoughts and feelings to myself.

I remember reading a science fiction book about this time. It was a short story about these two beings in this spaceship. I assumed they were human beings, but when the story ended, it described their long tentacles. All of a sudden, it dawned on me that they were aliens. When I finished the story, I was seized by this incredible feeling of unreality, like I was trapped in this hideous body with these ten little scrawny things at the end of these blobby, fleshy knobs. I can't describe it. I felt like an alien. I was seized with this very alien sensation. Maybe this was an alien body. I felt repulsed by my own body.

It was also during this early period that I first discovered girlie magazines and bondage magazines like the ones in the abandoned building in Panama. Having already become a voracious reader by that age, I went through the entire collection quickly. I remember being alternately perplexed and excited by all the strange and new ideas that I was exposed to while reading those magazines.

One Friday night after my parents had gone out for the evening, I walked a couple streets down to the home of a girl I liked. I cut through the jungle—this was Panama, remember—came up behind her house, and climbed a nearby tree. I could see her lying on the bed reading a book. I cannot begin to describe the mixture of intense conflicting emotions which raged through my mind at that moment. I felt as if I were teetering on the edge of a precipice. My heart was beating wildly. After watching her read for a short while longer, I could stand it no more. I climbed down and went home in a daze. That night, as I lay in bed, I felt extremely guilty about what had happened. I wasn't even sure why I had done it, but I knew it was wrong and resolved never to let it happen again.

But in the following weeks, again and again my thoughts gravitated back to that night. I couldn't seem to get it out of my mind. I couldn't control it. One night I found myself crouched up in that tree again, trembling, near panic. She entered her bedroom, undressed, and changed into her nightgown. Once more the emotions came roaring through my head. I felt as if I were about to explode. After that night, I couldn't bear to look her in the eye at school. I felt guilty and ashamed. I never went back to her house again.

Several months after this incident, I began to date girls for the first time. I was around thirteen. It was the sort of thing where one would hold hands while walking to class, eat lunch together, and perhaps even steal an occasional kiss if one were feeling particularly bold that day. There were a few different girls I liked and with whom I spent time while at school. And I knew they liked me. But even after I got to know them and became more or less comfortable with them, I still found myself holding back in a way I can't really describe. It wasn't due to a lack of self-confidence. Though certainly no Romeo, I was a fair-enough-looking boy and I knew girls liked me. In fact, at one time a girl who was considered the most popular in school and who was a grade above had a thing for me. My friends were positively green with envy. But for some reason, I still could not completely loosen up around girls. I had to hold a part of me close and tight. Why, I didn't know.

It was at a party while going to Augusta College that I had my first full sexual experience. She was visiting from out of state and had come with a girlfriend. I was also there with a friend. The party began dragging, so I asked her if she would like to go pick up some more beer with me. We ended up at the lake, half drunk, and then had sex. I don't think one could really call that making love. Later on we returned to the party, became separated, and I never saw her again. It made me sad.

It was about the time I went off to Georgia Tech that I began to lose control.

One day, as I headed from the student union to class along the main sidewalk there, I spotted a pretty coed walking across the central campus field. As I watched her, I became tense and felt confused. I wondered why I was stopping and watching this girl. I didn't have anything to say to her. I wasn't going to ask her out. But doesn't every guy turn and look at a pretty girl? I felt myself stopping and, with all of the confusion and the doubt, my head started to hurt. The girl came walking by me—she was very pretty—and I was feeling more and more confused.

Then suddenly I was seized by an irresistible urge to follow her. And I did. I had a class to go to. And yet I followed her. I walked behind her and followed her all the way back to her dorm. I stood out there for a minute. I felt confused. It didn't make any sense. Then I turned around and walked off, back to my class.

You have to understand, I had no reason to follow her. I had no conscious fantasies about following girls, and I had a class to go to. Why was I following this girl I didn't even know? Was I going to go up and introduce myself to her? It troubled me. I didn't want to be doing it, but I was doing it. And it began happening more and more frequently.

In the ensuing weeks and months, this bizarre compulsion became a burning, uncontrollable obsession. I would see a pretty girl and then follow her, on campus, off campus, even in my car. I began missing more and more classes, and when I did attend them, I found it almost impossible to concentrate. I fell behind in my studies. Eventually, I quit school and moved to California, hoping that the change of scenery might have a positive effect on my problem.

Soon after I got to California, though, I decided to return to school with the goal of completing my studies. But that was a wishful dream and I should have known it by then. San Jose State University had an abundance of beautiful coeds. I couldn't get away from them. They were everywhere and I was forever following them.

One day I was driving home, and, as I approached a bridge at the intersection of Routes 7 and 680, I came up to a red light and this girl drove up beside me. I glanced over at her, and she was pretty, very pretty, with long, dark hair.

And immediately I can feel it. It just starts. It's like a slow, dull headache. It starts to build right here in my head. It's not like a migraine, not localized. This feels like my whole brain is engulfed in it. My whole head. A dull pain. I begin to get tense, because I know what's coming next. I get that panicky feeling. I'm sitting there in the car, and I start to panic because I know it's coming. I'm trying to stop it. I start to get queasy. I feel like I'm going to throw up, and I feel the dull pain in my head getting more intense. And then, for lack of a better description, I feel reality changing.

My head turns. I can see the girl sitting in the car. She turns off to go down 680 south, so I pull in behind her and start following her. Why, I don't know. I follow and follow and follow her all the way down 680, all the way down 17, all the way down to the Santa Cruz mountains, all the way past Santa Cruz, forty-five minutes away, just following her, before finally turning away and returning home over three hours later.

This sort of thing happened more and more frequently.

In later years, I was to learn that driving alone in a car was one of the most dangerous places for me to be.

37

Gerry would never forget the day Danny announced he was going to marry Heather. They had been dating on and off for no more than a year. He was at Georgia Tech while Gerry and the rest of the family were doing their second tour in Panama. Then they returned stateside, and there was Heather. When Danny introduced her, Gerry's reaction was surprise that he seemed so fond of her. She wasn't the kind of person Gerry had expected Danny would be attracted to—not seriously anyway. Gerry had always pictured Danny with a girl who read a lot, who enjoyed deeper conversation—who was, in other words, more like him.

Heather was just about Danny's absolute opposite. Whenever Gerry heard the song "Don't Worry, Be Happy!" she thought of Heather. Danny called her "big-hearted, wholesome, and likeable," and that was probably all true. She certainly had a sweet, bubbly personality, and she was pretty in a kind of California beach-bunny way. Most important, Danny seemed to really like her.

But they couldn't have been more different. Danny was such an intellectual, always reading, always arguing, always worrying about politics. Heather never seemed to worry about anything more important than the color of her nail polish. There just had to be some conflict between two such different people. On the other hand, Gerry thought, maybe it was for the better. Maybe Heather's calmness and serenity would be a nice balance to Danny's hyperactivity. Finally, she decided to take her cue from Heather and not worry.

The problems started not with Gerry and Richard, but with Heather's parents. They had converted to Mormonism when Heather was still young, and although Gerry didn't have anything against Mormons—Richard's parents, after all, were Mormons—she sensed immediately that Heather's family was trying to pull Danny away from her. First, they tried converting him, taking him to their ward house, telling him how wonderful it would be if he joined the church and raised his children as Mormons. Because of his father's Mormon heritage, they pointed out, and because he didn't smoke or drink (alcohol, coffee, or caffeinated beverages), he was "already halfway there."

That didn't bother Gerry nearly as much as their effort to lure Danny to California. Before the wedding, Heather's father found a new job in San Jose and moved his family there. Soon he had found a summer job for Danny, who was still in school. It paid a huge amount of money for a college student, and Danny jumped at it. Before long, he quit Georgia Tech and made California his full-time home. Neither move made Gerry happy. Four years later, he returned to Augusta, but to lure Heather along, he had to promise her she could visit her parents twice a year for long periods, including Christmas. When Gerry heard that, she knew their relationship was headed for trouble.

The trouble started when Heather announced she was pregnant.

From the moment she started showing, it seemed to Gerry, Danny's attitude toward her changed. Whereas before he was always attentive and affectionate—touching, hugging, kissing, calling her "my little sweetie," and other endearments—suddenly he started pulling back. His entire repertoire of physical affection, as far as Gerry saw, was reduced to a peck on the cheek at night and another in the morning.

Then Heather started to gain weight, maybe 30 or 40 pounds. She lost her shapely figure. She also lost her sense of humor. Danny would tease her about her weight, and she would do a slow boil. The least thing could set her off. She complained to Gerry that Danny never "touched" her anymore—code, Gerry assumed, for bedroom activity. Gerry tried to assure her that Danny was hardly the first husband to lose physical interest in his wife during pregnancy and not to worry about it. Lots of men were callous that way.

On March 12, 1987, Allison was born, and things went from bad to worse. Gerry would never have known how much worse if Heather hadn't come to her when Allison was only a few months old, with a startling—and embarrassing—admission. "Danny has lost interest in sex," she said, "at least normal sex."

Flustered and blushing, Gerry searched for an explanation. "You know, Danny was in the room when Allison was delivered. Maybe it was the sight of the birth that turned him off to . . ." She had read that explanation in a women's magazine.

"But he isn't turned off to *all* sex," Heather pointed out, to Gerry's great discomfort. "Now, instead of intercourse, all he wants me to do is give him a blow job." And that wasn't all. To Gerry's mortification, Heather went on to say that she didn't really like oral sex, and it didn't make it any easier that Danny wanted her to do it for*ever*—a half hour or more at a time. "The longer I do it," she concluded, "the more Danny seems to enjoy it." And no matter how much she forced herself, she could last only five or ten minutes before her tolerance or her jaw muscles gave out.

As a matter of fact, sex wasn't the only problem. It was Danny's whole idea of marriage, Heather complained. "You'd never guess from looking at us that *I* was the one raised in a Mormon household," she told Gerry bitterly. She and Danny had argued over her desire to get a part-time job when Allison was older. It would take her out of the house and bring her in contact with more people, she said, and she liked people. But Danny was adamant. He wanted her to "stay home, keep an orderly house, and prepare nutritious meals." He wanted Allison taken care of by "a traditional mother." He had said that one day, when he was elected to Congress, he was going to fight for a law to give a tax credit to women who stay at home and take care of their families.

Gerry found Heather's candor breathtaking—it certainly took Gerry's breath away. "Have you tried a marriage counselor?" was all she could think to say. To herself, she said: Isn't this just like Danny? He's always there to lean on when anybody in the family has a problem, but he doesn't want to lean on us when he has a problem. But what if he *had* brought this to her? What would she have said?

Heather claimed that she had tried repeatedly to get Danny to see a counselor, but he refused. "I'm not going to tell my problems to some stranger," he would say and shut off discussion of the subject.

Later, however, when Gerry approached Danny with the same suggestion, he couldn't stop complaining: about how "deeply disappointed" he was in their marriage—disappointed in Heather's "modern" ideas about marriage and her unwillingness to play the traditional housewife and homemaker; about how he felt betrayed by a Mormon girl who turned out to be an ambitious, independent-minded career woman.

Nothing Danny said about the subject surprised Gerry—except the vehemence with which he said it.

Fortunately, neither Danny nor Heather would have to confront their problem immediately. Christmas 1988 was drawing close, and Heather would soon be leaving with Allison to spend the holidays with her family in California.

Despite their marital problems, the prospect of Heather's departure made Gerry very sad for Danny. Christmas had always been such a special time for him, ever since he was a little boy. And Christmas for Danny meant family.

She tried to console her son. "Look, Danny," she said, "Heather only wants to go home twice a year. We have them the rest of the time.

Ours is the better end of the deal." But Gerry, too, was thinking what a bad time this would be for Danny: Not only were his wife and daughter gone for Christmas, but they were gone for so long before and after— five or six weeks sometimes.

All that time Danny would be alone in his house, thought Gerry, alone with his headaches, alone with his brooding. And that worried her more than anything else.

38

My second year at Tech, I met Heather. She was special. She had more love, kindness, and gentleness in her than any girl I'd ever met, and that was exactly what I so desperately needed then. Somehow, when I was around her, I didn't feel so out of control. I didn't feel as if I was standing on the edge of a precipice. We began to date, although because Heather lived in Augusta and I went to school in Atlanta, we could see each other only on weekends.

Meanwhile, my problems continued—the obsessive habits, the headaches, the compulsive following of girls, and, worst of all, the thoughts. The thoughts which came from nowhere. By the summer of '81, I was terribly depressed. My schooling was in shambles. I thought I was secretly going crazy. My parents had moved back to Panama for another two-year stay, and our home in Augusta was being taken care of by an aunt who kept a .22-caliber handgun in her nightstand for protection.

On more than one occasion, I sat on her bed when no one else was home and held the gun to my head, wondering what would happen if I pulled the trigger. Would I go to heaven or hell, or would I merely go to eternal oblivion? Each time I squeezed the trigger a little harder, but never all the way.

Heather was the only thing keeping my head above water during that time. I would never have made it without all the love and support she gave me.

We were married in September 1982. At that time, we had sex about three or four times a week. I was happy about the way we made love, and I think Heather was, too, although sometimes she complained about it. She would lie on her back with her right arm over her head and her left arm down her side. I thought this showed her breasts to better effect. Once she had assumed this position, I would initiate intercourse.

I can only remember two times when we did something different. Both times I asked her if I could tie her to the bed. Both times she agreed, although she said it seemed silly to her. I tied her hands and feet to the four corners of the bed with some of my neckties, leaving her spread-eagled on the bed. That was the best sex we ever had, I think.

But the headaches and the voices only became more intense. They always came together. I continued to follow girls—like at a mall—but somehow things were changing. The urges were getting stronger, more demanding. Things were happening that had never happened before. I started going to houses under the pretext of looking at merchandise advertised in trader-type magazines. I would go in, talk to the people, look at whatever was for sale, and then leave. I got this idea from something I saw in Executive Imports *magazine. I purchased handcuffs from the same magazine. It seemed to give me an immense feeling of control. Each time I went to a house, I felt sick, as though I was going to throw up. But I was always calm and cool.*

As these things happened, I began to withdraw more and more—just out of fear and fright—from everything and everybody. Heather and I became more distant from each other, and she began to feel her family was her only security. I felt as if I was abandoning her, I guess. We had a falling-out. She felt as though I didn't love her.

About this time, she got pregnant and gained a lot of weight, probably fifty pounds. I kidded her unmercifully about it. She would be coming through the door and I'd say, "Bring it on through." She would get so terribly upset. I didn't know that women's hormones run wild during pregnancy and she would get so bent out of shape. Even the smallest thing could set her off. But towards the end of her pregnancy, I was working twelve hours a day, seven days a week, so I would see her only about thirty minutes when I got home, and that went on for about three months.

Heather couldn't understand why I was withdrawing from her. She wanted me to go to a marriage counselor with her, and of course I said no. "I'm not gonna tell this lady my problems," I told her. "My problems have nothing to do with typical marital problems." I think she may have gone to see a counselor a couple of times by herself. I just told her that it wasn't necessary. I never complained to her about my headaches. I never told her anything, and she didn't ask. She just gave me words of comfort and encouragement; she never tried to delve into anything. She is a fairly private person herself. The psychological problems had a chain reaction, a snowballing effect, and they rendered me almost incapable of functioning with her.

At one point I wanted to try something new to jump-start our flagging love life. I told Heather that it was my fantasy to videotape us having sex. I had been obsessed with videotaping ever since Allison was born, so it didn't seem like such an off-the-wall idea, and after a while, she agreed. So I went and set up the video camera on a tripod and asked her to lie down on the floor. I stood over her, with my underwear pulled down around my ankles. Then I pumped my penis in and out of her mouth. Heather didn't like the tape when we played it back because all it showed was my penis going in and out. She said it was even more boring than doing it.

We used the videotape the same way three more times, and then Heather refused to do it anymore.

Before Christmas 1987, Heather took Allison to California for the holidays. On New Year's Eve day, I found myself in Columbia, South Carolina. I can't recall the drive up there, but that wasn't uncommon. I drove randomly. I was calling want ads and going to houses, something I'd done many, many times before. It always made me feel guilty when I did this, but I told myself it was really harmless. At worst I left behind disappointed sellers when I failed to return and buy whatever they were advertising.

I did this dozens of times, but the women were too old, or too young, or too ugly, or something wasn't right. I read up on various devices in the detective magazines—scanners, cameras, etc. It was all part of the fantasy. I don't ever remember using a scanner with any of the girls. I used the blue light once to stop someone. But they turned out to be older ladies, so I wasn't interested. I didn't even have to show my badge. I just told them something about driving too slow.

I never made obscene phone calls. They just never cut it for me. The fantasy wasn't complete over the phone.

Eventually, I pulled up to another house. A girl answered the door. I went in, looked at the appliance or furniture or whatever, and then asked to use the phone. That was strange. I had never asked to use the phone before. There was certainly no one to call. I took the phone off the hook and then, without any warning, reached out and grabbed her by the arm. Then I went into a complete state of shock. I completely blacked out.

The next thing I remember was coming down some stairs. I felt dazed. I didn't know what had happened, but somehow I knew it had to be bad. Panic. Terror. Horror. All three came flooding through my mind like a torrent of water through a broken dam. I stumbled out, barely able to walk. While crossing the lawn to the car, I thought I was going to be sick again, but I managed to keep from throwing up. I don't remember the drive back, or what happened most of that day, before or after. Only much later did bits and pieces return to memory. Yet even now I can't remember what happened upstairs, and I have absolutely no recollection at all as to what the girl looked like.

The ensuing days were a chaotic jumble of terror and despair. I desperately tried to withdraw as far away as I could. I didn't want to think about what I was doing. I hated myself. I felt so horribly ashamed. All my life I had been quite idealistic. I always believed that good would triumph over evil and the good guys would win in the end. And I thought that I was one of those good guys. I wanted to help people, not hurt them. Yet here I was, caught up in an unimaginable nightmare over which I had little control.

The next time it happened, I made only three calls before a girl that sounded right answered the phone. I told her I wanted to see something. Maybe it was an appliance, I'm not sure. I got the address from her and drove over to her house. She was uncertain about letting me in. She was the first one that I ever took back to my house. I told her to do what I said and she would not get hurt. I pulled the gun on her and walked her to the car. I thought she was about fourteen years old. At the house, I tried to talk her into oral sex, but she wouldn't do it.

In the car on the way back, I did unzip my pants and put her head in my lap, but she wouldn't do anything. She just kept crying.

After that, I knew for certain I had gone too far. Unlike the first incident, I was aware of what I had done this time. I didn't know where to go or who to turn to. I felt hopeless. I felt desperate. I fought it every way I could. I tried getting in a carpool, because it was when I was alone in a car, when I was alone, period, that I was vulnerable. As long as I was around other people, I was safe.

39

Gerry worried most about Danny when Heather was away. His headaches always got worse when he was alone. Sometimes they would get so bad that as soon as he arrived he would head straight for her medicine cabinet and grab whatever aspirins and painkillers he could find, grab them by the handfuls and wash them down, desperately trying to get rid of the pain. Then he'd come back in and fall down on the sofa with his head in his hands. She'd say, "Danny, have you got another headache?" And he'd say, "Yes." Then she'd say, "Well, have you gone to see the doctor yet?" And he'd say, "No, but I'm going to, I'm going to."

Gerry shared her concern with Richard, but all she got in response was another lecture: "Danny's headaches aren't migraines," he would say. "His are like internal-pain headaches, not stress-pain headaches. You can take things for migraines. Rubbing and relaxation help. But this is like an inside pain: Touching increases the pain. He can't stand the light. He has to have the door shut. He doesn't want anybody around. Those aren't migraines."

Gerry didn't care what they were; she just wanted them to go away. But with Heather and Allison scheduled to depart soon for Christmas in California, she feared the worst. She knew how upset Danny was that they were leaving. This would be Allison's second Christmas, and it pained him not to spend it with her.

True enough, as the day of departure approached, Danny grew more withdrawn and irritable. He called late one night and asked Gerry to take care of Allison for a while so he and Heather could "go out" one last time.

"Son, I would love to," Gerry answered, "but I have to get up in the morning. I'm sorry."

Danny responded with a huff—"No problem. Heather and I will just do it some other time *next year*"—and hung up.

Shocked, Gerry told Richard what Danny had just said. "I don't understand it. This isn't like Danny at all," she said.

After Heather left, Danny went from bad to worse. He would come in, flop down on the couch, turn on the TV, and just sit there holding his head. Danny had always been the most lively, most active, most involved member of the family: Danny, who made sure the family got together every weekend to cook out and play badminton, Danny, the good listener who always wanted to hear what everyone had to say, who was always bursting to put his own two cents into every conversation. *That* Danny had turned into a couch potato.

On the rare occasions when he did join the family around the dinner table, he would sit there, barely participating, shading his eyes, rubbing his head, sometimes even putting it down on the table and resting. In the kitchen, out of Danny's hearing, everyone was asking the same question: What has happened to Danny? Where is the old Danny, the Danny who had to bite his lip to keep from interrupting? We miss him.

Then one evening, after Danny had fallen asleep on the sofa, Gerry went to wake him up—and she couldn't. She didn't know if he had drunk something when she wasn't looking or taken too many pills. Whatever the reason, she couldn't rouse him no matter what she did, and the feel of his limp body as she shook it brought her closer and closer to panic. Finally, just as she was about to call an ambulance, he opened his eyes.

That wasn't his first blackout, or his last. Several times Danny's boss called Gerry and told her that Danny had blacked out at work. Some of the episodes she saw were only brief, passing attacks—more like brownouts than blackouts. He would get a distant, blank look in his eyes. If he was talking, he would fall silent; if moving, freeze. Suddenly, he would go from looking his usual bright, effervescent self to looking dark and gray and hollow. Sometimes, he would mutter something in this state but, when he broke out of it, couldn't remember what he had said.

That gave Gerry something new to worry about: Danny was losing his memory. Danny, whose memory had always been fantastic; Danny, who never failed to remember every important date—birthdays, anniversaries—for the whole family. That Danny was beginning to forget the most obvious things. He'd forget what day the family had agreed to meet for dinner, what time he was supposed to meet his mother at a restaurant, who had given him what present for Christmas last year—the very things that he used to remember with astonishing clarity.

And then there were the times when he just disappeared. One moment, he would be sitting there with the rest of the family, and the next thing Gerry knew, he was gone—without so much as a word of explanation or leavetaking. The next time she saw him—maybe not until the next day—and asked him why he had left so suddenly or where he had gone, he might have a perfectly good explanation, or he might just stand there awkwardly, eyes downcast, hemming and hawing. Even as a small boy Danny had always looked her in the eye and given her a straight answer. Now he would just avert his eyes and mumble something unintelligible.

It had to be those headaches, Gerry concluded, or maybe the medication he was taking for them.

40

Christmas of '88 was just around the corner. It would be my little Allison's second. I thought for sure Heather would stay this time. But she didn't. She took my baby and left me alone again. Summers weren't too bad, but at Christmastime it was very hard on me. From early childhood, I'd always gone overboard for Christmas. It was the most important and exciting time of the year to me. Not so much because of the gift giving, but because of the effect the season seemed to have on people. Everyone was happy. Everyone was nice to everyone else. There was magic in the air. But this Christmas there would be no happiness and no magic.

When they left, I was enraged and hurt at the same time. I didn't want to spend Christmas by myself. I now knew that whenever I was left alone, bad things were bound to happen. And so I secretly called the travel agency and made my own reservation for a round-trip ticket to California. Nine hundred dollars in airfare was more than we could afford, but I knew I had no choice. I planned to surprise Heather by suddenly showing up at her parents' house a couple of days before Christmas. I would be safe, for a little while anyway.

The evening after I took Heather and Allison to the airport, I went to visit the battered and abused women's and children's shelter, as I had done the year before. It was a small house located on a back street in Augusta. Once again I was outraged at the inadequate facilities they were forced to make do with. Visions of a national program for funding the construction of clean and safe housing for abused women and children in cities and towns across the nation came to mind. The profound and bitter irony of that thought, in the face of what had happened during the previous twelve months, was not lost on me.

The day for my flight to California drew near. I was excited, but I felt uneasy at the same time, almost as if I were expecting something to happen. As I drove home from work one afternoon, it did. I saw an attractive girl pull up next to me. She looked over at me and smiled. I felt instant panic. I hadn't carpooled that day. I was alone in my car. I followed her all the way to her home. Then I returned to my empty house, sat down, picked up the phone, and canceled my reservation.

That night, I went to a secret place I had discovered many years ago in a dark and lonely stretch of woods along Clark's Hill Lake, not far from Augusta. I went there that night, as I had done so many nights in the past, to find God and ask him why. But God wasn't there. God was never there. First, I would beg. I would beg on my knees in the dark. But there was no answer. Then I would curse. I would stand and curse up through the trees. But there was still no answer. And then it would be silent and I would go home.

Several days later, alone and without hope, the driving began again. But then Jeannie and I found each other, and life changed forever.

It began, as it always did, with looking things up in The Carolina Trader. *I called and got directions to the girl's home. The girl who answered the door was Jeannie McCrea. I said, "I'm here to see the bedroom furniture." She let me in. I couldn't believe how they always let me in. Jeannie led me upstairs, where the furniture was. I don't remember what it was. As she showed me the furniture, she was almost flirting. I instantly took a liking to her.*

I pulled out a gun and said, "This is a stickup." Jeannie reacted with stunning calmness. I took her back down the stairs, where I tied her hands and told her, "Stay here for a minute." Then I went back out to the car I had rented and got my video camera. As I was closing the car door, I changed my mind. Instead of doing it at Jeannie's house, I would take her back to my house in Martinez.

At this point, I felt sick to my stomach. I felt as though I was going to throw up. I went back in the house and said, "This is a kidnapping for ransom."

She didn't fight back. She was acting like she almost expected things to turn out this way. It was almost as if I had invited her out for a weekend date and had just dropped by to pick her up.

"Just let me pack some things," she said, seemingly unfrightened by what was happening. I watched her collect her things: some clothes, some hairbrushes, a purse, and a book she was reading. Then I took her out to the rental car, opened the trunk, and told her to get in.

When we got to the house, I took her to the closet in the third bedroom and locked her in, tying a chain through the hole in the bottom of the door and padlocking it around her ankle. Then I ran around cleaning up the house of any traces that might let Jeannie know where she was, or what my real identity was. As I did this, I was feeling more and more guilt-stricken over what I was doing. I liked this girl. It was so hard to distance myself from her, as I had the others, because she acted so normal—so unscared, so accepting of everything that was happening, so much more like a friend than a victim.

When I let Jeannie out of the closet, I asked her if she wanted anything to eat, and she said she wouldn't mind an apple and a Coke. I got us both a snack and then tried to reassure her that she would benefit from all that was happening to her: "When we get the ransom money," I said, "you're going to get $5,000 or $10,000 of it."

"That's great," Jeannie said, "because I'm going on a school trip to New York and I want to go shopping."

I couldn't get over the fact that Jeannie still didn't seem frightened. When I asked her why she wasn't scared, she said, "I expected this would happen. I think I know what's going to happen with us, don't you?"

I asked her where she went to school, and she said, "I'm a senior at Irmo High." She seemed so mature. I thought she acted more like a college sophomore. I liked the fact that she was so independent—that she wasn't easily persuaded by peer pressure.

At some point, I suggested that we play cards. Jeannie asked me if I liked to play solitaire, and I said I didn't know how. She started to show me but, after a while, I stopped her. I told her I didn't think I had the patience to play solitaire.

I was getting more and more worried through all this. Sooner or later I was going to want her to give me a blow job. But I liked her more and more and, to my amazement, she seemed to like me, too.

At some point, I asked, "Do you want something to drink?"

And Jeannie said, "Well, I like peach wine coolers."

Then I asked her what she liked to eat, and she gave me a list, which included Pringles in the silver can and some other stuff. I apologized that I couldn't go to the store without locking her back in the closet, but I told her I'd be right back. Jeannie didn't put up much of a fuss. All she said was, "Why don't you rent a movie while you're out?"

I asked her if she had any particular movie in mind, and she told me to pick whatever I wanted, that it would be all right with her. It was all very polite. Except for the closet and the leg chains—and my wife and daughter in California—this could have been any guy spending a quiet weekend with his girlfriend.

I got in the car and headed first for Kroger's, where I filled the grocery list, then to the video rental store. I walked up and down the aisles and ended up with Monty Python and the Holy Grail. *When I got back, I let Jeannie out of the closet, and we sat down and watched the Monty Python movie and munched on potato chips.*

When it was time to go to bed, I put chains on Jeannie's ankles, but I didn't lay a finger on her. There was no end to the surprises this evening was bringing.

The next morning, we got up and I offered to fix Jeannie some breakfast. She said some cereal would be fine.

Before we started eating, I turned on the TV. But almost immediately I realized I had a problem. Each station had local commercials, and all Jeannie had to do to locate me for some future law-enforcement official was to remember the ads. She would know damn well that we weren't in Charleston. So I sat there with the TV on, but with my hands on the channel changer, ready to switch channels before she could see any revealing commercials.

After breakfast, I asked Jeannie if she wanted to play a

game. She suggested Monopoly. It wasn't long into the game before I realized that she was playing it all wrong. She kept skipping over property when the best way to win Monopoly is to buy all the property you can. Soon afterwards, I landed on Boardwalk and Jeannie had a fit. Then I landed on Park Place, and she really had a fit. "Okay," I said, wanting to be nice, "I'll sell it to you." That really made her happy.

I got hungry again, so I suggested that we go out to the back patio. I took her into the kitchen, where I made some sandwiches, which we took outside with us. There was only one chair on the patio, so I said, "You take the chair. I'll sit on the ground." Then we went inside to get something to drink. I got myself a rum and Coke, but Jeannie wanted one of her Bartles & Jaynes wine coolers.

Then the moment came that I had been dreading. I couldn't wait any longer. I told Jeannie that I wanted to have sex with her.

But Jeannie didn't seem at all upset at the idea. She didn't seem to mind at all. Except when I started the camera. And then she cried like crazy. I said I wouldn't use the video camera and she seemed happy again.

So she gave me a blow job.

Then I suggested another card game.

After a while, Jeannie said she wanted to see some more movies. She also said she needed some shampoo, some makeup, some more Pringles—in fact, a whole list. As I was getting up to leave, Jeannie said, "You know, you really don't need to lock me up. I'm not going anywhere." So I didn't lock her up in the closet. I just locked the bedroom door.

I could feel myself falling in love with Jeannie, and I felt that she was doing the same with me. As far as I could tell, she was treating the whole experience like an adventure. I even admitted to her that I didn't think any ransom money was in the picture, but assured her that I would give her some money to spend on her trip to New York. At one point, I asked her, "Would you like to stay here until you go to New York?" And, to my surprise, she said she would.

We had sex several more times, and Jeannie seemed to like it.

One night, we played Pass Out and I got completely wasted. Jeannie suggested that we have sex and got upset when I couldn't get an erection. She started pouting. I tried to turn it into a joke. I told her it was her fault for letting me drink too much.

Jeannie told me about her previous boyfriends, but also said she had never had sex with any of them. I was the first person she had ever had sex with.

I tried to bring up a lot of serious topics: politics, religion, etc. I asked her what she thought about abortion.

"I think it's up to the woman," she said.

"I used to believe that," I said, "but now it troubles me. I think people are defining life as beginning at the moment of birth, and I'm not so sure."

But Jeannie didn't seem convinced.

When I brought up politics, Jeannie said, "My dad voted Republican, and my mom voted Democrat."

"Then they just canceled each other out. What about you—are you a Republican or a Democrat?"

"I'm probably Republican," she said.

"Do you believe in God?" I asked.

"Yeah, I do."

"You're very mature for your age," I complimented her.

"I don't like school very much," she confided. "I don't fit in with the in crowd."

"Well, you're not a conformist," I said. "I like that about you. It means you're secure in your own self-worth."

"I've gotten into some arguments with my teacher," Jeannie said.

It was getting colder, so I made a fire and we took the first of several naps together in front of the fireplace. In be-

tween we played Parcheesi and talked. At one point she said that she had always known that we were going to meet someday. That sounded eerie and made me feel strange about the whole thing.

Eventually we were hungry again, so I ordered a pizza, and we sat in front of the fire munching on pizza and cheese sticks. Jeannie liked junk food even more than I did, and that worried me. I got her some vitamins and insisted that she take them because she liked junk food so much. She thought that was funny.

For Christmas, I went out and bought her a fancy dress and some earrings. She really liked the presents, but said she was a little sad. She said she was worried about her parents, and she knew they must be worrying about her. I offered to call them and tell them that she was okay. But Jeannie didn't think that was a good idea.

No wonder she was having such a good time, I thought. I was practically waiting on her hand and foot. All she had to do was ask for something, and I'd run and get it for her. I brushed her hair, scratched her back, massaged her feet. Whatever she wanted.

"You should feel really honored," I told her. "The only other person whose feet I rub is my mother's."

That reminded me that I was late for Christmas dinner at my mother's house. I locked Jeannie in the closet before I left.

41

Gerry didn't see much of Danny that Christmas. She thought he was working the week before, until Helen reminded her that he had arranged to take that week off—hoping, perhaps, that at the last minute he might be able to persuade Heather to spend Christmas at home. That meant he was probably alone most of the week, a thought that filled Gerry with dread. She knew how upset he was about Heather and Allison's departure. Christmas had always been *his* holiday. Everybody in the family knew that.

Danny had always been her Christmas child. Every child loves Christmas, but none of Gerry's children loved Christmas the way Danny did. From the time he was old enough to say "Sandy Claws," he was the first to catch the holiday spirit. The minute December rolled around, he would start decorating. There wasn't a spot that he didn't fill with greenery or ribbons or candles.

And the tree—no one could decorate a tree the way Danny could. He'd take construction paper and cut out bells. He'd take pictures of Santa Claus and reindeers and elves from coloring books and stick them on the walls nearby. He'd string popcorn and cranberries and leave half of them on the floor on the way to the tree. He made all kinds of odd little things to hang on the tree that didn't look right at all. Just crazy stuff. He would spend days looking for holly. It would take Gerry forever to clean up after some of his projects, but there was nothing she could do to stop him. He just really, really loved Christmas.

He loved it because Gerry was always baking something delicious, and the sugary aromas would waft through the house, drawing him to the kitchen, where the sheer hustle and bustle of Christmas preparations made him break out in peals of happy laughter. Even now, years later, whenever Gerry went into the kitchen to make Christmas cookies, she could hear that laughter.

He loved the lights of Christmas. As soon as he was old enough, he absolutely *had* to string lights all over their house—wherever it happened to be—even in Panama. And as soon as the first Christmas tree lot opened, Danny had to be the first in line to get the best tree. Thanks to Danny, no matter where they were, the Starretts were always the first to have their lights up at Christmas.

Danny may have grown up, but his delight at Christmas never changed. He still enjoyed putting the wreath on the door, stringing the lights around the house, getting out the tree stand, hoisting the tree, decorating it, picking the presents, wrapping them, writing cards, stuffing stockings. He took special pleasure in everything: from eating holiday foods to greeting holiday friends and family, such as Gerry's mother and father, who always came up from the farm to preside over the celebrations.

But this year was different. Through all the holiday preparations, Gerry had hardly seen Danny at all. In fact, it wasn't until the day before Christmas Eve that Danny finally showed up. And he looked terrible. His hair was messy, and he was wearing a wrinkled undershirt and a pair of dirty jeans. Was this the same Danny? The Danny who took four showers a day? The Danny who couldn't stand to wear the same shirt two days in a row?

"I'm here for dinner," he announced.

"That's tomorrow night," Gerry corrected him gently. "Remember? That's what we decided. Everybody will be here."

Danny turned sheepish. "I didn't remember that."

Gerry said to herself: It's Danny's memory again. This was getting worrisome. And she could tell from the fatigue and anxiety on Danny's face that he was worried, too.

The next night, Christmas Eve, Danny came back but stayed only a few minutes. Gerry asked everyone what time they wanted to open presents later that night, and as soon as everyone agreed on a time, Danny mumbled something about "having things to wrap," and then disappeared— so quickly that no one saw him go.

When he didn't return by the designated time for opening presents, everyone was surprised—"This isn't like Danny at all"—and a little irritated. Everyone except Gerry. She was worried.

42

Jeannie said she was getting bored staying around the house all the time. She thought it would be a nice idea to go somewhere for New Year's. When I suggested the beach, Jeannie thought that was a great idea. So I made reservations at Jekyll Island, off the Georgia coast.

Before we left the house, though, I put tape over Jeannie's sunglasses.

By now I had returned the rental car I had used to pick Jeannie up, and I didn't want to spend the money to rent another car for the trip. So, when we got into my red Camaro convertible, I just told her I had rented another car in another city up the coast from Charleston. When we got to I-16, far enough from Augusta, I let her take her sunglasses off.

Jeannie loved the new car. She immediately wanted to put the top down, so I pulled the car off the road and put it down. She put the music on real loud and opened one of the wine coolers I had brought along on the trip. Before long, she was getting a little high, holding the bottle up in the air and screaming.

"You better stop that," I said. "Otherwise the cops could pull us over for having an open container in the car."

When we got hungry, I decided to risk just stopping at some fast-food place. I pointed to a Waffle House and asked Jeannie if that was all right. The whole time we were there, I worried that Jeannie might yell, or scream, or do something to get help. But she acted as if there was nothing wrong in the world—that we were just two normal youngsters out for a quick, cheap bite to eat. I didn't even have to threaten her.

When we arrived at the motel where I had made the reservations, I told Jeannie to stay in the car while I went in and got the keys to the room. We unloaded our things in the room and then decided to take a walk on the beach. It was a cloudy day, and her mood as we began to walk matched the weather.

"This makes me a little sad," she said. "I was here once before, and it was with my parents."

I offered to take her home if she wanted. She said it was okay, as long as she got home before the New York trip. I said, "Well, at least this is the best excuse you ever had for missing school."

When we got back to the room, Jeannie complained that she didn't have a change of clothes, so I offered to take her into town to buy some new clothes. There was a big shopping center there, and we went to a dress place. Everything she liked was black. "I like black," she said. "Some people think I'm morbid." I told her I thought she looked great in black. She did.

Next she needed some black hose to go with the dress, so I suggested that we go in different directions, look for a place to buy the hose, then meet back at the grocery store. After fifteen minutes or so apart, she showed up, just as she said she would, hose in hand, and we went back to the motel together.

When she put on her new clothes, I took her to a nice restaurant, the Pirate's Inn. I soon realized, to my amazement, that instead of worrying that Jeannie might do something that would get me in trouble, she was more likely to do something that would simply embarrass me. After we had already sat down, she decided that she didn't like the table we were at. She wanted a view of the ocean. So I had to call the waiter and ask for a change of tables.

A little later, Jeannie pointed to a group of waiters and said, "I think they're queer." She was speaking awfully loud, and I was afraid some people might have overheard her. I was more than a little embarrassed.

Finally, she settled down and we ate until we were stuffed.

That night, we decided to stay in the motel room, even though there were booths set up in town to watch the countdown to the new year. Back in the room, we watched Die Hard *with Bruce Willis on the pay service. By the time the movie was over, we were both hungry again. I ordered some pizza from the Pizza Inn, which was next door to the motel. We also had a lot to drink. Then Jeannie started to complain that her neck and back were hurting, so I gave her a massage.*

The next morning, we packed our things into the car and I paid the bill. On the way home, Jeannie asked to stop at St. Simon's Island because she had been there once with her family, and she wanted to see it. "There's a pier somewhere there where people go fishing," she said. I was able to find the exact spot she was talking about, and we got out and walked around. Then we got back in the car and headed back to Augusta.

We stopped to eat at one fast-food place, and Jeannie brought her Coke out to the car. She almost spilled it, and I nearly had a heart attack. I thought, "I'll never be able to get the Coke stains off my seats!"

When we got back to I-16, I put the tape back on Jeannie's glasses so she wouldn't be able to tell where we were going.

Back at the house, we watched some more movies and ate some more junk food.

Throughout this two-week period, I was in contact with my parents several times. Every workday, I called in sick. There were no time sheets or clock-ins where I worked. One day, I actually did go in to work—I put Jeannie in the closet—but I got sick and went home almost immediately. My boss called my mother and told her that I was going to go home early.

One night, I built a fire and got both of us drinks— Bacardi for me, wine coolers for her.

We got on the subject of her family. Jeannie started telling me about her mom and her dad and her stepdad. "I get into lots of arguments with them," she said.

We started playing Pass Out, but I developed a particularly bad headache, so I went into my bedroom and got some pain pills. When I came back, we resumed the game. Jeannie was smoking one of her Marlboro Lights, and I started in telling her again how bad smoking was for her and how she needed to quit. Jeannie said, "If you'd just try it, you'd see how great it is." With that, she took a puff of smoke and blew it in my mouth. I almost choked to death.

By now we were both pretty drunk. The Christmas tree was still up, and we knocked some of the ornaments off it. We started talking about getting together again. Jeannie got a piece of paper out of her pocketbook and told me that it was the list of vacation days at Irmo High School. We tried to figure out which ones would make good times for us to see each other.

Jeannie told me that she was going to Myrtle Beach the next summer. I suggested that we meet each other there. Jeannie thought that was a great idea. "Where would we meet?"

The only place I knew there was the Holiday Inn.

Then Jeannie said maybe we would get married there someday.

I told her I thought I was too old for her. That upset her. She said, "You're acting like a brat."

You see, I hadn't told Jeannie that I was married. Even as I was falling in love with her, I didn't feel it was a betrayal. I guess I didn't really believe that she loved me. "Marrying you would be crazy," I said—especially crazy given the circumstances under which we had met and fallen in love.

"No, it wouldn't!" she said. "We could write a book about it and get rich!"

"Yeah, and make a movie, too," I said.

When I said I wanted to take a shower, Jeannie said she wanted to join me. We started arguing over who was going to have to stand in the front of the shower. I suggested that we go to my bedroom because it had a bigger shower. I grabbed some towels, and we headed off to my bedroom.

Jeannie had never been allowed inside my room. There were letters and bills that might give my real name, and there was all of Heather's makeup. When Jeannie saw all the makeup in the bathroom, she wanted to know who it belonged to.

I lied. I told her it was an old girlfriend's stuff. I wanted to tell her about Heather, but the way I saw it, Heather didn't love me anymore. It was only a matter of time before we would be divorced.

Jeannie laughed. She asked if she could have it.

I turned the shower on but then remembered that I still had my contacts in, so I got out of the shower and started looking for my contact-lens case. I opened one drawer where Heather and I kept our toothpaste, thinking the case might be there. My gun was in the drawer. I had put it there thinking that if the police ever showed up at the door, I could run to the bathroom, lock myself in, and blow my brains out.

Meanwhile, I heard Jeannie coming out of the shower after me. I reached for the blue towel that was lying on the toilet and quickly covered the gun with it. I didn't want Jeannie to see the gun—I knew guns scared her. I turned around, expecting to see her brushing her hair, but she was sitting on the toilet looking at me.

The next few moments are a blur—but I can see her grabbing for the gun, and I can hear the gun go off. The noise was so loud, reverberating in the small bathroom. My ears actually hurt. I watched as Jeannie stepped back and fell down against the wall.

With my ears still ringing badly, I ran to put the gun under the bed in my room. I ran back into the bathroom and saw Jeannie in the shower, lying there as if she had passed out. There wasn't any blood—the shower had drained it away. I tried to wake her up, but she wouldn't wake up. I figured she was drunk, so I made the water hotter—I didn't want her to get cold—and I tried to hold her up under the spray.

For a moment, I just stood there in the shower with her motionless body draped over me. I had a sudden irrepressible desire to see a picture of Allison. I lowered Jeannie's body to the floor. I decided to leave her in the shower so she would stay warm. I went into Allison's room and held a framed picture of her in my hands. First I felt shock—absolute, numbing shock; then absolute, terrifying desperation.

Then I went back to the bathroom and looked at Jeannie's unconscious form. I dragged her into the bedroom and laid her on the bed. I couldn't stand looking at her face, so I covered it with a shirt. Then I covered her body with a green blanket. Green was her favorite color.

Then I started drinking nonstop. I tried to blot out everything. This went on for a long while. I lost track of the time, but it seemed as if it could have been a day or two. Finally, I took Jeannie's body out to the car and put it in the backseat. I didn't have any idea where I would go. When I got an hour or so away from Augusta, somewhere in South Carolina, I decided to dump her by the side of the road. But then I thought about how much Jeannie liked the water, and so I decided to find a stream somewhere. I was crying most of the time.

Eventually, I found a stream at the end of a dirt road. I reached into the backseat and, as gently as possible, pulled her body out of the car. I looked over at the stream, found a spot that looked suitable, and dragged Jeannie's body to it. I sat down next to her and had almost lost myself in thought, when I was startled by the sound of some cars coming down the dirt road.

I had brought a gun with me and I wanted desperately to have the courage to use it on myself, so that I could stay there forever with Jeannie. But I didn't.

When I got back in the car, I looked back at Jeannie and said, "I want to stay here with you."

But then I drove away.

43

Gerry knew something was wrong. Before Christmas, she barely saw Danny—and when she did, he looked terrible. Then, after Christmas, he disappeared altogether. He said he was going on a business trip, but Gerry thought that sounded strange: a business trip between Christmas and New Year's? It wasn't like Danny to take time away from his family, especially holiday time. More and more often, she caught herself thinking, and saying to other family members, "Danny just hasn't been himself lately."

He did call her on New Year's Eve, but he sounded distant and distracted. He had also completely forgotten about the family outing she had planned for New Year's Day. When she reminded him, he complained that he had a headache—and, in fact, he sounded in pain. "Do you think you'll be able to come?" Gerry asked.

"It all depends on how I feel," Danny said.

The next day they talked on the phone again. He didn't sound any better.

"Well, are you coming?" Gerry asked. "Has your headache gotten any better since last night?"

"I'm still not feeling so great," Danny said.

"Well, why don't you come up with us?" Gerry pressed. "You'll feel a lot better once you get there."

He told her he would think about it.

Gerry thought: "That's not like Danny."

Around six that night, Danny did show up, but he seemed tired and withdrawn. While everybody else threw darts, ate, and played a board game called Scruples, Danny sat in a chair by the window, looking very distracted, tired, and desperately in need of a shave. The one time he got up, he almost fell and had to steady himself on the back of a chair. Maybe it was the drive, Gerry thought.

"Are you all right?" she asked.

Danny just shrugged his shoulders and mumbled something about having a headache. By now this complaint was so commonplace, she didn't give it another thought.

It wasn't long before Danny announced that he was going to bed. "You'll feel better in the morning," Gerry reassured him as he left.

What Gerry really thought would make Danny feel better was Heather's return with Allison from California on January 14. When she hadn't heard anything from either Danny or Heather for weeks, she assumed the storm had passed. Then, one day in early February, she got a call from Heather. She wanted to have lunch.

From the moment Gerry sat down, all Heather could talk about were her problems with Danny.

Their relationship had been going downhill for a long time, even before her trip to California. But since her return, things had gotten even worse. They had never been as distant as they were now. "We never talk anymore," she whined. "Most of the time I don't have any idea what's going on in his head. I don't really *know* him anymore." That complaint sounded eerily familiar to Gerry.

According to Heather, Danny was spending almost all his time at home lying around the house, complaining of migraines. As bad as his headaches had been before, they were far worse now. "He says it feels like his whole head is going to explode," Heather said. "He can't sleep. He can't even think. He says Allison's crying drives him crazy, and he won't talk to me because his head hurts too much." He had even suggested that Heather and the baby move in with Gerry until he felt better.

And he was missing work. One day Danny's boss had called her and told her Danny was coming home early because he had blacked out at work. When Heather asked him if this had happened before, Danny admitted that it had—many times.

According to Heather, Danny agreed to let the neurologist do a scan, but it didn't show any sign of a tumor. When the neurologist suggested more tests, Danny balked. He recounted his terrible experiences with testing back in West Virginia and again insisted, "If I have any major blemish on my medical records, it could mess me up politically."

So the headaches continued, and the memory lapses, and the unexplained absences. Just in the month since her return, Heather had twice called members of the family late at night, looking for Danny. Gerry remembered the calls because they worried her, too. "I was hoping he was with you," Heather had said, "because I don't know where he could be."

"Didn't he tell you where he was going?" Gerry had asked.

"He just told me it was none of my business."

That didn't sound like Danny, either, Gerry thought.

"Just the other night," Heather said, "I called him to find out what time he would be home from work. He said six o'clock. But he didn't show up until nine. I asked him where he had been. All he said was, 'At a friend's house.' " Later that night, they had tried to have sex, but Danny couldn't get an erection. They kept on trying, two more times later in the evening, but Danny still couldn't get an erection. "What was really strange," Heather said, "was that it didn't seem to upset him too much."

When they finished lunch, Gerry invited Heather and Danny to a spaghetti dinner later that day. But when Heather called Danny, he said he had a headache and wanted to stay home and lie down. "No problem," said Gerry brightly. "Come by yourself."

On the way home, Gerry stopped off at Danny's house to let Heather change. Gerry stayed in the car and watched as Heather went to the door and knocked, and knocked, and then banged madly. A few minutes passed. Then she went to a window around back and knocked on it. Suddenly, the door flung open and Danny came out. Even from the car, Gerry could see how haggard and angry he looked.

When Heather came back to the car, Gerry asked, "What was he doing?"

"He was on the couch drinking."

"Drinking by himself?" Gerry started. "That's not like Danny."

"Well," said Heather, "it is now."

The next day, Friday, February 3, Heather called Gerry. Her voice was trembling. Gerry thought she sounded like she had been crying. Then, in brief, whimpered fragments, she told Gerry her story.

Danny had taken her out to dinner the night before.

At some point during the meal, he turned to her, looked her straight in the eye, and said, "Heather, I think I'm going crazy."

She didn't know what to say.

"If I go crazy, will you come visit me?" Danny said.

Heather tried to laugh, but she could only think of one question to ask, and finally she asked it: "Are you seeing another woman?"

"No," he said.

The next morning, Danny had dropped an even bigger bomb on her: He wanted her to take Allison and go back to California for a while. "I love you and Allison," he said. "But I need you to leave for a while. I need to get my head together, and to do that I need to be alone." He called the trip a "separation" and said she could return to Georgia when he felt better.

But he wasn't *asking* her to go. He had already bought her a ticket. And the plane left *the next day*.

Heather broke into sobs.

Gerry didn't know what to say except, "That doesn't sound like Danny."

The next day, Danny drove Heather and Allison to Augusta's Bush Field for a 1:30 P.M. flight from Augusta to San Francisco. He walked them to the gate. When they got there, he kissed them both good-bye and waved at them as they walked to the plane.

44

I wanted desperately to stop them from leaving. But I knew that Heather would have left me eventually anyway. She would leave me and take the baby with her, and I would look like a fool and an idiot. She never did anything I told her to. I wanted her to work less and spend more time at home with the baby, and she couldn't care less. She didn't love me, and knowing that made it impossible to be in the same room with her sometimes. Too hurtful.

Of course, I couldn't tell her anything. I couldn't tell her about Jeannie. I couldn't tell her that I had fallen in love with Jeannie. I couldn't tell her that I had spent two glorious weeks with Jeannie. I couldn't tell her I had shot Jeannie.

One day, after Heather left for California, I just up and left the house and headed to Jekyll Island. I went to all the restaurants where Jeannie and I ate. I walked to all the stores we had shopped at. I even stayed at the same motel.

On the way home, I considered just driving to Jeannie's home in Columbia, knocking on the door, and telling Mr. McCrea what had happened. Then Mr. McCrea would shoot me, and it would all be over. But I kept on driving home instead.

Next, I tried finding another Jeannie where I had found her, in The Carolina Trader. *I thought all I needed to do was answer a few ads, and a Jeannie would be at one of the houses I went to. But I would knock on the doors, and it wouldn't be a Jeannie who answered, so I would just turn around and leave. There was an ad for a dresser, a side table, and a mattress, and another ad for a double bed and a mirror priced at $850. Neither panned out. Then there was an ad for a stereo cabinet. I called the owner, and she sounded fairly young. I went to see her and measured the cabinet, but she was wrong. She wasn't Jeannie. I told her that I didn't think all my stereo components would fit into her cabinet and left. No matter how many houses I went to, Jeannie was never there.*

Then I saw an ad on page 19 of the January 31– February 6 issue of the Trader. *It read: "Waterbed by Sona, full size, brand-new," and it gave both home and work numbers. I guessed that someone with a brand-new waterbed was probably young. I called and got directions to her house. When I arrived, this girl came to the door. She said her name was Chrissy Blake.*

"I'm here to look at the furniture in the ad," I said.

She invited me in.

When I got inside, I felt like I was going to be sick to my stomach, so I asked to go to the bathroom. When I came out, I pulled out a gun and said, "This is a stickup. Come with me." I told her that I was kidnapping her and holding her for ransom.

I took her to the car, told her to get in the backseat, and then told her to cover her face with a blanket so she couldn't see where we were going. When we got to the house in Martinez, I took her to a closet, chained her ankles together, and forced her inside. I went in and cleaned up everything so Chrissy wouldn't be able to remember anything that could be traced to me. When I brought her out, I told her, "I don't want to hurt anyone," and asked her if she would like something to eat or drink.

She said no.

I said I wanted to have sex.

Chrissy said, "I would rather die."

We spent the night together in the bed.

The next day, I asked Chrissy to play cards. She agreed and even managed to smile a few times. The cards had pictures of girls on them, some in two-piece bathing suits, others half naked.

I asked her if she wanted something to drink. "How about a wine cooler?" I said. She said she wasn't thirsty.

Then I said I wanted sex.

I set up a video camera to film the event and forced Chrissy to perform oral sex on me. I was having a lot of trouble with the camera. It was very hard to focus properly. So I didn't always use the videotape—sometimes it didn't even have tape in it.

When we were finished, we played cards again even though Chrissy was very upset. I tried to console her, but she said she was a virgin.

I unchained her except when I was sleeping or I went to the store to get something to eat.

She began to complain of a stomach flu. She told me that she had gotten a bug from her mother. She told me that she couldn't hold anything down. I went and got her an Alka-Seltzer, but when I handed it to her, she said, "That won't help." So I went and got her some fresh fruit and some vitamins.

We had sex a few more times over the next few days.

Chrissy stopped eating because she was so sick. That made me more and more worried. I made a chicken potpie for her, and when she tried it she threw up.

I suggested that she take a warm bath, or maybe a shower. I told her it would make her feel better. She did.

When she got out of the shower, I told her she should drink something, that she needed something in her system. She said she wanted some chocolate ice cream. So I went to the store and got some. She ate a little, but still she was sad. She was breaking my heart. I desperately wanted to see her smile. "If you smile, just once," I said, "I'll give you $300."

She did, and I handed her $300.

I suggested that we play cards again, and I taught her a few games. She seemed to like one of them. At least she called it a "fun game." I was beginning to like her, even though she clearly wasn't anything like Jeannie. For one thing, she liked soap operas.

"They're garbage," I said. "You really should be watching something educational—like C-Span."

"I don't want to watch C-Span," she said. "I like soaps."

I agreed to let her watch soaps, but only on the condition that I sit there and watch for commercials with the channel changer, so that I could change the channel every time a commercial came on so she wouldn't see a local commercial and figure out where she was.

Chrissy began to ask when she was going to get to go home.

She wasn't having a good time, and her illness was beginning to worry me more and more. She couldn't hold down food and was always throwing up. So I decided to take her home Saturday, after I rented another car. But after I rented the car, I changed my mind and decided to keep her around a little longer.

That night, I taught her how to play poker. I took a

thousand dollars, kept half of it myself, and gave half to Chrissy. I let her win the first game. I thought maybe it would make her feel better. It did, at least by the expression on her face, which lightened up a little.

"What are you going to do with the money?" I asked.

"I'm going to buy some clothes for my mother," she said. That thought seemed to make her even happier.

"Well," I said, hoping to improve her mood even more, "I'm going to give you $10,000 out of the ransom money." But, having said that, I remembered that there wasn't any ransom money—that was just a ruse I had come up with to get her to cooperate.

By this point, I really didn't know what I was going to do. I didn't want to let her go, but I was getting more and more scared about some real harm coming to her. So I started drinking. I stretched out on the carpet and stared at the ceiling, trying desperately to figure out what I should do.

I must have fallen asleep, because the next thing I knew, Chrissy was gone.

I looked for her for as long as I could, but I knew it was only a matter of time before the police arrived. I got out my gun fully intending to use it on myself. But I decided to drive around for a while and look for Chrissy instead. I thought about driving up to the lake—Clark's Hill Lake—one last time before pulling the trigger. This was the place I had always gone to be alone. But I didn't. I thought about calling the police—they were going to find out soon enough, anyway. But I didn't do that either. After driving around for a while looking for Chrissy, I drove back to the house and the police were already there.

And to think I actually aspired to living a normal life. I even aspired to run for political office—perhaps even high political office. At that moment, the sheer idiocy of it all consumed me.

I also realized that I would probably never have sex again. My life was over.

Part Three

45

Gerry Starrett straightened her blue-and-white print suit, smoothed her hair, and checked her reflection in the window of Sheriff James Metts's office door one last time before knocking. She had come with one purpose only: to get her son out of the Lexington County Jail. She knew she couldn't win his freedom altogether, but at least she could get him moved to a better hell.

She had been to see him just the day before. He looked terrible. Worse, he looked miserable. Did Metts know that Danny's weight had dropped from 165 to 145? She asked Metts what he was planning to do about it without giving him a chance to answer. She had rehearsed this confrontation again and again in her head.

Did Metts know how terrible the conditions were in his jail? Danny was being kept in one of two holding cells that were designed to keep a drunk overnight—someone gets drunk, has a fight with his wife, gets depressed, gets suicidal, they put him in this little cell to dry out. The light stays on all the time, and there's a little window in the door so the guards can keep an eye on him, make sure he's not trying to hang himself or something. That's what these cells were supposed to be for—keeping an eye on someone while he sobered up overnight.

Did Metts know how long Danny had been in that holding cell? *More than two months!*

Metts's mouth said he would look into it and his hand made a note, but his eyes said, "Why should I care?"

Did Metts know that Danny's life had been threatened?

He didn't.

That's right. Another prisoner had threatened to kill him. Danny had told her about it himself.

Metts made another note but looked skeptical.

Gerry flared. Whatever the papers were saying about her son, he didn't lie, not to his mother.

Metts tried to explain that inmates sometimes took reprisals against one another, "especially when young people are involved as victims." He explained this matter-of-factly, without a trace of outrage or regret.

"But he hasn't been tried yet! Isn't he supposed to be innocent until proven guilty?"

"I'm afraid some of these people don't put much stock in our judicial system, ma'am," Metts explained with a little "that's-the-way-it-is" smirk that made Gerry's cheeks burn under her mask of makeup. "They won't wait for judge and jury to determine if he's guilty."

Gerry couldn't hold it in any longer. "My son is a human being!" she cried, trying to tap her anger without yielding to her tears. "There are people who love him and believe in him, who know what kind of person he is and don't buy into all this garbage in the papers. This is a human being you're dealing with, not a monster. My son is a *human being.*"

Gerry Starrett had always been fighting one battle or another. She didn't look like a warrior, of course, with her flawless makeup and perfectly cut, curled, and frosted hair. Nor did she act the way a warrior—of either sex—was supposed to act. She didn't hurl challenges or berate the faint-hearted or vainly parade her power. That wasn't her strategy. Gerry Starrett didn't look or act like a warrior because she chose—had always chosen—to fight her battles in the more private and favorable terrain of the heart.

Gerry never could figure out where she picked up her warring ways. She was the eldest child, after all, the responsible one. Of all her brothers and sisters, five in all, wasn't she most likely to follow in her parents' footsteps: believe what they believed, want what they wanted? Shouldn't the rebel of the family have been one of her younger siblings, one of the ones who went to a big high school where they met other people with other ways of thinking? Gerry didn't have any of that exposure. Her entire childhood, it seemed, had taken place on the little farm in Appling County, Georgia, where her father grew cotton and sweet potatoes and tobacco as well as some feed for his animals.

Yet somehow she knew from early on that there was something wrong about it all—the little farm with its rich soil and long fences and black laborers working the fields. Something just plain wrong about the fact that her father owned a farm—modest as it was—and other people worked it. Or that during the Depression, he was one of the lucky few in the area who got to keep his farm. And whenever she heard someone in her family running down other people because of their race or their religion, or some other accident of birth, and saying it wasn't any surprise that *they* were poor, it made her bristle and ache inside.

For a long time, the only blacks she knew were the ones her father hired to do farmwork and odd jobs—picking cotton mostly. She could remember the first time she saw a black person up close. She was standing behind the screen door before school one morning when a group of them came up the road on their way to work. They were mostly women, a few men, and lots of children, and they were laughing and singing.

Gerry was especially transfixed by three little girls in the group. They looked about her age—as the eldest child on an isolated farm, she had no one her age to play with. She smiled at them and they smiled back. She beckoned them up to the screen door and then scratched a timid welcome as she gazed at their black faces through the screen. She had never seen faces like that. The girls giggled and made little gestures back at her while the older people collected the empty bags that had been laid out on the porch in preparation for the day's labor.

Suddenly, Gerry's mother appeared from the kitchen and saw what was happening. Shrieking, "Oh, my God!" she rushed to the door, jerked Gerry away, and latched the screen as fast as she could. "You get back," she commanded. "Don't you stand near that door, you understand me? You stay away from them."

Gerry wanted to go with them.

Later, when she was attending school in nearby Baxley, she saw the same girls again—or at least she thought she saw them. The state of Georgia had just passed a law that black children had to go to school, too—Gerry's father thought this was a great waste—but they had no way to get there. The only school buses were being used by the white students. So the blacks were transported in an old cleaning van, a big metal box on wheels with windows that didn't open and no place to sit down. On blazing September days, of which there were many in Appling County, Gerry would watch the van go by and think, "It must be as hot as an oven in there."

Every day the van would pass by the white school in Baxley during recess, and every day someone would yell, "They're coming, they're coming!" At the call, all the kids on the playground would run out to the dirt road, clamber onto the wire fence that ran alongside it, and, as the old van rattled by, yell and scream and make faces, hurling the insults and ridicule they had learned from their parents. It was a daily ritual of which the white children of Baxley never seemed to tire.

Then one day, when her place at the fence was closer than usual, Gerry got a particularly good look at the cleaning van and actually saw the faces in the window of the van that day. And she thought she recognized them. They were the same girls who had come onto her porch and shared hellos through the screen door.

More than forty years later she could still see the quilt of their faces pressed against the glass and all of her schoolmates lined up against that fence hurling insults for no reason. "Something clicked," she recalled later, "and it just didn't make sense. It didn't seem right. I went away and I never, ever went back to that fence again."

She was the only one in her family who felt that way, though, and as far as she could tell, she was the only one in her church who felt that way, too. She heard her preacher use Scripture to "prove" that whites were superior to blacks, but that didn't make sense to her, either. She would sneak out at night to look at the sky—this was before electricity dimmed the stars—and ask herself how a creator of so much beauty could have such narrow, mean-spirited thoughts. It just didn't fit, she told herself over and over. She realized for the first time that sooner or later she would have to leave Baxley.

When she was a teenager, Gerry visited relatives in the big city, Savannah, and discovered whole new ways in which life was unfair. She realized that there were not only people far worse off than she but far better off as well. And her sense of the world as a place of wrongs—big and little wrongs, wrongs within wrongs, all in need of righting—was confirmed.

No wrong seemed more unjust to Gerry than the way she was treated because she was a girl. Her father made no effort to hide his disappointment that his eldest child wasn't a son. "I shoulda known a puny woman like your ma couldn't birth no boys," he would say, his lip curling with contempt. Not that she didn't work as hard as any boy: canning food, cleaning, ironing, washing.

But that was nothing compared to what the women in the fields went through. More than once, Gerry had seen the mother of a newborn child do a full day of backbreaking work, pulling her infant behind her in a cardboard box.

No wonder the women she knew as a child were always tired, Gerry thought. No wonder men's work always looked much more interesting to her than women's work. No wonder, when she read books about knights and dragons and damsels in distress, she never wanted to be the princess waiting somewhere for someone to discover her and kiss her and wake her up. Just waiting. That didn't sound right to her. She wanted to be the knight who went off and found his fortune or slayed the dragon.

No wonder, like a lot of girls, she loved school so much. It was the one place where she was doing something to better herself, not just choring. Her idea of heaven was going to school every single day, Saturdays and Sundays included, forever. Gerry's father, however, thought education was wasted on girls. Whenever Gerry brought homework home, her father would thunder, "I send you to school during the day! When you get home, you have chores to do, not schoolwork!"

At times like that, Gerry felt her resolve stiffen. The day would come when she could no longer tolerate the injustice of her father's control.

When that day came, Gerry was fourteen and up before sunrise to help the men drag their heavy loads of tobacco down to the tobacco barn and string them up to dry. Somehow her father found out that she had a date with a boy from school that night. She hadn't told him because she knew what he would say: Girls—good girls, anyway—don't go out on dates; they get married. Period. So when the boy showed up at the door that night, her father chased him away and then turned on her.

She knew she was in trouble as soon as she saw him pull off his belt with the Indian-head buckle. It was the same belt he used on his mules.

One time, she had seen him beat an old mule that wouldn't take the harness, beat it so badly that it couldn't get up. It was pretty much ruined after that, so one day Pa pulled out a gun and shot it.

Now it was her turn.

The blows fell so hard her knees nearly buckled and she urinated down her leg. She screamed and begged him to stop. She fought the pain by thinking of something, anything else. Her first day of school. She was riding next to her father on the front seat of the wagon. They were late for the school bus. He was whipping the mule to go faster. Whipping harder and harder. Suddenly a voice broke her reverie. "Think you're ready to git down on your knees and say you're sorry?"

"No, Pa," cried Gerry through sobs of pain.

So he went back to whipping her, flailing away with righteous abandon.

And Gerry went back to thinking. She thought about her first sight of a shooting star. She thought about how it zoomed through the sky, absolutely silent, at some impossible speed; how it seemed to part the night in its wake; how it seemed to be coming straight toward her. Coming to take her—take her away from Appling County, away from her father.

"Think you've had enough, girl?" she heard him say. "Think you can say you're sorry now?"

But now her mind was set and the pain didn't seem to matter anymore. "Never, Pa," she screamed. "Never!"

Eventually, the pain stopped. Her father, winded and covered with sweat, leaned against the banister and fought to catch his breath, and then stormed out of the house in disgust and defeat.

Not long after that night, Gerry left home. She found a job with a doctor in town and moved into his house while she worked and finished high school. A year later, she was living in Atlanta, working at the Federal Reserve Bank and going to Georgia State College on a scholarship.

When she arrived in Atlanta, she didn't know how to take a bus, had never seen a taxi, and when she walked in the Reserve Bank for the first time and saw the guards, she thought she had mistakenly wandered into a police station. Six months later, she was at a sorority mixer filled

Top, left: Danny at age three. Gerry never had to discipline Danny; he disciplined himself. Of all her children, Danny was the only one who kept his room neat—not just neat, impeccable. And he was the same way about his appearance.

Top, right: After years of hyperactivity—constantly running, jumping, climbing (and falling), and tearing through the house—Danny suddenly disappeared into his room. For days at a time, no one saw him.

Above: Danny with his older sister, Helen. "That's not my brother," said Helen when she heard what Danny was accused of. "If they told me, 'Helen, *you're* being arrested because *you've* done these things,' that's how surprised I feel. There's just no way."

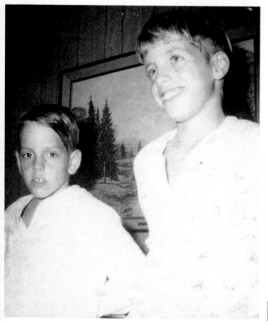

Top, left: Danny (right) with his brother, Robert. It had always puzzled Gerry that Danny was the only one of her kids who had problems in school. He was, after all, at least as bright as any of the others—maybe brighter.

Top, right: Danny suffered two major head injuries as a child. The doctors performed some tests and said there was no permanent damage. "Kids are resilient," they told Gerry. But now, she wonders how they could have been so sure.

Left: At the senior prom. Danny confessed to being "a romantic." "I thought I would find my true love, sweep her off her feet and onto my waiting stallion," he said, "then gallop away to live happily ever after."

with Southern belles and men who smoked—the pretty blond country girl in a party dress whom all the boys wanted to meet.

One of those boys was Santiago.

Only Santiago wasn't like the other boys. At twenty-seven, he didn't seem like a boy at all to Gerry. He had come from Bogotá, Colombia, to visit a cousin at Emory. To a girl who had always thought of Atlanta as a faraway place and New Orleans as unimaginably exotic, South America seemed like a distant universe. He was charming, handsome, rich. He told her how wonderful she was, how beautiful. He took her to a restaurant. She had never been to a restaurant. Whenever Santiago returned her to the church-run home where she lived, the other girls would peer out the windows and hang over the banister to catch a glimpse of him. They, too, had never seen any man quite like him before. He made all the men they were dating seem so young, so plain, so boring. And now he had come for Gerry; come, like the shooting star, to take her away.

When he returned to Bogotá, he called her every night. One night on the telephone, he said something she had never heard before: "I love you." Then he asked her to marry him.

The next thing she knew, she was on a plane—a plane!—to South America. When she arrived, the people who worked at his family's house brought baskets of wild orchids and laid them down as she stepped off the plane. He celebrated her arrival with wine and food and singing and dancing. For a girl from Appling County, Georgia, who had never been dancing—in her church, dancing was a sin—the nightclubs of Bogotá were a brave new world. Even in the countryside, when they drove by a little cantina and she heard music coming out, she made Santiago stop the car. She had to see what was going on inside. When she walked in, all the locals would stare and smile at the pretty blond gringa in the party dress. And then she would dance.

Gerry loved to dance. If dancing was a sin, it was one she embraced with abandon. She wasn't a good dancer. What she cared about was the letting go. When the music started, she did whatever she wanted. She didn't care what anybody else was doing. She just did what the music told her to do. And if Santiago was embarrassed, she didn't care. She was going to dance the way she felt like dancing.

Years later, she heard a country song that made her think of her month in Colombia, and the music drifting out of the roadside cantinas into the tropical night, and dancing her dance:

You got to sing like you don't need the money
Love like you'll never get hurt
You got to dance like nobody's watchin'
It's gotta come from the heart if you want it to work.

The fantasy ended when Gerry returned to America to tell her family about Santiago. "What in the world are you doing?" "How could you live there?" "You don't know his family!" "You have no idea what it's like to be married to one of them!" "You're not really in love, you just think you are!"

Gerry fought them all. Even when her grandfather wrote a letter—the first and only time he ever wrote to a grandchild—telling her that she was dishonoring the family by marrying a Catholic, and that if she went through with it she would never go to heaven, Gerry would not be stopped. She flew to Miami and waited there for Santiago. As soon as he could get away from his business in Bogotá, he would come and take her away.

Only, he never came. She had fought her family, fought her church, even fought her own fears, and won every battle, and he never showed up. Only a few weeks after she abandoned the wait in Miami and returned to Atlanta, she met a reserved young engineering student, a Mormon from Wyoming named Richard Starrett. Six months later, she married him.

46

Gerry was never defeated, and she never surrendered; she just moved the battle to a different field. Now it was work. First, she worked to finish putting Richard through school. Then, as soon as Richard started

Top: Richard and Gerry Starrett on their wedding day. Danny called his parents "loving but typically middle American in their attitude about sex. They weren't prudish...but sex was still something secret."

Middle: The Starrett family in the sixties; Gerry holding Danny. "When people talk about Ozzie and Harriet families," said Danny, "they think about families like ours."

Bottom: Gerry, Gail, Helen, and Danny, far right. "I think ours was an incredibly loving, normal family," said Danny.

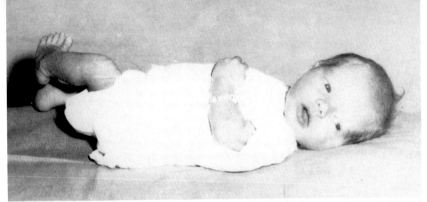

Top: Richard Daniel Starrett, newborn. Gerry still remembers her shock when she saw Danny for the first time, his head black and purple with bruises.

Right: Danny as a baby. Twenty-nine years later, his mother would strain to remember if Danny been "different from other babies."

To his sisters and brother, Danny (far right) was "the one they could always count on." "If he had a cookie," said his sister Helen, "and you wanted some of it, Danny would give you the whole thing, not just half."

Left to right: Officer Mike Adams, who reached kidnap victim Chrissy Blake just after her escape. COURTESY OF CAPT. MIKE ADAMS

Prosecutor Michael C. Eubanks believed "with vivid clarity" that the death penalty was justified. "Some people are just terrible people," he said, "and for them, the only logical outcome is death." COURTESY OF MICHAEL C. EUBANKS

Prosecutor Donald Myers dismissed defense claims that Danny was mentally ill. "He's just a serial criminal," Myers insisted. "He planned. He schemed. He made sure everything was right." Said another prosecutor: "He's a glad dog, not a mad dog." COURTESY OF DONALD MYERS

Left to right: Jack Swerling was a fast-talking defense lawyer from New Jersey who had come south to law school, married a local girl, and decided to stay.
COURTESY OF JACK SWERLING

A military brat, former Green Beret, and Vietnam vet, defense attorney August F. "Bud" Siemon was a warrior—like Gerry Starrett. COURTESY OF AUGUST F. SIEMON

"We all come from dysfunctional families in one way or another," said Dr. Robert Storms, chief forensic psychologist at Georgia's Central State Hospital. "We don't even know what normal is." Yet nothing was more abnormal, Storms felt, than the Starrett family's droning insistence that everything was normal. COURTESY OF KEVIN G. KEISTER

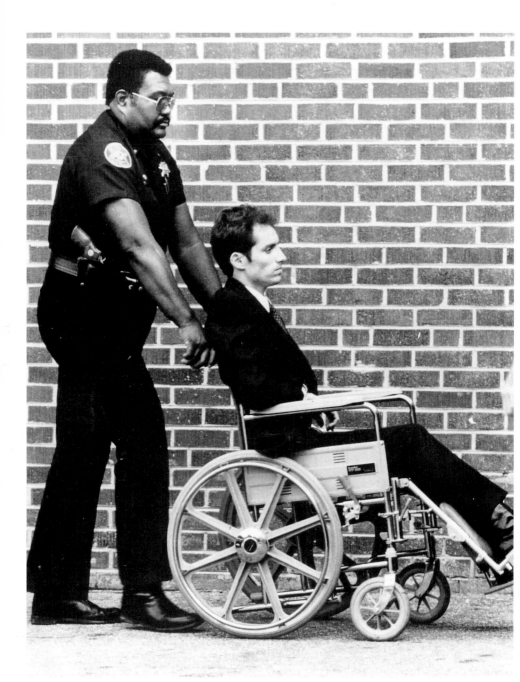

As they rolled Danny into the Lexington County Courthouse for yet another hearing, Gerry thought he looked as pale and thin as a cadaver. He stared absently straight ahead the whole time, into the middle distance, and never said a word. COURTESY OF DOUG GILMORE AND THE STATE-RECORD CO.

his first job, she turned her energies to his work. She thought it would be good for his career to entertain, so she went to the library and read every book she could find on "what upwardly mobile people did and the right look and everything."

But that wasn't good enough. Unlike Gerry, Richard was a reluctant student of upward mobility. "He considered socializing a chore, unless it was golf with his buddies," she later told a friend. "I never had to set the alarm for that." Besides, Gerry's ambitions demanded a bigger stage than candlelight dinners and backyard barbecues. So she started a fashion business in Panama, designing and marketing clothes, mainly to the wives of other army officers, and doing "color analysis"—determining exactly what hues were right for people's makeup and clothing.

When she moved back to the States in 1975, Gerry started visiting spas around her home in Monmouth, New Jersey, offering her color-analysis expertise "for one day only." More and more, she found herself doing not just makeup, not just color, but the "total look"—everything from shoes and handbags to body proportions and posture. Years before the term came into vogue, Gerry became a "personal shopper." A local department store gave her space in one of its stores, and customers made appointments to see her. She helped them with everything: wardrobe, accessories, makeup, hairstyle.

Business boomed, and before long Gerry had the whole family involved. Helen shopped, Gail manned the reception desk, Robert learned how to do color analysis, and Danny helped with the accounting. When the store objected to having nonemployees on the premises, Gerry packed up and moved to a competing chain. Only this time, she kept moving—from store to store—rather than setting up shop in one place. Her "team" traveled with her: a hairdresser, a clothing expert, and usually one of her children. She herself did the color analysis. They were constantly on the road: South Carolina, Alabama, Virginia. In anticipation of her arrival, Gerry insisted that stores advertise—"Gerry Starrett Will Be Available"—and take reservations as well as advance payment. If a minimum number of people didn't sign up by a certain date, the visit was called off. Gerry insisted on that, too.

In 1987, she opened up her own shop. In a leased space on Boy

Scout Road in Augusta, she laid out all the trappings of a traditional beauty salon: two chairs, three hairdressers, one nail technician, and two makeup artists. But that was just the beginning. After years of buying every different line of makeup for her customers, Gerry had come to realize that one brand was pretty much like another. How well it sold depended on who was selling it and how it was presented. So she might as well sell it herself. After all, no one was better at presentation than Gerry Starrett.

That was the start of her own line of cosmetics, skin care, and hair-care products, all sold exclusively in her salon and all emblazoned with her company's new name: The ImageMaker.

But that wasn't enough, either. Gerry wanted The ImageMaker to be about more than just cosmetics and hair. She wanted it to be about "helping people feel better about themselves," she said, "not just the way they look, but inwardly." Thus, anything that could make a person feel more comfortable and more competent *belonged* in her shop. So she started giving classes: in etiquette, in body language, in interpersonal behavior, in ordering food and wine. Soon ladies' groups were calling, asking her to talk at their luncheons. She spent more of her time giving speeches than doing color analysis.

So many customers showed up, in fact, that Gerry opened an even bigger shop. She called it her "dream shop": four thousand square feet of image making, and every square inch of it designed by her personally, right down to the special cabinets at the hairdressing stations that hid all the unsightly clutter. "Nothing is borrowed from someone else or somewhere else," she said proudly, "but created from my own head, piece by piece. It is beautiful."

Beautiful to Gerry was sterile and clean. She wanted her salon to look as if "a physician could come in and perform surgery," because she had always been appalled by how dirty most salons were. The "hair technicians" wore lab coats. Each technician had his or her own enclosed area where nothing was allowed to sit out, not even a pair of idle scissors.

Champagne and wine were served—one drink per customer—as well as unlimited quantities of soda pop and specially prepared fruit drinks. Now and then, the staff dietician would bring around special muffins and hand out copies of the recipe. Everything was complimentary, of course. This was a spa, not a salon, and the price was all-inclusive.

Here, finally, Gerry could serve all of her clients' needs. In addition to eight hairdressers and the registered dietician, the staff included nail technicians, makeup consultants, skin-care experts, personal shoppers, physical therapists, massage therapists, and, of course, color consultants, plus a manager, a secretary, and a receptionist. Fifteen people in all. Classes were going on all the time in everything from menu preparation to speech making.

But it was still very much Gerry Starrett's business.

Clients who just wanted a shampoo, cut, and style might never see her. But for those who wanted a "complete image consultation," Gerry always took a personal interest in designing a program that suited their needs and budgets.

But it still wasn't enough for Gerry. Something was still missing. No sooner was everything in place than she began to wonder if she was "just patching things up, not doing anything permanent." Sure, some people came in just because they were tired of their current hairstyle, but what about the others? Gerry could spot them because she had been one herself once. What about the people who came in because "they had a deep-seated need that stemmed from a lack of self-esteem"? What about the woman who was recently divorced and blamed herself? What about the college student who was about to graduate but didn't know what to do with her life? All the color consultations and skin-care products in the world were "only putting Band-Aids" on people like that.

So Gerry added a clinical psychologist to her staff. After all, she told herself, the business really was born out of her desire to help people feel better about themselves. Just as a little farm girl out of Appling County could overcome her insecurities and learn to like herself, so could they. And she started thinking, "What would it be like if there were a school where you could learn the things you needed to feel both comfortable in polite society and comfortable with yourself?"

That's what Gerry had created at The ImageMaker. Not a salon, not a spa, but a school: a school for reassurance, a school for self-respect, a school for security, a school that was making a quarter of a million dollars a year—and just getting started.

Then came the call from the police in the middle of the night looking for Danny. After that, Gerry barely thought about the business again. The battle moved to a new field.

47

Only days after her visit to Sheriff Metts's office, Gerry won her first battle: Danny was moved out of the Lexington County Jail. The governor of South Carolina signed a special order permitting him to be placed in a state prison prior to his trial. Sheriff Metts swore out an affidavit declaring Danny both "a security risk," because of the death threats he had received, and an "escape risk." Any prisoner that risky, said Metts, had to be transferred to the Columbia Correctional Institute, or CCI, in the state capital, for "safekeeping."

At last, Gerry thought, they'll start treating him like a human being.

She couldn't have been more wrong. If the Lexington County Jail was the fifth circle of hell, CCI was the first. A huge, brooding pile of gray stone dating from the Civil War, CCI was a relic of an earlier, sterner time. With tiny, cold, block cells and huge, echoing cell blocks, it had never been a pleasant place, even when new. Now, with decades of accumulated grime and neglect, rotting plaster and rusting metal, it had taken on a dark air of almost medieval grimness.

At the darkest, grimmest heart of this place was the death-row cell block where they put Danny Starrett. They called it a "safekeeping cell"—a place where special prisoners could be isolated from the main prison population: because they were dangerous; because they were likely to be hurt; paradoxically, because they were waiting to die; because they needed to be watched. In short, the death-row cell block was, in another grim paradox, the safest place at CCI. As a prisoner who had not yet been convicted of anything—and therefore technically innocent—Danny needed a safe place. And, even more, the state of South Carolina needed a safe place for him.

Starrett's cell, on the third floor of the block, was a six-by-nine concrete cubicle with rusty bars at one end, a small barred window at the other, water-stained walls, a seatless toilet, and a little sink, all ancient and encrusted, filthy and swarming with roaches. And a TV. Previous occupants had spent unnumbered hours scratching obscenities on every wall except one. On that wall, the words "Jesus Saves" had been etched with care, and the space around it left reverently blank.

Out the wall of bars at one end, Danny could see into the large common area onto which the three tiers of cells opened. On the other side were big windows, barred from floor to ceiling. Through those he could see across a field, past several prison buildings, across a fence, and past a parking lot to a little green park, far in the distance, where people walked their dogs and children played in the afternoons after school. Danny would spend hours gazing, as if through a telescope, at the activity in this speck of real life.

There wasn't much else to do. There were forty other men in the death-row block, but, as an inmate in safekeeping, Danny wasn't permitted any contact with them. He was taken out for walks by himself, escorted to the showers or to the phone in the courtyard by himself. He could hear them, though, as they stood against the bars and yelled back and forth at one another like dueling echoes. He could hear their curses and their TVs. At night, after the TVs were ordered off, he could hear someone in a lower tier reading a Bible to the man in the neighboring cell who couldn't read.

Idle and restless, Danny started a diary. He called it his "jailhouse journal."

(2/24/89) *I'm in an alien world. I'm sitting in a death-row cell block, me, Richard Daniel Starrett. One of the good guys. I'm in an alien world. The whole thing is—none of it is real.*

Gerry came as often as they would let her to the little visitors' booth with its dirty windows and water-stained walls. She listened to

Danny's accounts of the indignities of life on death row. She heard how the guards refused to let him shave or put on clean clothes before court appearances. How they handcuffed him through the bars before taking him anywhere—"So he's *never* free," Gerry reported to Richard, "not even for a second!" How they came with search warrants and plucked samples of his pubic hair. How they forced him to take mood elevators—"happy pills"—before meeting with prosecutors. "That's just so when they attack him their consciences won't bother them," she fumed.

When she tried to bolster Danny's sagging spirits by sending a minister to see him, not only was Danny handcuffed behind his back the whole time, but the guard who brought him in refused to leave the room. As soon as Gerry heard the story, she stalked into the warden's office. "This is totally unnecessary," she charged. "How is Danny supposed to talk to his minister with his hands behind his back and some stranger sitting in the room? Why should he have to suffer this way? He has his dignity. He has his pride. He's a human being!"

The warden promised halfheartedly to look into her complaints, but within days Gerry faced a new crisis. Danny refused to eat. He had stopped eating on and off for a few days at a time ever since his arrest, at one point losing almost twenty pounds before starting to eat again. Every time, the reason was the same: He was depressed—more depressed than usual—and wanted to withdraw from the world. He never actually said that, but Gerry could tell. She would come to visit and *he wouldn't talk to her.* Danny—who loved to talk, who couldn't wait to tell her what had happened at school that day, who would sit on the kitchen counter and talk for hours, wouldn't talk to her. She didn't need to hear from the warden that Danny wasn't eating to know that something was terribly wrong.

This time, he didn't break out of it. His weight dropped from 165 to 140, then to 120, and he still wouldn't eat. As she watched her son wasting away, Gerry pleaded with the warden to do something. "He's trying to kill himself," she wailed. Every day she made phone calls to prison officials, prosecutors, and police investigators.

Finally, when Danny had shriveled to 105 pounds, prison officials capitulated. They moved him out of the death-row cell block at CCI and into the infirmary of a new state prison, Kirkland Correctional Institute, or KCI, on the outskirts of Columbia. Then they sought a court order to feed him intravenously.

Gerry thought she had won the battle, that someone was finally treating her son like a human being. Then she discovered why Warden Bill Wallace had ordered the transfer. Like Danny, he had read a book about serial killer Ted Bundy that described how Bundy stopped eating and lost weight in order to squeeze through the air-conditioning grate in the ceiling of his cell and crawl to freedom. Wallace wasn't about to let that happen in his prison. Just to be sure, he also ordered that Danny be chained hand and foot while in the infirmary and stationed three guards at his bedside.

When Gerry visited the infirmary and saw the guards and the chains, she was apoplectic. "What do they think he's going to do in his condition, tear the place apart?" she railed at Richard when she returned. "It's like they expect him any minute to turn into a monster!"

But at least he was safe, she told herself.

Later the same evening, the infirmary staff inserted an IV needle in Danny's arm so incompetently that he bled through the night. The next morning his gown and bed were soaked with blood.

48

Gerry Starrett sat in Jack Swerling's busy office in downtown Columbia amid a crowd of lawyers: little lawyers in plastic and wood, gathered in knots around little plastic judges, haranguing from little wooden lecterns, weeping before little porcelain juries. Everywhere Gerry looked she saw these little frozen comic vignettes of life in the law, and all she wanted to do was cry.

She had talked to what seemed like a hundred lawyers in a hundred offices like this one, trying to find someone to represent Danny. In fact, it had only been a few, but the prospect of retelling her story—Danny's story—to yet again another stranger left her despondent.

First there was the disappointment of Henderson Johnson. He was a nice man, Gerry thought, and undoubtedly a good lawyer, but they couldn't afford his $50,000 fee. Eventually, Johnson referred her to Richard Allen, a former district attorney in Augusta. But at first Allen offered only to act as a go-between, to talk to the D.A. in Richmond County, South Carolina, where the first charges would be brought. Just for that he wanted a $1,000 retainer. When she asked him about representing Danny, he said he, too, would need $50,000—up front. Now they were a thousand dollars poorer, and Danny was still without an attorney.

It wasn't that they didn't have the money. Between their savings, Richard's salary, the equity in the house, and the money coming in from The ImageMaker—although business at the salon had already begun to slump as a result of the notoriety—they had enough to pay a lawyer. But only enough for *one* lawyer for *one* trial. Danny was facing charges in three counties in South Carolina and one in Georgia. That meant at least *four* trials—long, complicated trials—and maybe more, depending on what revelations lay in store. Every morning, Gerry picked up the paper with a prayer on her lips.

She also knew that the last of these trials, the one in Georgia, was the most important. That was the murder trial, the capital trial, the trial at which the state would do everything in its power to put her son to death. If they had only enough money for one lawyer for one trial, Gerry decided, they should save it for that. In the meantime, they would have to take a public defender.

But when Gerry applied to the court to appoint a public defender, she faced another battle. Danny Starrett had the money to hire his own attorney, prosecutors argued, citing his wife's frequent trips to California, his frequent car rentals, and the nearly $1,300 found by investigators in his $400-a-month rented home. "I just don't think my tax dollars, or those of anybody in South Carolina, should go to hire him a lawyer," one of the prosecutors complained to a reporter. "Had he not been arrested last week, he would not be filing for bankruptcy or for food stamps today, and that's what you think of when you think of an indigent."

Then one day at an arraignment, a big, burly man stood up and declared that *he* would represent Richard Daniel Starrett. He was Jack Swerling, a very un-Southern, fast-talking lawyer from New Jersey who had come south to law school, married a local girl, and decided to stay. In the ten years since, he had made a considerable name for himself in high-profile, high-paying, high-publicity cases. Henderson Johnson had called Swerling "probably the leading criminal defense lawyer in South Carolina right now," and early on recommended that the Starretts take their case to him. They had, but found his fees, like everybody else's, prohibitively high. Now, in a rare stroke of luck, a judge had appointed Swerling to take the case as a public defender—at no fee.

The next day, Gerry was back amid the crowd of play lawyers, trying to concentrate on Swerling's detailed explanation of his strategy for her son's case while biting back the sobs that threatened to erupt at every mention of Danny's name.

The trial in Georgia was the one to worry about, said Swerling. Every decision in the South Carolina cases had to be made with Georgia in mind.

Like what to plead.

"Under normal circumstances," Swerling said in his deep, reassuring voice, "I would recommend Danny plead not guilty by reason of insanity." Then there would be a hearing to determine if Danny met the legal definition of "competent": Was he able to understand the wrongness of his actions? Was he able to control those actions? Was he able to participate in his own defense?

The prosecution would call doctors to say he was competent, and Swerling would call doctors to say he wasn't. Then the judge would probably call it a wash, throw out the experts on both sides, take one look at Danny, and say, "This man looks competent to me," and not accept the plea. Then Danny would either have to enter a straight guilty plea or go to trial. "And you know Danny's attitude about that," said Swerling.

Gerry did, indeed. Danny had told her many times: "Under no cir-

cumstances do I want to put the victims in the position of having to testify in court."

But Swerling was more worried about the effects of a competency
hearing on the Georgia case. If Danny was found competent—"and
chances are fifty-fifty that he would be," said Swerling—then a smart
Georgia prosecutor could use that against him in the murder trial:
"Your Honor, a South Carolina court has already rejected Mr. Starrett's
insanity claim."

"What about a not-guilty plea?" Gerry ventured, her mind adrift in
the sea of possibilities.

"Mrs. Starrett," Swerling instructed in words that Gerry would re-
play over and over in her mind through the next few months, "I'm afraid
you don't understand. Your son has signed confessions to all of these
crimes. The police have forensic evidence from his house and statements from the girls. No, if Danny is ruled competent, then I either
have to enter a straight guilty plea or go to a jury trial. In a jury trial,
the victims would have to testify. Danny says he won't let that happen.
So we have no choice: We have to plead guilty."

Unless.

Swerling had another idea. He wanted Danny to plead "guilty but
mentally ill," a relatively new plea that South Carolina and other states
had adopted in response to the public furor over the acquittal of John
Hinckley, the attempted assassin of Ronald Reagan. Previously, the
only plea available to a "crazy" person was "not guilty by reason of insanity." But thanks to aggressive defense attorneys, who could produce
"experts" willing to find almost any defendant insane, and public outrage over not guilty verdicts in high-profile cases, the old rule was
crumbling. When Hinckley was found not guilty by reason of insanity,
it collapsed. Justice still demanded some allowance for insanity pleas,
but the public demanded accountability and the result was "guilty but
mentally ill."

Gerry didn't like either part of that formulation: either the "guilty"
or the "mentally ill." Part of her still wanted to believe her Danny was
neither of those things.

Swerling sensed her hesitation. "Believe me, Mrs. Starrett, that's the only defense I can see. You can hope for a miracle if you like, but I have to go on what I see."

Gerry gazed out the window of Swerling's office for a long time before answering. Since their last conversation, she had talked to the doctors who were examining Danny. They had recommended that he see a private psychiatrist. She had also read part of the autobiographical sketch he had written in jail. In it, she learned for the first time about the pornography and the drawings and the stalking and the voices. This wasn't an opinion of some doctor who didn't know her son; this was from Danny himself. She thought she knew him so well, yet this was a person she hardly recognized.

"Guilty but mentally ill," she repeated. "I agree."

The next day, Swerling went back to Danny and explained the plea.

"I am not crazy," Danny said with finality. "I am *not* mentally ill."

"The only alternative," Swerling warned ominously, "is a trial. And that means the victims will have to testify."

"I won't have that," Danny said again and again. "I won't put those girls through the . . . the . . . the whole thing again."

Gerry arrived at the Lexington County Courthouse a few days later and sat in the front row, to be sure Danny saw her. He was brought into the courtroom in a wheelchair. Emaciated after two weeks of once again refusing to eat, he looked like a cadaver: thin and pale and barely there. When the indictment was read, charging him with two counts of kidnapping and sexual assault, and the judge asked him, "How do you plead?" he responded in a voice as distant and disembodied as a sleepwalker's, "Guilty, Your Honor."

"Guilty, but mentally ill," Swerling clarified.

The judge accepted the plea without argument.

Swerling allowed a smile of victory. But to Gerry, it hardly seemed like a victory.

Then the judge pronounced sentence: "Two life terms to run consecutively."

And Gerry wept.

49

She didn't stop fighting, though. She wasn't prepared to give up that easily, even if her son was. Outside the courthouse, she confronted the prosecutors in dueling interviews with reporters.

"Richard Daniel Starrett is not mentally ill," declared prosecutor Donald Myers. "He's just a serial criminal. He planned. He schemed. He made sure everything was right. He's extremely dangerous."

On another occasion, Myers said, Starrett put a blue police light on his car and stopped two women near Lexington. "But he didn't bother them because they were too old. If he had uncontrollable urges, it wouldn't have made any difference what they looked like." Finally, Myers claimed that if Starrett had attempted to plead mental illness, "we would have had probably twelve witnesses to show he's not mentally ill."

When reporters brought those quotes to Gerry, she wiped her eyes and lashed back at Myers. "And we could stack up hundreds of people who have known Danny all his life who could prove that isn't true. My son is definitely mentally disturbed. He couldn't have committed the crimes otherwise. No one can be in a position of always helping and never asking for themselves. That was our Daniel. He was the one in our family who had no problems. I guess that should have been a warning that something was wrong. Since the arrest, I have heard psychologists say they worry when parents tell them their children have no problems."

"So Danny had no problems growing up?" someone shouted.

"None," said Gerry defiantly. "Danny was the perfect son."

"But now you believe that he's mentally ill?"

"Absolutely," Gerry heard herself say. "My son is mentally ill."

Of course, Gerry had known for years that her son was "sick," although she preferred to think in terms of headaches and pills and good nights' sleep. Even after she added a psychologist to the staff at The ImageMaker, she never allowed herself to think that anyone in *her* family needed that kind of help—least of all Danny. She knew he had been seeing a doctor at the Humana Hospital in Augusta, but he never made clear—and she never asked him to clarify—exactly what his complaints were or what the doctor was prescribing for them. Whenever she ventured near the subject, all he had to say was the magic word *headache*, and whatever little passing shadow of fear she felt was instantly dispelled.

After Danny's arrest, when she finally allowed herself to believe that her son needed help, she couldn't find it. His doctor at Humana, fearing a lawsuit, wouldn't talk to her. The police, who had drafted her into their manhunt with promises to "get Danny the help he needs," wouldn't return her calls, or, if they did, turned a deaf ear to her pleas for help. "I'm no psychologist," one of them told her bluntly, "but in my opinion, your son's not sick. He was smart enough to get a good job with the Department of Energy. He had security clearances, which means a big background investigation. He was smart enough to use a rental car instead of using his own car, smart enough to make those girls lie down in the backseat and cover up, smart enough to realize when Chrissy Blake got away that he'd better get the hell out of there, smart enough to go by his storage bin and destroy all the evidence of his other crimes, and then smart enough to make it from here to Texas without any money. In my opinion, if he's sick, he didn't get that way until after he got caught and realized he was in big trouble."

Gerry's hopes were raised briefly when, on Henderson Johnson's recommendation, a forensic psychiatrist visited Danny in the Lexington jail. Everett Kuglar was the director of Georgia Regional, a public mental hospital in Augusta, and an old friend of Johnson's. A straight-backed, stern-faced colonel in the Georgia reserves, Kuglar interviewed Danny several times, looking for a personality disorder that could be the basis for an insanity plea. But before Kuglar could find anything, Gerry decided they couldn't afford Johnson's fee, and when Johnson dropped out of the case, so did Kuglar.

Not until Danny was transferred to Kirkland Correctional Institute in March did Gerry allow herself to feel hope again. At KCI he was placed in Gilliam Psychiatric Hospital, a separate unit within the prison where inmates were treated for psychological problems. "Finally," she told Richard, "he'll get some real help."

She was wrong again.

Less than an hour after he arrived, Danny was in trouble with the staff psychiatrist assigned to his case. As Gerry later heard the story, Danny had arrived at Gilliam with some paper and pencils he had been using to write his journal. The psychiatrist, Dr. Rose Lawson, ordered that they be taken away. She also took away all his books except for two. That was the maximum allowable, she said.

When Gerry heard this, she immediately went to see Lawson. "You have to understand," she said, "the most important thing in the world to Danny is not cigarettes, it's not food, it's not a television, it's not talking to people—it's reading, and writing, and thinking. When you take his books and pencils and paper away, you hit right where it hurts most."

"That's the policy," said Lawson curtly. "He can't have a pencil because he might hurt himself."

The next time Gerry visited Danny, though, he had forgotten the pencils and paper. He had a new complaint: the noise.

The hospital cells were arrayed in a semicircle around an open bay, two stories high, overlooked by a central control room where guards kept watch from behind bulletproof glass. In the middle of the bay stood a metal contraption that held five huge televisions arranged in such a way that every cell had a clear view of at least one screen. The sound on all five sets was turned up full blast, all day long, and the big open bay would rock, the cell doors vibrate, from morning until night, with the sounds of *Wheel of Fortune* or *Big-Time Wrestling*, punctuated now and then by the unsynchronized moans and hoots and screaming fits of the captive audience.

Danny closed the door to his cell, but it did no good. The thunderous noise poured through a big screened slot in the middle of the door "like water through a net," he told his mother. "It's just torture for me."

Much more serious was another run-in with Dr. Lawson. For their first interview, she had him brought into a room wearing leg irons and belly chains, and there were two other people with her, a guard and a nurse. Danny refused to talk to her with anyone else in the room. Dr. Lawson refused to ask the guard and nurse to leave. She wondered why he found their presence disturbing. "After you have been here a certain time and are at a certain level," she tried to explain, "and we determine that you are not dangerous, hallucinating, or actively psychotic, then we will let you out of the chains so that you can talk to me alone in my office. But until then the chains, the guard, and the nurse stay right here."

Danny still refused to talk. "If you are concerned about your safety," he told her, "I can understand that and I can deal with having these leg irons and belly chains on. But I can't deal with these two people sitting here listening as I pour out my deepest, darkest secrets, my most painful and personal experiences, to you."

Still, Lawson refused to ask the others to leave.

They had reached an impasse. After a few more minutes of silent confrontation, Lawson ordered the guard to take Danny back to his cell. The next day, when he was brought back to try again, the guard and nurse were there again—only they were a *different* guard and nurse. Danny complained to Lawson: "After a year here, every guard and nurse in the place will know every detail of my private life. Why don't I just get on a loudspeaker and tell it to the world?"

That was the end of that session.

When Gerry heard the story, she, too, was indignant. How dare they not permit her son to speak privately with his psychiatrist? How did Lawson expect to get open and honest responses from Danny in front of an audience? As soon as she returned home, she called the public defender's office to express her outrage. "Did you know they won't let Danny speak to his psychiatrist in private?"

The next day, Dr. Lawson called Danny back into her office.

She was furious.

"I just got a call telling me that patients should be able to talk privately with their psychiatrists," she said bitterly, biting back her anger. "How dare you question the way I run my therapy session?"

"All I did was talk to my mother about it," Danny said.

"Don't lie to me, Mr. Starrett," Lawson exploded. "You orchestrated this whole thing. You're just trying to manipulate me, manipulate the therapeutic environment, just as you've manipulated everything and everyone else in your life."

Danny remained calm. Infuriatingly calm. "I would have thought that, as a psychiatrist, you would be pleased that now you're permitted to have more private conversations with your patients."

"Well, let me tell you, sir. When I took this job, I promised my husband that I would *always* have someone in the room with me. He was concerned for my safety, and I promised him."

"I understand completely," said Danny. "But by the same token, you have to understand—"

"Understand this," Lawson snapped. "You need at least a year in psychotherapy—*at least!*—if I'm going to have any chance of helping you with your problems."

Danny wanted to know what problems.

"Well, to begin with," said Lawson, "you are a narcissistic, sexual sadist."

Stunned, Danny thought for a long time before responding. "I guess it can't get much worse than that," he finally said.

(3/2/89) *How could she conclude something like that? A narcissistic sexual sadist? First, if she would talk with anyone—family, friends, coworkers—none of them would characterize me as being a self-centered, selfish, narcissistic kind of person. There is no evidence for that. That's point one.*

As for point two, that I was sadistic, I know enough of what went on to know that there were no overt acts of sadism. I know that she could read the police reports and find no evidence of any sadistic acts.

Plus, outside of those incidents, I have other relationships in which there is not any element of sadism. I have been married for five years, and I have never laid a hand on my wife. There is no evidence anywhere to support narcissism or sadism.

So how in the hell did she come to such a terrible conclusion about me?

The next time Gerry visited, Danny recounted the story of his confrontation with Dr. Lawson and especially his revulsion at her diagnosis.

"I can't tell you how much it hurt me to hear Dr. Lawson say something like that," he muttered, looking very sad. "Imagine. Me. I can't think of anything worse that you could call somebody. A narcissistic sexual sadist loves to love himself and loves to hurt other people. How could she see me as some manipulative, narcissistic, self-centered person who wants everything his way?"

Gerry had no answer.

50

After that, Danny refused to talk to Dr. Lawson again. He also refused to eat or to go outside. Before long, Dr. Lawson came to him. "Mr. Starrett, you know, I'm sorry," she said, summoning all the limited supply of contrition at her command. "Perhaps sometimes I am a little hard with you. That's my manner. I am a direct person. That is how I believe in dealing with problems, confronting them directly. I don't always think that it is good to tiptoe around on eggshells. I don't mean to hurt you, but you have a hard, defensive shell to crack."

Danny smiled benignly and said, "I understand," but still refused to talk to her.

He did, however, speak to Lawson's underling, a staff psychologist, Wanda Tarpley. He had liked Tarpley ever since the day in Lawson's office when Tarpley fearlessly volunteered to see Danny alone—without benefit of guard or nurse or even chains. Danny liked Tarpley's directness and warmth. She always called him "Daniel," while Dr. Lawson never called him anything but "Mr. Starrett." (" 'Mr. Starrett, tell me all of your deepest, darkest secrets, Mr. Starrett,' " he would mock her. "I feel as if I'm talking to my boss.")

A middle-aged mother of three, Tarpley wrapped Danny in motherly compassion. "It's as though she's saying, 'I trust you,' " Danny told Gerry. " 'Regardless of what terrible things I may have read about you, I think there is something decent in you and I'm going to trust you.' "

Not coincidentally, Danny also thought that Tarpley perceived that he was not crazy—"I think rightly so—but that there is a lot going on underneath the surface, and I think that she is concerned for me."

When Tarpley finally got around to telling him exactly what she thought was "going on underneath the surface," however, it did not please Danny at all. He was suffering from "a dissociative state," she told him, "which is usually the result of a psychotraumatic childhood." She wanted to know if he had had some kind of childhood sexual trauma.

Danny was aghast. "Absolutely not," he insisted. While it was true that whenever he read an article about childhood abuse, he "got this queasy feeling," he was certain that "if something like that had happened to me, then I would know it." So he had dismissed that possibility a long time ago, and he thought Tarpley should too.

But Tarpley wouldn't. "Isn't it conceivable," she pressed, "that you could have been raped as a child or something?"

For a moment Danny was too shocked to answer. "Why wouldn't I know something like that?" he said when he found his voice.

"Well, people do block it out, you know."

"I . . . I . . . just don't think that something could have happened to me that was so traumatic that I could not remember it." Danny stammered some more, until his rational defenses kicked in. "And besides, even if there was something like that, why didn't I exhibit these behaviors earlier on? Why didn't they show up until I was a teenager?"

"Actually," said Tarpley, "a common time for split personalities to appear is in late adolescence. They can be sublimated during the childhood and early teenage years; then they manifest themselves in your late teens and twenties."

But Danny was firm. "I have racked my brain for anything in my childhood like that," he insisted even more loudly and stridently. "But there's nothing. Nothing! I had a *wonderful* childhood."

Tarpley wasn't convinced. She wanted to put Danny's memory to the test. She wanted to hypnotize him.

Both Danny and Gerry balked, but before the battle over hypnosis and control of Danny's past could be joined, Dr. Lawson ended it: She was sending Danny back to CCI. She had finally had enough. She was tired of his complaining, frustrated by his unwillingness to talk to her, fed up with his hunger strikes and other blackmail, his questions, his back talk, his endless "one-smart-person-to-another" chatter and self-serving theories about himself. He was making her look bad: assigned to her but not talking to her, talking instead to her underling— a mere psychologist.

(3/21/89) I'm sure most of the people that [Dr. Lawson] is exposed to are uneducated, illiterate, not the cream of the crop, mentally speaking; people who are institutionalized in passing. They answer yes or no to questions. Then someone comes in here who shows real intelligence and starts questioning her, questioning the policy of the place. No wonder her reaction is, "Who the hell do you think you are?"

I talked with her, I questioned the policy about pencils, about having someone in the room when I'm talking. I can see how it all came together for her, how she could come to think, "This man clearly thinks he's special, and he is clearly a narcissistic criminal. He wants everything his way, he's trying to manipulate everything, he's trying to make things happen his way, and I want him out."

Maybe it's just as well. I have grown to hate this place with a passion, and I am ready to go to any prison rather than stay here. But I will miss Wanda. I doubt if I will find anyone like her again. She is like a life preserver, and it is as if I am drowning in the ocean.

51

When Gerry heard that her son was being transferred back to the hellhole of CCI, she could hardly contain her rage. He didn't get a fair chance, she railed at Dr. Lawson. They didn't give him enough time. He had just begun treatment. How could they expect to make a meaningful evaluation in such a short time? They had only started investigating the possibility that Danny's problems were related to "childhood traumas"—blows to his head from falling off the slide and tumbling out of the car. Skull X rays and a CT scan showed nothing. "There's no tumor growing in there," Tarpley had told her, "so we don't need to worry about that." But surely there was more they could do, Gerry insisted. Danny said he needed an EEG, for example, but now there wouldn't be time.

All Dr. Lawson could say was, "Don't worry." Danny would continue his therapy as an outpatient in the psychiatric unit at CCI, she assured Gerry, and would continue to get the best care. Gerry laughed bitterly. "Obviously, doctor, you've never spent any time at CCI."

Because the discharge report from Gilliam concluded that Danny "was not a threat to himself or others," the doctors at CCI took their time in adding his case to a patient list already overloaded with certifiably psychotic and dangerous inmates. When he finally did make it to the psychiatric ward, his case was assigned to a graduate student. "Hi, I'm Tiffany," she said brightly when they met. "I'll be doing your psychotherapy." Tiffany had a bachelor's degree and was working on her master's. She was a student in training. Danny described her in his journal as "a sweet girl."

Appalled at the way Danny was being bounced around from one inadequate evaluation to another, Gerry began a telephone campaign to get him transferred to the Hall Institute, a psychiatric facility in Columbia that routinely did forensic psychiatric examinations for the state of South Carolina. But even when she succeeded in convincing a judge to order an evaluation at Hall, Danny got short shrift. Unlike every other inmate undergoing similar evaluations, he didn't go to Hall; the doctors from Hall came to him. When Gerry demanded to know why, she was told that her son was too much of a security risk to move.

Sitting on hard chairs on opposite sides of a big table, in a room at CCI more suitable to parole hearings than soul barings, Danny and a succession of psychiatrists from Hall explored Danny's world and why it was caving in. Danny came to the sessions disheveled and unshaven. He rarely looked his examiners in the eye, mumbled his answers, refused to talk about the crimes of which he was accused, and repeatedly broke down in tears. Before each session, the doctors informed him that he could stop the evaluation at any time, that anything he said could be used against him in court, and that the doctors could be called to testify against him. "How do you feel about your situation?" one examiner asked, and Danny started to cry. When asked, "Why are you crying, Mr. Starrett?" Danny moaned loudly and threw up his hands as a reminder that he was, after all, in prison for the rest of his life.

Eventually, even the doctors from Hall realized that an adequate diagnosis was impossible under such conditions, and they did what Gerry had been demanding all along: They transferred Danny to the Hall Institute. Finally, Gerry thought, he'll get the help he needs. The nightmare was ending.

In fact, it was just beginning.

As soon as he arrived at the Cooper Building, in chains and accompanied by a police officer who never left his side, Danny was stripped of his clothes and possessions, given a paper gown that barely covered him, handcuffed, tied to a wheelchair hand and foot, and then rolled into a large room.

(9/17/89) *The first time they saw me, it was incredible. There was a whole room of them—there must have been about seven or eight psychiatrists, social workers, and a couple of psychologists. I felt like a guinea pig being wheeled out into the scientific observation room where they were going to do this operation or something. As usual, I was handcuffed. Then they started asking questions right away about things that would tear my heart out. And they asked them as if we were all talking about the weather, like, "Gee, how is the weather out today?" "So, exactly how many people have you raped?"*

Their cavalier attitude just amazed me. It was as if they were operating on me without anesthesia. When those psychiatrists came into the room, they just took out their scalpel and said, "Let's start cutting." I got the feeling that they were thinking, "We've got a monster on our hands." Monsters have no feelings, so I don't think it occurred to them that the questions they were asking could be painful to me. They were just throwing these questions at me, and they quickly reduced me to a very bad state.

Finally they stopped, gave up on me, and left.

This all lasted an hour or so, it's hard to tell. They thought I was some kind of superhuman monster. I wanted to say, listen, I'm not going to hurt you. I'm really human, no matter what I may have done.

The next time Gerry visited, Danny recounted the experience to her with tears in his eyes. To see him cry set her lip quivering. More so than ever in this long, grotesque nightmare, she felt helpless to help him. How easy it is when they're babies, she thought. You pick them up, you change their diapers, you feed them. When they're children, you bandage their wounds, and when they get older, you talk them through the pain. After an entire childhood, you begin to think that there's no hurt you can't make go away, no wound you can't mend, no crisis you can't get them through. But this was beyond her healing powers.

Still, she was his mother. She had to try.

She thought of a story she used to tell Danny when he was a boy. It was about *The Wizard of Oz*. Of all the characters in the movie, she loved the Cowardly Lion best. She could describe the scene where Dorothy and her little dog, Toto, the Straw Man, the Tin Man, and the Cowardly Lion are all walking through these scary woods at night, afraid of being attacked by the Wicked Witch's flying monkeys. The poor lion, who wants the Wizard to give him some "c-c-courage," is holding his tail in front of him and wringing it nervously, wiping the tears of fear from his eyes. Every movement, every shadow, frightens him. "I *do* believe in spooks," he stammers, "I do, I do, I do."

But what Gerry saw in that scene wasn't the frightening, batlike monkeys or the spunky Dorothy, but the Cowardly Lion's *feet*. Even as he was wringing his tail and moaning in fear, scared to death, his feet were moving forward, slowly but surely, one timid, relentless step at a time, moving forward in spite of his fear. "I realized that I wanted to be that Cowardly Lion," she would tell Danny, "that I was in search of courage, too, and that I wanted to be able to move forward even when I was scared to death."

So she told him that story again. Only she added a new ending. "I don't care how frightening it is," she said. "I want you to keep moving forward, even if the going is slow, even if you fall down and get up again and again—just keep in mind that you're moving forward."

And he wouldn't be doing it just for himself. "You would be doing it for us, too," said Gerry. "I mean, we really need rescuing, too, the way Dorothy and Toto did. We need you to get through this."

52

But every day, it seemed, brought new trouble. No sooner was one crisis avoided or endured than a new one took its place. By now charges had been filed against Danny in two more South Carolina counties. To Gerry, that meant yet another tortuous round of hearings, yet another media humiliation of her family, yet another heart-wrenching battle with Danny over his plea. And it meant yet another lawyer. Every county had its own ambitious prosecutors and its own public defenders, so each time another county announced charges against Richard Daniel Starrett, like bells tolling across the state, Danny's case passed into yet another in-basket and Gerry found herself in yet another lawyer's office.

"We ought to fight every charge," said Pat McWhirter, a short man in his fifties with flames of silver streaking his hair.

The words came as such a shock that Gerry took an extra second to process them. Then she realized how long it had been since she had heard words like that: words of optimism, words of encouragement, words of hope. Fighting words.

She responded in kind, putting into words a question she had kept locked away, unspoken, in the remotest recesses of her thoughts. "Do you think that maybe Danny might get out of jail someday?"

McWhirter leaned back in his squeaky chair and hedged. "We certainly can minimize the sentences."

That was good enough for Gerry. "So you don't think he should plead guilty?"

"Right now," said McWhirter, putting his hands behind his head, "from what I know, I would say he shouldn't plead guilty to *anything.*"

"What about those things he signed?" She couldn't bring herself to say "confessions."

"There's a question about whether or not those would be admissible," said McWhirter. "We can contest them on the grounds of Danny's mental state at the time. And then if those get thrown out, it'll just be his word against the victims'."

Gerry didn't want to think about what he meant. She could only think of Danny.

"Even if we lose," McWhirter added, "there are always appeals. You know, Mrs. Starrett, human beings being what they are, they're going to make mistakes. The prosecutor is going to say things and do things he shouldn't, the judge is going to say and do things he shouldn't, and then we'll have all kinds of appeals. You can overturn sentences. You can bargain for reduced sentences."

For a brief moment, Gerry allowed herself to feel a new and strange sensation: hope. Then another thought came to her. "What about Danny? He doesn't want to have a trial. He doesn't want to make the victims testify."

"Don't worry about that," said McWhirter. "I'll talk to him."

(6/12/89) *Pat McWhirter came to see me today. He is the public defender for Lexington County. He is a very hard-nosed, very caustic fellow, to the point, no beating around the bush. I didn't like him very much. I just got the impression he was a cynical, jaded person who had seen it all and didn't give a damn who I was or what I was or what I had done.*

We had a bad start, a little run-in. He was mad that I've

*been talking to the investigators again. He couldn't under-
stand it. He said he didn't want me to talk to anybody, to keep
my mouth shut. He was obviously thinking, "This guy's a
fool." He told me, "They'll try to play the nice guy to you and
buddy-buddy and befriend you to get you to talk to them." I
told him he was wrong. They aren't playing any games with
me. I think they realize that I'm intelligent enough so that
they aren't going to be able to play any games on me. They're
being very up-front and professional.*

*I told him I wrote a letter to one of the victims and her
family. He got very mad. Like red-in-the-face mad. He raised
his voice. He said that he didn't want me to write any letters
to anybody because if the victims turned them over to the
prosecution, the prosecution would find some way to use
them against me. He was real put out. He said, "You're being
so stupid. Don't you realize they're playing you for a fool,
blah, blah, blah." He said, "You're doing more talking to the
police than to your own lawyer."*

*He just doesn't understand my motives. Here I am coop-
erating with the police, doing the very opposite of what he's
telling me to do. I feel as if the lawyer is trying to help the bad
guy, and I'm here trying to help the good guys defeat the
bad guy. What I'm doing is logical.*

*Some of the things he said were just terrible. Terrible
things that confirm every bad opinion I've ever had of a defense lawyer. They are willing to do anything to try to get a
guilty man off. He made some suggestions and said some things
that I couldn't believe I was hearing, ways of doing things to
help my case legally, things that were just morally reprehensible to me. He wants to attack the reputation of the victims. I
told him I don't want to go into that. It's just one of those
things that I can't do. I refuse to do that.*

So right from the very start the relationship went badly.

53

It only got worse.

A few days later, McWhirter visited Danny again. "We think you should plead not guilty by reason of insanity," he said as soon as he walked in.

"I am not insane," said Danny, very quickly and calmly, as if he had been waiting ever since McWhirter's last visit with just those words.

"Look, Mr. Starrett," McWhirter said. "If you can qualify for a not guilty by reason of insanity, maybe we can possibly get you off this charge."

"But I did it," said Danny. "I deserve to be punished. Don't be doing any of that legal mumbo jumbo. I am not crazy."

"Don't think of it as crazy. Think of it as incompetent. Mentally ill."

"I am not mentally ill. I don't want anyone to label me incompetent or mentally ill or *anything*. I am not crazy. I am a very logical person. I have been my whole life. I'm like my father. He's very logical, too. I would rather die than be labeled mentally ill."

"Listen, Mr. Starrett," said McWhirter, trying suasion first, "I'm not your psychiatrist. I'm your lawyer. Right now I'm concerned with what plea would be in your best interest. What plea might get you the least number of years in prison. What plea might make it possible for you to have at least one more day of freedom when you're seventy or eighty. What plea might even save your life."

Danny paused for a moment, as if pondering his next response. "I am not crazy," he finally said.

McWhirter took a shot in the dark. "Is it your family you're worried about? What they will think of you if you plead insanity?"

Now it was Danny's turn to flare. "Leave my family out of this."

McWhirter could see he had hit a nerve. "Are you afraid they might feel humiliated?"

"I am not crazy!" Danny screamed.

McWhirter started to speak, but Danny put his hands over his ears. "I don't want to hear any more about it," he said.

After a minute of awkward, frustrated silence, McWhirter stood up and left.

(6/16/89) *McWhirter visited again, trying to influence me to do what he says. He just can't understand where I'm coming from. I guess he thinks I'm engaged in self-defeating behavior, suicidal.*

54

After Danny's horrific experience at the Hall Institute, Gerry wasn't surprised when the report came back from Dr. Donald Morgan, the head of the institute's forensic division, concluding that Danny "was capable of understanding the nature of the charges and was capable of assisting counsel in his own defense, and also that he did have the capacity to differentiate right from wrong at the time of the alleged offenses."

In legalese, he was "sane," "competent."

The report was much more than a clean bill of mental health, however; it was a devastating indictment. It described Danny as a "usually clean and appropriately groomed" young man who "always speaks in a very low voice" and "is able to smile." His speech was "clear and coherent"; his thinking, "clear, logical, and goal directed"; his intelligence, "above average." In fact, the report noted, his IQ had tested at 124. Moreover, he had "an excellent fund of general information," "good insight into the nature of his problems," and, most damning of all, "good judgment."

In light of the crimes he stood accused of, it was a chilling portrait. This was no lunatic, the report seemed to say, no blameless victim of disfiguring abuse or mental handicap, no lost soul in need of reclaiming, no wronged child in need of righting. This was the worst of all criminals, the nightmare of every law-abiding citizen—the pervert in the guise of a normal man, the smiling killer, the monster next door—a smart, poised, self-possessed, articulate, cold-blooded rapist and murderer.

*　　*　　*

Gerry fought the report, of course. With only a week left before the hearing at which it would be presented, Gerry and McWhirter scrambled to find a private forensic psychiatrist to conduct yet another evaluation of Danny. Dr. Harold Morgan—no relation to Dr. Donald Morgan at the Hall Institute—visited his new patient in a dirty little office on the death-row cell block at CCI. At first, Danny refused to speak to the balding, bespectacled Morgan about the crimes, about his childhood, or about anything else except "philosophy"—especially free will and predestination. But when Gerry heard that, she threatened that if Danny didn't speak to Morgan, *she* would, and she would show him the autobiographical sketch that Danny had written.

After that, Morgan came every day and spent at least an hour each visit. He was soft-spoken, considerate, polite—a careful listener and an even more careful talker. "He's very cautious about telling me what he's really thinking," Danny told his mother. "I think he's afraid of setting me off."

Because of Morgan's professional reticence, Gerry Starrett didn't know what he thought about her son until two days before the court hearing, when she saw the letter he had written McWhirter. At the time it didn't seem odd, but later she would recall that when McWhirter handed her the letter, she whispered, "Please, God," by which she meant, "Please God, let my son be mentally ill."

Her prayers were answered.

"Your client has atypical paraphilia," she read. "This is a mental disorder which is characterized by unusual or bizarre fantasies or behavior as a means of sexual excitement. These urges are involuntary, repetitive, and have a strong driving force.

"At the time of the act, Mr. Starrett had the capacity to distinguish right from wrong and to recognize the act as being wrong, but because of the mental disease he lacked sufficient capacity to conform his conduct to the requirements of the law.

"Incidentally, atypical paraphilia has been accepted as a basis for the guilty but mentally ill plea in South Carolina."

Gerry felt as if Morgan had given her son back to her.

And then Pat McWhirter took him away again.

*   *   *

Gerry knew from the moment she walked into the conference room of McWhirter's office that something was wrong. It was the day before the court hearing, and, as far as she was concerned, they had cause for celebrating. But McWhirter didn't see it that way.

He held up the Hall report in one hand and Dr. Morgan's letter in the other, as if on a set of scales. "The problem with these," he demonstrated to Gerry and the members of his staff who had been working on Danny's case, "is that they cancel each other out." He dropped them both on the table at the same time. "And Danny won't plead not guilty because he doesn't want the victims to testify." There was a wave of negative muttering around the room. "So that leaves us with a guilty plea."

Guilty? Where was the optimism? The enthusiasm? The hope? How had they fallen so far so fast?

"My son is not guilty," she heard herself say.

McWhirter was undeterred. "It won't make much difference to the sentence," he argued, trying unsuccessfully to sound positive, "and we already have the GBMI from the first hearing to serve as a precedent in Georgia."

But Gerry wasn't listening to the arguments. She was listening to the thoughts of the people in the room, and she didn't like what she heard. The same muttering of negativity filled their eyes. And then she realized what it was, what had struck her wrong when she walked in the room. *They* had already found Danny guilty. Everyone in the room had read both reports and decided that the first one was right; that Danny *was* a cold-blooded rapist and murderer.

She stood up and straightened her dress. "Well, if you have so little faith in my son," she said as she turned to walk out, "I don't know why you're bothering to defend him at all."

"Mrs. Starrett," McWhirter called out, bringing Gerry to a stop in the doorway, "it's the rare defendant who gets the kind of time and attention that Daniel has. So many cases come through our office, we sometimes have to identify clients by picture just to remember who they are."

"You know," said Gerry, measuring her words with all her might, "if I had decided that there was no reason Danny did what he did, if he was just plain evil, I don't think I could defend him. If I thought anyone had done those things just because he was an evil person, I wouldn't want to have anything to do with him."

Then she walked out.

That evening, Gerry visited Danny one last time before the hearing. She looked yet again at the filthy cell, recoiled yet again at the toilet encrusted with dried urine and the cobwebs between the bars. Danny was lying on his bunk, an IV needle in his arm, even more disconnected than usual. He couldn't or wouldn't talk. He didn't even seem to know who she was. All she could do was cradle his head in her arms and, under the cold, watchful eyes of the guards, sing softly in his ear.

While she was there, McWhirter arrived. He wanted to try one last time to talk sense into Danny. He knelt down next to the bunk and put his hand on Danny's bony shoulder. "We think you should plead guilty," he said loudly, as if calling to someone from a distance. Danny's eyes didn't move. "Danny, Danny?" McWhirter said as he shook Danny's shoulder. "Danny, do you understand me? Do you understand what I'm saying?"

No response. Not even a blink.

Gerry had seen all she could stand. "You don't really think he's in any condition to go to court, do you?" she demanded.

"Well, Mrs. Starrett," said McWhirter, struggling to be both sympathetic and professional, "unfortunately, the doctors say he is, which means we don't have much choice."

Gerry felt the tears choking her yet again. "But he doesn't even know who he is!"

The next day, they rolled Danny into the courtroom in a wheelchair. He looked as pale and thin as a cadaver. Two barrel-chested officers had to lift him out of the wheelchair and plant him in a chair at the defense table. He looked absently straight ahead the whole time, into the middle distance, and never said a word.

Sitting in the front row of yet another courtroom, Gerry felt a huge knot of anger and frustration gathering in her stomach. It was a new feeling, and all the more terrifying for being new. Through all the battles and heartbreaks of the last months, the clashes with lawyers and police and prison officials, she had somehow maintained some faith in the judicial system. Now she could feel that faith slipping away, leaving a festering hole where the nausea gathered. The judicial system wasn't about justice; it was about punishment, about revenge, about politics and public opinion and careers and looking good—and just about everything else *but* justice.

A month ago, she wouldn't have thought it was possible for things to look worse. But now they did.

Gerry listened as Dr. Harold Morgan testified for the defense. "Danny's disorder transformed a normally mild-mannered young man into a Dr. Jekyll and Mr. Hyde," he said. "He knew these things were against the law, but the drive is stronger than the legal and moral standard." (Sometime later, after his role in the case was finished, Dr. Morgan told a colleague that he found Danny Starrett to be "the most reprehensible person I ever met.")

But Morgan was answered by the prosecution's witness from the Hall Institute. "Mr. Starrett may have suffered from paraphilia," testified Dr. Richard Ellison, "but it didn't render him incapable of controlling himself." Then the prosecutor himself argued that Danny "was in control enough to go to great lengths to avoid detection by renting cars and wiping away evidence." Besides, he continued, if Danny was truly sick and unable to control his actions, how was he able to stop himself when faced with a woman not to his liking? But when faced with a pretty fifteen-year-old girl like Jeannie McCrea—

"Don't say her name!" a pained and plaintive voice cried out.

Everyone looked around to see who it was. But Gerry knew. She knew her son's voice. She had seen him slumping lower and lower in his chair as the prosecutors beat him down with their words, the same prosecutors who had called Danny "a glad dog, not a mad dog."

"Don't say her name!" The pain in his voice was like a knife in Gerry's heart.

"Don't say her name!" Grimacing in agony, Danny clasped his hands behind his head and slid out of his chair onto the floor under the

defense table. He pulled his knees up toward his chin and writhed back and forth with his hands behind his head, crying out between heaving sobs of pain.

Gerry leapt up from her seat just as the tears exploded out of her. She stretched over the rail, reaching as far as she could, trying to touch her son. "Oh, Danny, baby," she called out to him in one great maternal sob. "Danny, my *baby!*"

Then she turned to the prosecutor with fire in her eyes. "You leave my son alone!" she screamed in a scalding voice. "You don't have to say those names. You leave my son alone!" Then she turned back to her son, who lay weeping on the floor with his hands over his ears, rocking back and forth in fetal agony. "Oh, Danny, baby."

55

As Gerry made her way out of the courtroom, she passed an artist from a television station in Augusta putting the finishing touches on a sketch of Danny curled up on the floor. It reminded her of that awful portrait she had seen in the store—and everywhere else—in those first, numb days. They had taken her Danny and made a cartoon out of him. Out of him and their nightmare.

The reporters had started calling almost immediately—on the phone, at the door. At first, she always answered. It was the only polite thing to do. They had lost their son, not their civility. "It's a terrible thing," she would say, or "It's a shock," or "This just isn't Danny." If they persisted, she would try to cut them off with a gentle "I have nothing more to say right now. Thank you." Sometimes, if they continued to push, Richard would appear to deliver the same message in a harsher tone. "We have nothing to say right now." Or just a curt "No comment." Gerry always regretted when Richard had to be harsh. She felt even that was giving away too much. It was, in a way, a surrender to the meanness of it all.

Once, a reporter came to their door, and neither Gerry's civility nor Richard's harshness could discourage him. He pushed and pushed—"What's it like to have a rapist in the family?" "When did you first realize your son was dangerous?" Finally, Richard lost his composure. "You ghoul!" he shouted. "You get paid for this, don't you? We have no further comment. I can't tell you anything more. To you, this is a story. To us, it's our son."

Then the courtroom journey began, and, wherever Danny was, there were swarms of reporters and cameras and microphones and questions. At first, the lawyers told them to say "just a little bit," but that was almost impossible, because little answers led to more little questions. So Gerry tried giving big answers—she gave the *Augusta Chronicle* an entire interview—but those, too, only led to more questions. So she started not saying anything, just ignoring the questions altogether. But that was hardest of all. She had spent much of her professional life flirting with the public eye. In her years of giving talks and advising clients, she had made many friends in the media. They had seen her build her business from nothing into The ImageMaker. Now, in her hour of trial, she would trust them to be fair.

But the media's eyes were focused elsewhere: first and foremost, on the victims. Chrissy Blake's disappearance had started a flood of stories—most of them accompanied by the victim's winning high-school photograph—that combined mystery, sex, crime, and local color. One article described a sign on the door of the Blakes' family business: DUE TO A TRAGEDY IN THE FAMILY, WE WILL BE CLOSED FOR A SHORT PERIOD OF TIME.

> The tragedy is that 17-year-old Chrissy Loren Blake has been missing since Monday. The family business is a short walk through a field from the Blakes' home, which is set back from the highway near a small pond.
>
> Folks say it's full of bream and catfish. But nobody was fishing Thursday morning, and only the wintery wind made ripples on the surface of the black-blue water.
>
> Earlier this week, authorities dragged the pond bottom for a body. Nothing was found.

As soon as reporters uncovered connections to other crimes in other counties (and pictures of other attractive young girls), the stories took on a new and ominous tone: TROUBLED MEMORIES RESURFACE AMID MYSTERY OF MISSING TEEN.

> Day by day, as the mystery of Chrissy Loren festers, an uneasy feeling among folks in Lexington County festers, too. "They're starting to get scared," said Daisy Hicks, who had stopped along Rural Route 2 to deliver mail.

Within days, a local story of doubtful newsworthiness had been transformed into possibly the state's biggest crime drama in a decade. Stories referred darkly to earlier serial rapists and murderers and sent readers to the inside continuation of a front-page story with the injunction: "See Fear."

Then came the huge, breathless headlines—CHRISSY BLAKE ESCAPES. Within hours of the escape, Lexington Sheriff's Department was deluged with calls from TV and radio stations across a three-state area, newspapers, wire services, and a dozen print agencies. For a few days, media attention was riveted on the manhunt for Danny Starrett. But as soon as he was arrested in Texas, the media eye turned back to the victims to satisfy the public's insatiable hunger for details.

First, they were treated to the heartwarming spectacle of Chrissy Blake's return, including a front-page picture of a sign placed by friends in the driveway of the Blake home: "Welcome Home, Chrissy. We love you." The occasion was made even more poignant, the victim even more sympathetic, by the stories that appeared at the same time and often on the same pages about the videotapes Starrett had made of his victim and the ordeal of degradation they revealed.

For a fleeting moment, Blake's return raised the public's hope that the other missing girl, Jeannie McCrea, would be found safe. The media was there when Jeannie's worried parents visited Chrissy's jubilant family. A police spokesman described the encounter to a group of reporters: "They knew Chrissy was okay, and they were hoping that Jeannie was okay, too." But she wasn't okay. And when Danny Starrett led police to

Jeannie's body in a watery ravine near her house, readers and listeners throughout the Southeast shared her parents' shock and grief.

Jean Taylor McCrea, 15, was remembered on a cold, gray Sunday as a "sometimes stormy, sometimes sunny, never dull" teenager and a strong-willed crusader for what was right.

Family members and friends—about 1,000 in all, many wearing black ribbons—filled the sanctuary of Ashland United Methodist Church to overflowing.

Many wept openly as her silver-colored casket bedecked with yellow flowers entered and left the Lexington County church for a 30-minute funeral service.

The Rev. Robert Borom, Miss McCrea's pastor, spoke. "If you have come today with the expectation of hearing from me some profound words that will help make sense of this tragedy, I fear you will be deeply disappointed," Borom told mourners. "I have no answers. I am heartbroken."

Borom remembered Miss McCrea, an only child, as a bright and energetic student and loyal friend.

Miss McCrea's life often took on a crusading quality if she saw some form of injustice, Borom said. Had her life not been cut short, he said, many thought she was headed for a career as a lawyer, helping the downtrodden and disadvantaged.

Borom quoted a note that hung on the bulletin board in Miss McCrea's room. He said it summed up her feelings toward herself and others.

It read: "No one has the right to pressure you into anything that hurts your body, clouds your future, or robs you of your self-esteem."

Next the spotlight fell on Carl and Cora Thornton, the Martinez couple who lived next door to Danny Starrett. It was to the Thornton house that Chrissy Blake had fled the night of her escape. "If it were not for Carl and Cora Thornton," claimed one paper, "Chrissy Loren Blake might not be alive today." That claim, and the media attention that went with it, was confirmed when the Georgia Sheriff's Association awarded the couple its Meritorious Service Award "for their contribution to the field of law enforcement."

The media followed every detail of the Thorntons' trip to Jekyll Island, Georgia, to accept their award, as well as a thank-you visit to the Thornton house by Chrissy Blake herself. "They strongly deserve the award," Blake told reporters. In the face of so much attention, the Thorntons were winningly modest. "It's very gratifying to receive this award, but we just tried to help her because you could tell she was in trouble," said Mr. Thornton. "She is a remarkable young girl." "I'm just glad we were here," said his wife.

Then one day Gerry Starrett turned on her television and watched, along with millions of her neighbors, as South Carolina governor Caroll Campbell took Chrissy Blake by the arm and led her up the steps of Air Force One to a private meeting with President George Bush. Campbell, like everyone else, had been following the Starrett case in the media. The day before the president's visit, the governor had crossed paths with Chrissy Blake in the Columbia airport and arranged the presidential audience. "It was a very quick and private thing," Campbell told the throng of press on hand to cover a rare presidential visit to South Carolina. "That little girl's been through hell."

If Chrissy Blake was the media's new darling, Danny Starrett was its new devil. Every time Gerry turned on the TV or opened a newspapers, she saw pictures of her son—they had gotten pictures somehow—always accompanied by the same words, in block headlines or voice-over: "SUSPECT," "KIDNAPPER," "SERIAL SEX OFFENDER," "MURDERER." Danny had always photographed well, Gerry thought: handsome and serious with big, warm eyes and a kind mouth. Now, whenever she saw that familiar face staring back at her from the television screen or the front page of a newspaper, she closed her eyes or turned away. That was not her Danny.

In the weeks following Chrissy Blake's escape, the portrait of Danny only got darker, especially when Governor Campbell, eager to turn public interest into political hay, dispatched his personal plane to bring

Danny back from Texas. Normal means of transportation were not enough for such a sinister, devious criminal. Every day, it seemed, investigators issued new and ever more colorful descriptions of "master criminal" Danny Starrett: "a professional rapist who has done extensive reading and a lot of planning on how to carry out his various crimes and ways to possibly reduce the evidence he was leaving behind, looking for ways to make his crimes look like missing-children cases instead of abductions."

The media eagerly reported every official innuendo and then filled in the blanks with its own tabloid speculations, calling Starrett "another Ted Bundy or Hillside Strangler."

By the time of Jeannie McCrea's funeral, the public consensus about Danny Starrett was expressed by Rev. Robert Borom, the pastor who delivered Jeannie's eulogy, when he said he "couldn't begin to understand or explain how a sick and depraved human being chooses an innocent victim."

Three days later, Gerry Starrett saw another picture of her son, larger than usual this time, on the front page of the *Columbia Sun.* Under it, an article, THE ANATOMY OF A SERIAL CRIMINAL:

There walk among us men and women who are in but not of our world. . . . Often the sign by which they betray themselves is crime, crime of an explosive, impulsive, reckless type.

Richard Daniel Starrett. Young . . . attractive . . . intelligent . . . educated. He was good at his job. He was a husband and father. He came from a good family, had a good education.

Richard Daniel Starrett. Alleged kidnapper and murderer. A serial criminal.

Richard Daniel Starrett. An enigma, a stranger to those who knew him, his family . . . his friends, maybe . . . even to himself.

Inside, these people are basically angry. Those who rape or commit other sexually oriented crimes are usually angry at women or females in general. Offenders who pick on younger girls seem to have lots of problems with female authority figures.

These men have insecurities in dealing with adult women. A case in point would be Ted Bundy. He grew up in a home with a domineering mother.

Psychopathy, possibly more than other mental disorders, threatens the safety, the serenity and the security of American life.

After that, and dozens of articles and TV stories like it, even Gerry Starrett wasn't surprised at the public reaction to Danny's first hunger strike. When a judge ordered prison officials to force-feed him, a cry of outrage went up. "If that guy wants to get closer to God," one person told a reporter, "why in the world are we trying to stop him?" Capitalizing on the public mood, a state legislator from Lexington County angrily introduced a bill that would make it illegal to force-feed prisoners who refused to eat. "That's perfectly all right if Starrett wants to starve," he thundered. "He ought to be allowed to." Besides, if Starrett starved himself to death, the lawmaker went on to say, just think of the money the state would save on appeals.

The only public voice in Danny's defense came from a newspaper editorial—"Why force-feed?"—and it was the best argument anyone could think of for keeping Gerry Starrett's son alive:

> If Starrett were allowed to starve himself to death, it's possible that the crimes would go unsolved. Besides, in the course of trials or psychiatric examinations, we might learn something about why a seemingly normal, middle-class person like this goes off the deep end and commits serious crimes against adolescent females.
>
> *Like it or not,* Richard Starrett must be kept alive.

56

Gerry Starrett didn't consider this fair at all. Like the police and the prison officials and even the doctors, the media treated Danny like a monster. Didn't they realize he had a family? That there were people who loved him, people who had seen his kindnesses, enjoyed his playfulness, shared his sadness, felt his affections? Didn't they realize that the victim isn't the only one with a family? That the accused has a family, too?

One night Gerry and Richard tried to escape the ordeal by going to a movie. Without thinking, they walked into a showing of an unusually violent action film. The first time one of the villains was killed, the audience laughed and applauded. Gerry and Richard got up and left. On the way home, Richard turned to Gerry and said, "You know, we've spent our whole lives watching bad guys getting blown away in movies and never stopped to think: Maybe that bad guy had a mother and father who loved him and tried to raise him right. And maybe they didn't understand why he became a bad guy. Think of the agony they will go through when they find out he was killed by the good guys."

That night, Gerry resolved to take her side of Danny's case to the public. A few days later, after some plaintive but insistent phone calls to old friends, she appeared on *News Talk*, a local news-magazine show on WBE-TV, Channel 67, in Augusta. The host was Charlie Britt, a blandly handsome, sandy-haired man in his forties.

Britt began brightly. "Good evening, it's March 20, and this is *News Talk*. Much has been said about the victims of crime, and well it should be, for crime is rampant in our country. Much has also been said about the effect crime has had on the families of victims. That also is totally justified. But what about the innocent families of those who commit heinous crimes? Are they not also deserving of our concern? Up next, we speak with Richard Daniel Starrett's mother."

Gerry appeared in a pale blue suit—she knew she looked best in blue—and did her own makeup. She looked collected and confident and deserving of Britt's fulsome welcome. "Ms. Starrett, we think it's very courageous that you have come to do this interview, and we appreciate it very much. And I want to say out front this is not easy on you. The past months have been awfully stressful, so, once again, let me thank you."

Gerry nodded appreciatively.

"Ms. Starrett," Britt began, "we hear about victims' rights, the families of victims, how everybody has suffered. Tell me just for a moment how it feels to be in the situation you are in."

"I think I'm a victim, too," said Gerry, talking quickly, nervously. "But unlike most victims, we have no place to go for help. Of course, we have our friends and our church, but as far as any formal group that we can identify with—where we could go and say, 'This is how I feel. This is what is happening to me. I understand you had a similar experience. How did you handle it? What can we do?'—I know of no such organization. There is no organization for families who have loved ones in the situation that our Danny is in."

Britt put on his most concerned voice. "Tell me," he said, "what is your purpose in being here today?"

Gerry, in contrast, was all business. "I have two purposes," she said brusquely, keeping track on her manicured fingers. "One is to help my son—although I honestly don't see how this could do that. The other is to shed some light that might help someone else. If someone heard me and became interested enough to ask the right questions, perhaps they could prevent this from happening in their own families.

"That's my reason for being here. And when I go anywhere to talk from now on, that will be my purpose. Because no one expects to find themselves in the situation that we are in. Absolutely no family expects *this*"—she gestured broadly enough to embrace the world—"especially not a family where you have a child that has had no problems with society in any way. Then, all of a sudden, this is cast upon you. You're lost."

She looked directly into the camera. "I know there are people who are listening to this program and saying, 'That couldn't happen to me. That couldn't happen to my family. Well, it *could* happen. It *has* happened to other people. It happened to us. And it will continue to happen to unsuspecting families, to families that have nothing in their backgrounds to cause them to think that it would happen to them."

Britt conferred another sympathetic smile. "What can people do to prevent this from happening in their own families?"

"We need to learn how to spot when someone in our family is having mental problems," said Gerry. "I always thought, and I think many other people do, that if someone has mental problems you can tell easily. I had this image of someone who's never coherent, who's always drooling. It's all very obvious. But that's not true. That's not true at all."

Britt decided to change the subject. "If this isn't too delicate a question—tell me if you don't want to answer it—but looking back on your son's life, is there anything that you would advise parents to look for, anything that you saw then but didn't give a second thought to until now?"

For the first time, Gerry looked genuinely uncomfortable. She had wanted to talk in generalities: Danny is sick. Like any sick person, he needs help and sympathy. She did not want to lay out her own life or her son's for public scrutiny. But she had come this far. "In my particular case," she allowed, "I would have paid more attention to his physical illness instead of brushing it aside. I think I would have sought more medical information than I did."

Somewhere deep inside, alarms went off. She thought she felt the beginnings of a sob gathering in her throat. The thought of losing control terrified her. "I suppose," she said, stanching the flow of confession, "that's the main thing I would do differently. If there were any kind of physical ailment, anything unusual, I would say don't stop until you find out what it is. Just don't stop. No expense, no time, nothing could be more important." She breathed a sigh of escape.

"Let me move on, then," said Britt, looking for another opening. "For every mother sitting out there, tell us, how does it feel to have your son judged as being mentally ill?"

Without thinking, Gerry said the first word on her mind—the word, in fact, that was always on her mind but rarely uttered: "Guilt." As soon as it was out of her mouth, she regretted it and she scrambled to take it back. "I should have known that something was wrong, even though, at the same time, I know I couldn't have known."

Britt persisted. "How does it feel to have your son sentenced to life in prison with no possibility of parole?" he asked with even more sincerity. "How does that make you feel?"

Gerry found the question offensive. How does it feel to have your leg cut off, or your heart cut out? How does it feel to have your child run over by a car or stricken by a fatal disease? "Terrible," she said in a voice edged with anger. "It makes me feel terrible." But she couldn't leave it there. She was determined to end on a positive note. She had done it so many times for Danny, by now it was second nature. "But what I substitute for the hopeless feeling," she added, "is a funny kind of hope. I keep thinking, well, maybe Daniel can be treated. Maybe he can be okay again—even in an institution. People have done amazing things in unusual places and in unusual ways. And Daniel is an unusual person."

She had hit her stride. "Hope is very important. I hope through his being in an institution we can learn more. I hope we can understand more so we might be able to help someone else. If we can help just one someone in the future to prevent this from happening again, just one, that would be enough. . . ." She trailed off, not sure that it was enough.

It was enough for Britt, who was almost out of time. "Let me close with a rather unusual question," he said. "If you can, Ms. Starrett, what would you like to say to the families of the people that Daniel has wronged?"

Gerry was ready for this one. "I would say to them, please remember that if you had a family member that was dying of cancer or anything else that you could not control, you would have compassion for them. Daniel cannot control his illness, and I would ask you to have compassion for him."

"I think that's a lovely note to end on," said Britt, "and, once again, let me thank you for coming."

57

Gerry's pleas fell on deaf ears.

For a few days after Danny's name appeared in the papers and on TV, her daily life hardly changed. Crank callers forced her to request an unlisted number at home, but otherwise her routine remained eerily the same: the ImageMaker during the week; friends, family, and church on the weekends. She wondered how it was possible that her emotional life could be in such upheaval and her daily life remain so normal.

All that ended the day the Augusta paper printed the name of the business.

Up to then, there hadn't been much trouble at The ImageMaker. Until Danny was caught, the police sat outside the door in unmarked cars, hoping, apparently—despite Gerry's indignant denials—that Danny would walk into his mother's shop in broad daylight. Once, they even raided the place because they saw a man enter who very roughly fit Danny's description. They charged out of their cars, barreled past the receptionist, and stormed into the serene salon space Gerry had created, only to find that the man they were after was a minister—a friend of one of the employees.

Then one day a regular client came into the shop and complained that she had received a call from someone identifying himself as an FBI agent. Then another client called with the same complaint. It wasn't long before Gerry realized that investigators were systematically calling all of her customers. They had seized boxes of her business records from Danny's house, where they had been stored, and were now going through those files and calling everybody listed. Clients wanted to know how the police had gotten their names. Some canceled. A few stopped coming altogether, but not enough to make a difference at first. Then somehow the FBI's list leaked to a paper in South Carolina, *The Star,* and soon clients were complaining about calls from reporters. Looking back, Gerry realized she should have seen then that the business was in trouble.

The next day, Gerry called the staff together and told them the bad news. Now that the papers had the name of the business and a list of customers, anything could happen. Clients could cancel, TV cameras could show up at the door. Certainly reporters would pursue staff members, as they were already pursuing Gerry and her family. "Now is the time we have to stick together," she told them, fighting back the threat of tears. "I really need you. There's no way I can maintain this business without you."

Everyone seemed sympathetic. One young hairdresser, Robert, whom she had only recently hired, came forward and hugged Gerry tightly. Public displays of affection always made her awkward and uneasy. But, she said later, no hug ever felt better than that one. She thanked him with tears in her eyes. Then another hairdresser, Nancy, walked to the front of the room. "This is from all of us," she said to Gerry, and then hugged and kissed her. That meant a lot to Gerry, too. Nancy had been her special project. She had come to The ImageMaker with a bad job history, bad references, and a bad attitude. But Gerry believed in her and worked with her and gave her a chance. Now here she was, a first-rate hairdresser, pledging the staff's support for Gerry's fight—Danny's fight.

Almost immediately, though, the desertions began. First, it was her two star hairdressers, the ones who had been with her the longest, the ones with the longest client lists, the ones who brought in the most business for the other services. Gerry begged them to stay. "If the two of you go, I don't think we can make it," she pleaded. "We're that close." But they left anyway. It was the only way they could keep their clients. They had to think of themselves first, they said.

They, at least, were nice enough to come and tell Gerry before leaving. Robert, the one who had hugged her, just didn't show up one day. And she never heard from him again. He had talked once about moving back to his hometown to be with his parents, and Gerry assumed that's what he had done. Then one day she discovered that he was working at another local salon. That hurt, too.

Eventually, gradually, they all abandoned her, even Nancy, her special project. The gleaming new salon was operating with a skeleton crew. Gerry's biggest dream was dying. She tried to find a buyer for the business, but nobody would touch it. She auctioned off all the nearly new equipment for a fraction of its value. The landlord tried to find someone else to rent the space, but nobody wanted it. When the real-estate agent asked one potential renter why not, he said simply, "Bad karma."

58

Gerry sat in an old chair in the dining room of her parents' farmhouse in Appling County, Georgia, looking out the window at the fields where she had played as a girl and recounting, a little distractedly, the story of her business's collapse. That, at least, was something she could talk about. More than once she had tried telling her family what was really on her mind: Danny. But except for her mother, and one or two others, it only made everybody feel awkward. They were used to tragedies, all right—deaths and accidents were a part of everyday life in rural Georgia—but they didn't know what to make of this. Or what to do. Or what to say. More often than not, they resolved their doubts by doing and saying nothing. No matter how many anguished stories Gerry told about Danny's suffering, about her family's suffering, about *her* suffering, all she ever got from most of them was, "I really don't know what to say."

This time, when she finished telling them about The ImageMaker, she didn't even get that. There was a long silence around the table before somebody tried lamely to start up a conversation by asking, "What's planting this spring?" Finally Gerry's mother, Arline Williams, a slight, sinewy woman with steel-gray hair, responded to the pain in her daughter's story in the only way she knew. "Why don't we read?" she suggested. She meant from the Bible.

She opened the well-worn book to a passage from Psalms and handed it to Gerry to read:

> For thy name's sake, O Lord, pardon mine iniquity; for it is great.
> What man is he that feareth the Lord? Him shall he teach in the way that he shall choose.
> His soul shall dwell at ease; and his seed shall inherit the earth.
> The secret of the Lord is with them that fear him.

Gerry's mother smiled. "Don't the Lord's words make you feel good?" she asked, although it wasn't really a question at all.

Gerry, who had barely held on until the last word, shut the Bible forcefully and sprang up from her chair. "No, they don't!" she snapped. "How am I supposed to be comforted by that? 'Fear this, fear that!' I want a loving God, not a God I have to fear."

Her challenge plunged the room into astonished silence. One sister-in-law began clearing dishes, the other fled to the kitchen. The men folded their arms and exchanged glances. Arline floundered for a moment in stuttering disbelief, then stood up and left the room.

None of it surprised Gerry. What good was organized religion anyway? Twice she had persuaded her minister to visit Danny at CCI, and both times he had come back complaining about the noise and the congestion. "I just can't handle it," he said over and over. "I just can't handle it." If God couldn't handle it, Gerry wondered, who could?

Still, she went every Sunday morning to church, and when the minister asked if anyone needed a prayer, she asked for a prayer for Danny.

More and more, God was the only one Gerry *could* turn to. One by one, more fallible friends fell away. Some just stopped calling. Some, like the majority of her relatives in Appling County, had nothing to say. Some said the wrong things. No one was deliberately cruel, but inadvertent cruelty could cut every bit as deep. The words that hurt the most (and she heard them in a hundred variations) were these: "You know, if my child had done all these terrible things, I'd love him, too. I'd stick by my child no matter what he did." That was exactly what Gerry didn't want to hear. *"But Danny didn't know what he was doing,"* she wanted to scream.

One day in the shop, a customer suggested—helpfully, she thought— "When an apple is rotten, you should cut it away from the tree and just leave it alone. You only make things worse if you refuse to cut yourself away from the rotten apple." By which, Gerry suddenly realized, she meant Danny. Normally, she would never argue with a customer, but this was different. "I want you to tell me," she said, reining in her anger, "just exactly where a parent should draw a line? Just how evil does a child have to be before you stop loving him? Where would you draw the line for your child?"

Even among friends and neighbors, Gerry found little consolation. Now and then, someone might venture a few words of encouragement—bromides bobbing on a sea of awkward silences—"The press always makes it sound worse than it is," or "Hope everything turns out all right," or just "We're thinking about you." But most, not knowing what to say, said nothing. A regular bridge group dissolved without a word, and not a single neighbor wrote a card, called, or paid a visit.

When a reporter asked Gerry what effect the water torture of daily news reports was having on her family, the candor of her response surprised even her. "It's hard coping every day," she admitted, "trying to keep up hope, just trying to *live* almost, trying to find a reason to live and encourage other family members to keep going."

It hadn't been like that at first. In the weeks after Danny's name took up permanent residence on the front pages of every newspaper in two states, everyone in the family had followed Gerry's lead, matching her bravery with their own, advancing the image she was determined to project of a solid, wholesome family solidly behind its most wholesome member. "It's a shock to all of us," Gail had told the papers in those first days. "This is not Danny." Helen and Gail and Robert had been "fantastic," Richard boasted in the same interview. "The way these kids have been supporting Danny, if it was only serving Danny's need, they wouldn't be able to keep it up for long. It's got to serve some of their needs, too." Even the in-laws, Conrad and Pat and Sally, were portrayed as ardent supporters of Danny's cause, lest it appear that blood was the only issue. "This crisis has brought everybody closer together," Gerry told a reporter. "We were a close family anyhow. But as you talk to each one, you will find out that when one is in danger, the rest of them fly immediately to help the one in danger."

Perhaps, but it wasn't long before cracks in Gerry's united front began to show. Within several months, two family marriages (not including Danny's) were themselves in danger. At one point, Gerry felt the need to counsel her younger son, Robert: "If you ever have to make the choice of who to let go—your family or Danny—there should not be any question in your mind if it comes to that. You've got a wife and a baby—and you've got a life."

But most distressing to Gerry was Richard's increasingly profound silence. At work, people had newspapers delivered to their desks and would spend their lunch hours reading huge headlines like STARRETT INDICTED ON MURDER CHARGE, but no one ever said a word to Richard. And, of course,

Richard never said a word to them. Every Tuesday, he continued to meet for his weekly poker game, but nobody ever mentioned Danny, and neither did Richard. He continued to play golf with friends from the church, but the name Danny was never uttered. When Gerry asked him about it, he would say only, "I really don't talk to anybody about my private life much."

Gerry wasn't surprised. She had known for some time—perhaps since before they were married—of Richard's inaccessible emotional life. Whenever she would get mad at him for not playing more of a role in their kids' lives, he would say, "I'm perfectly satisfied with them getting Cs, and you demand that they get As. That doesn't leave me any role." When she said she wanted him to play more of a role in *her* life, his response was the same. "Well, you like to do different things than I do. That doesn't leave me any role."

One time she did succeed in coaxing him into a therapist's office. For a few minutes he filled the air with his usual mix of philosophy and anger, but as soon as the therapist criticized him, he got up, walked out, and never came back. The therapist had broken the rule of silence.

As she thought about the trials ahead, for Danny, for her, and for her family, Gerry couldn't help but wonder what use Richard would be and how he would ever make it through.

The only person Gerry was sure she could rely on, the only person who would never fail or abandon her, was Danny. Every visit brought her new hope, gave her new strength. "People can change anything about themselves," she told him one day, "if they want to change it enough, if they recognize it as something that needs changing." She knew Danny believed that, too. If nothing else, she had given him that.

She knew Danny enjoyed her visits. He was always trying to reassure her, the way he'd always done, that her parenting was good after all. He knew how much she needed to hear that. Wasn't that just like Danny: always trying to help everybody else with *their* problems. She had tried often to think of a time when Danny came to her and said, "I have this problem." But he never did. Surely, he *had* problems, little day-to-day kinds of problems. But she had never heard about them. Like everybody else, she was so busy talking while Danny listened.

Now, here he was doing it again: trying to find the best in a bad situation—just the way she had taught him. More than anything else, she decided, that would get him through this nightmare—get *her* through this nightmare. Every time she came away from seeing him, she felt stronger. So unlike her times with Richard. That, she decided one day, was what love really meant.

> (6/20/89) *My mother and I talk a lot. I like to keep up and know what's going on in the family. I like to think that I can still make some healthy suggestions. I've done that with my father also, occasionally. My mother is a little more open in terms of talking about her difficulties than my dad. I haven't encouraged him to get into therapy. That would be a waste of my breath.*
>
> *I think that what's happening to me has brought some stress to all of my family's lives, but I think my family really is an incredibly loving, normal, middle-American family.*

59

More and more often, when she came on her weekly or twice-weekly visits past the guarded gates at CCI, Gerry was seeing a change in Danny. As she waited in the sweltering heat on one side of the filthy glass, listening for thirty fleeting minutes to her son telling of his life on the other side of the glass—a life from which she was being excluded for the first time—Gerry thought she heard a familiar voice, the voice of the old Danny, *her* Danny.

Her Danny was helpful. Almost from the first day, he had offered to help the police in any way he could. He told them again and again, "I only want to make things right." He had been thinking about the victims, he said, and to prove it he offered to meet with the victims' counselors, if that would help. He offered to talk with investigators from other counties and states about any similar unsolved cases and put the minds of other victims' families at rest. When a representative of an Australian police department requested an interview with Danny in an effort to construct a profile of a serial rapist/murderer in that country, Danny eagerly agreed. Why? "Because I want to feel like one of the good guys again," he told them.

(7/5/89) *David Caldwell, who recently completed a special FBI course in criminal behavior, asked me to supply some information for the FBI computer in Virginia. He said that they were building this database and that I could help them understand the mind of the criminal. I told them I've had a firsthand seat to observe the workings of a criminal mind—an animal mind, really. I was just beside myself I was so excited about helping them—to think that all this traumatic, terrible stuff could be turned into something useful and positive. When you desperately want to be a good guy, and every time you pick up the newspaper they're showing a black hat on top of your head, you are desperate to do anything to prove that you are not what they are trying to make you out to be.*

It was Danny himself who suggested that he could help the police "design better preventative measures" to deal with other serial criminals like himself—criminals "who are organized and of above-average intelligence." Unlike so many run-of-the-mill, easy-to-catch criminals, Danny argued, *he* knew how to commit a crime. He knew the importance of going to another state, of maintaining a geographical spread, of using rental cars, of varying the M.O.—even though he never did—and of keeping victims away from identifiable items. With the benefit of his expertise, Danny maintained, the police would stand a much better chance of catching master criminals like himself and Ted Bundy.

What did he think about the comparisons being made in the papers between him and Bundy? "Well, the fantasies may be similar," he said, "but Bundy took pleasure in hurting people, and I never wanted to hurt anyone."

Danny also volunteered to help in the battle against pornography. After all, it was pornography that had gotten him into this mess in the first place, he told his interrogators. If it hadn't been for the horror movies he had devoured as a boy, movies showing "scantily clad damsels in distress," he would never have developed the destructive fantasies he had.

> (8/4/89) *Everything a person experiences, everything he sees or hears, affects the way that person is. And it really worries me that the kinds of movies I collected are so easily accessible to everyone, particularly younger people. I used to see young people, some of them twelve years old, renting some of the same videos I would rent. I think it is real dangerous for young people to see those kinds of movies.*
>
> *I want parents to say to themselves, "My kid is renting these horror movies, and it's creating a link between sex and violence in him when he's still in puberty, the most dangerous time of all. And my kid is renting 'em by the stacks. This Richard D. Starrett, when he was that age, only got to see 'em once a week. So what's going to happen to my kid in twenty years? Are we gonna have thousands of Richard D. Starretts running around out there?"*
>
> *You know, we outlaw child pornography because we recognize it as harmful to others. All I'm saying is that we now recognize, as many feminists have for a long time, that the line needs to be moved back. It needs to be shifted a little further back to include certain types of violent pornography. Playboy may be like marijuana—it is everywhere and easily accessible, but it has a marginal effect. This hard-core pornography is like crack—it may not be everywhere, but it will ruin you.*

To stop pornography linking sex with violence, Danny proposed suing the companies that produced it, turning over any settlements or awards to victims. He also wanted to make a video about sex and violence, a video that showed the crimes from the point of view of the victim, that showed the suffering of mothers and sisters and daughters. The video would train people in preventive techniques—like not opening the door to strangers, no matter how harmless they look—as well as convince legislators of the evils of pornography. "I want to help protect people like my daughter," Danny insisted.

> *(8/5/89) I also want to help prevent other would-be criminals and catch other criminals, particularly the ones who might read about or study what I did. I'm really afraid someone will get some ideas, as I did, from detective magazines, TV, newspapers, or wherever.*
>
> *You know, it's ironic. But I'm sure there is someone out there right now cutting out articles about me—like the ones I cut out on crimes and stored in my warehouse. My case is probably in those detective magazines by now—there are people out there right now reading about me.*
>
> *I lie awake sick at night just thinking about that sometimes. That someone's going to take one of my ideas and use it to hurt somebody else.*

If anything, Danny was *too* helpful. In the first few days after his arrest, in an effort to prove his innocent heart, he had given interview after interview to investigators Bill Galardi and David Caldwell. Before every session, the two would read Danny his rights, but he would always waive them and sign the Miranda form with a stoic flourish. "I was advised by an attorney not to discuss any aspect of my case with anyone," he wrote on one form.

> *But I decided quite some time ago that I would cooperate with the two investigators, whom I have come to have a great deal of respect for. With what is left of my humanity, I am determined that at least some small good shall come out of all the grief and suffering I have caused. Somehow I will find a way.*
> *Richard D. Starrett*

Once, his interviewers ran out of tape in the middle of a long session, and Danny waited patiently while they left to search for more cassettes. To make sure they were readmitted to the visitor area, he scribbled a note for them to present on their return:

I would like to meet with Bill Galardi and David Caldwell or both anytime from today 6/2/89 until I die or hell freezes over, whichever comes first.
                                                Richard D. Starrett

Danny's lawyers ranted and raged over their client's loose, irrepressible tongue. "Keep your mouth shut!" Pat McWhirter screamed at Danny once. Jack Swerling had even tried to recruit Gerry and the rest of the family in his campaign to put a muzzle on Danny. Gerry played along and clucked at her son several times about following his lawyer's advice, but she knew it was no use. Danny was a talker—a talker who wanted to be helpful. That was just the way her Danny was.

(8/13/89) My family was trying to influence me to do what my lawyer said. They just couldn't understand where I was coming from. I have this human need to get this guilt off my shoulders, which is true. And that's the central issue here. Defense attorneys should be there to defend people who are innocent of crimes they're accused of, or to guide guilty people through the process to see that their rights aren't violated. But not to help them avoid responsibility for their acts. That perverts the whole judicial system.

Whenever Gerry tried to warn her son to be wary of his interrogators, Danny would dismiss her concern with a little wise laugh, describing himself as lucky to be in the care of "two able, skilled, knowledgeable, experienced, tactful, considerate, sometimes humorous, but always professional law-enforcement officers."

I think Caldwell and Galardi should get a big raise out of this, because they've done an outstanding job in protecting the public. And if they don't get a raise, then I'll do something real nasty. That's a promise, not a threat. I think threats are illegal, aren't they?

Her Danny was thoughtful. For all his own problems, Danny never stopped thinking about other people's problems. And the death-row cell block at CCI gave him plenty to be concerned about. When he first arrived there, pale and gaunt from his first hunger strike, the old building was even grimmer and tenser than usual. For the first time in years, an inmate was actually scheduled for execution, and the nearness of it hung over every encounter. Danny met the condemned man in the little anteroom that led from the cell block to the main prison corridor. He was friendly, in his mid-thirties, and had been on death row for almost a decade. He had killed several people on some kind of crime spree—Danny never could get the details exactly.

In the few days the man had left, he and Danny became fast friends. They discovered their cells were adjacent—vertically, that is—and so they could hear each other at night when the usual din died down. It was in the quiet, dark hours that Danny heard the man's voice below him reading the Bible to an illiterate neighbor.

At Danny's suggestion, Gerry gave the man fifty dollars so he could buy pizza and candy for everyone on death row—a communal last meal. That was such a typical Danny idea, Gerry thought. He wanted to do something that would relieve the tension on the cell block but also brighten the condemned man's last days.

Her Danny was patriotic. Gerry never saw her son more agitated than the day after his lawyer had given him a stack of court papers to read. "You know what it says on these papers?" he said to her in an anguished whisper through the partition. "It says: 'The United States of America versus Richard Daniel Starrett.' Not 'The U.S.A. versus R. D. Starrett'—no, no, no. It's all spelled out. There's no doubt about it. *That's my name!* What are the chances that there's another Richard Daniel Starrett?"

He sprang up out of his chair and paced the tiny space, rubbing his forehead in vexation and despair. "Imagine. The country that I love . . . I know most people don't get emotional over politics, because most people are so cynical about that sort of thing, but not me. You know, I've read history. I know what this country stands for. I believe in truth, justice, liberty, freedom, pursuit of happiness." He flopped back down in the chair and braced himself as if waiting for the only jolt that could be more painful, muttering under his breath: "The United States of America against Richard Daniel Starrett."

Her Danny was sorry. Again and again he told his mother how determined he was to "make things right." And every time she tried to ease his pain by suggesting that "all the ugliness" was in the past and that it was time to start thinking about the future, he would fix her with that stern, instructive, but sympathetic gaze he had always used when expressing his deepest convictions to her, and explain how a person should be held accountable for his deeds. He should apologize. He should make restitution—financial, moral, whatever. Some things, of course, could never be made right, he would say with downcast, sorrow-lidded eyes, but that was no excuse not to try.

And try he did. He told the police he wanted the money they had confiscated from his house—$1,300 in cash—to be distributed to his victims: half to Jeannie McCrea's parents and half to the other six victims. If they refused to accept it, then he wanted it turned over to a victims-rights group, if there was one in the state. "There should be one in every state," he declared.

He talked about writing to raise more money. Not about his case. That would be capitalizing on the victims' suffering, and he refused to sink to that level. Furthermore, if anybody else tried to write such a book, he would sue them. He could not stand to see someone make a profit on the backs of the innocent. If, on the other hand, any of the victims chose to cooperate in a project that might help society and the proceeds from the project went to a victims-rights fund, he wouldn't object to that.

No, he would try his hand at science fiction—a genre for which he had always had an affection and a talent. He would become a great science fiction writer and make millions. Then he could give the victims money to help cover their medical and psychiatric expenses, maybe even set up a college trust fund. That would be nice. Then he could also pay back the states of South Carolina and Georgia and the city of Houston. He wrote a note to his interrogators requesting "that the people of South Carolina present me with a bill for the expenses that I have incurred as a result of my actions. I want a bill for all the costs, because I want to pay it back."

He also expressed a desire to write his victims letters of apology—a suggestion that gave his lawyer apoplexy. Even in this, however, he wasn't just performing a private act of contrition; he was setting a moral example for all to follow. "Please tell the victims that I am writing a statement of apology," he wrote in a note to prison authorities. "I plan to make statements of apology, which I think should be a standard act for anyone who wants to do right."

As for his punishment, Danny was unflinching. "If the McCrea family thinks I deserve the death penalty," he said, "then I'll demand the death penalty myself." Gerry tried to argue with him, but it was useless. She could never win an argument with Danny. One of the lawyers had told him that if the state of Georgia sought the death penalty, the case could be tied up in the courts for years, with a good chance of getting the death sentence overturned somewhere along the way. But Danny didn't want any part of it. "That crap makes me sick to my stomach," he told Gerry one day.

(9/7/89) *Philosophically, I identify more with the conservative thinking of people like Ronald Reagan and George Bush than with the liberal thinking of my own attorneys. The reason I voted for George Bush is that he was very tough on crime, and the same with Reagan. I see crime as getting out of hand in our society. I see it as robbing people of their liberty and their freedoms. We need tougher crime laws. We need to catch criminals and put them behind bars.*

I know Jesus would feel that the death penalty is wrong.

And you have to try to think like a Christian. But then I think about some of the things I've read about, and I have to agree that there's pure evil in this world. Some people are just sick. Some people may have problems, but others just enjoy it. And I believe that if we ever really institute the death penalty—I mean, in a meaningful manner, passing swift judgments, and then cutting short the ten years between judgment and execution—I suspect that we would begin to see a deterrent effect. And if it saves one innocent life, even if it means a hundred heinous murderers die, then I say it was worth it.

Sometimes a life sentence just isn't enough.

60

Nothing brought the old Danny back to life faster than the thought of his wife and daughter, Heather and Allison. Every time Gerry visited, he wanted to know what news she had from them. How were they doing? Had she talked to them? Did she have any pictures? No matter how tired, weak, or emaciated he was, no matter how distracting the legal battles, no matter how depressing the prison conditions or how uncertain his future, the mention of his family always seemed to bring a light to his eye and a smile to his face, and for a moment or two, he was Danny again.

So Gerry was thrilled when she heard that Heather was returning from California with Allison to see Danny. Of course, she insisted that they stay at her house, and she drove to the airport in Augusta hours early to make sure she was standing right there when they stepped off the plane.

Waiting at the edge of Bush Field's long, open concourse, Gerry had time—more time that she wanted—to think about her long, complicated relationship with her daughter-in-law. Danny's marriage had come as a shock to her. He had gone to California for what was supposed to be a summer job, but under pressure from Heather's family, had stayed much longer. Gerry wanted him to come back and finish at Georgia Tech; Heather's family convinced him to stay and enroll at San Jose State. Then, after he had been gone for a year, he called to say he was getting married.

Gerry tried to adjust. She and Richard drove to California for the wedding, and she played the marginal role of mother of the groom with poise and patience. The hardest part was hiding her anger with Heather's mother, Flo. All during Danny's year away, Gerry had sensed that something other than his love for Heather was keeping him in California. Now she found out what it was. Flo had pleaded with the couple not to return to Georgia, and she had found another job for Danny when the summer one ended. It was clear to Gerry, watching Flo and Heather together during the wedding preparations, that this was one mother who simply couldn't stand to be away from her daughter—which was why Heather took those long trips to California over Christmases and summers without Danny. They were the payments Flo had extracted for letting her daughter move away.

Still, Gerry was shocked to see Flo step off Heather's plane. No one had told her. For a moment, she replayed the tug-of-war she had been waging with this woman on the other side of the continent, and the sap of rivalry rose in her throat. Then she quickly put those thoughts away. She had to think of Danny first. And if it took Flo to get Heather to visit him, then it was worth it. Besides, she thought, if the situation had been reversed and it was Danny going to visit Heather, she would have done the same thing. She would have wanted to be there to help her child through this trial.

That night, at the Starrett house in Evans, after Allison was put to bed, Heather and Flo joined Gerry and her family in the living room with the Chinese figurine and the unicorn collection. As they had done so many times before, they formed a rough circle, joined hands, and knelt together to pray. Everybody in turn said something about Danny, some private memory, some secret gratitude, and a wish for his well-being. When her turn came, Heather spoke lovingly of Danny as a father and husband. Flo said something, too. With tears in her eyes, Gerry ended the prayer by thanking Heather for coming to Danny's side in his hour of need. It was everything she could do to cloak her excitement in the solemnity of prayer. She could hardly wait until the next day, when she would take Heather and Allison to the prison to see their husband and father.

The next morning, however, Gerry sensed almost immediately that something was wrong. Perhaps it was Heather's refusal to ride in the same car on the trip to Columbia. She and her mother had some business to transact, she told Gerry, that might put them at the prison late, so they would come in a separate car and meet Gerry there. Perhaps it was the stranger they brought with them to CCI: a dark-suited, unfriendly man with a briefcase. Gerry pulled Heather aside and asked, "Who is this person?" but Heather only mumbled something vague about "their house and property and papers to sign." Perhaps it was their body language: the way they avoided looking Gerry in the eye, the way they huddled by themselves in a corner of the visiting room while they waited for Danny. At one point, Gerry walked over to the man in the dark suit, extended her hand, and introduced herself. He took her hand tentatively, muttered his name, and then withdrew. And he never looked her in the eye.

It just didn't feel right to Gerry, although she didn't know why.

Finally, they brought Danny in.

He looked terrible. He hadn't been eating again, and the hours of interrogation had taken an especially heavy toll. His eyes were deeply sunken and heavy-lidded. He was so weak that a guard had to hold him up as he made his way to a chair on the other side of the glass partition. After the first wave of concern, Gerry felt a second wave of relief: at least Heather was there to bolster his spirits.

Heather looked to Gerry to go first—the guards would let only one person at a time talk with a prisoner—but Gerry waved Heather ahead of her. This was her day.

Heather approached the hole in the glass through which so much was expected to pass. There was no privacy; no partitions separated them from visitors to the right and left. After a few awkward words of greeting, Heather got right to the point: She wanted a divorce.

Before Danny could catch his breath, she rushed to say that she had brought the papers for him to sign. The man with her was a lawyer, she said, as she handed him a thin document with a blue legal backing. Danny's eyes slid over the first few paragraphs: "grounds for divorce . . . public exposure, ridicule and related facts stemming from defendant's arrest . . . Plaintiff seeks . . . all joint property . . . any personal property in banks, savings and loans and safe-deposit boxes . . . any stocks and bonds . . . any automobiles . . . custody of plaintiff's two-year-old daughter, Allison . . . maiden name restored to Heather Carlyn Carpenter . . ."

It was all too much for Danny, who could barely concentrate enough to understand the words he was reading, much less their implications. "I'll sign the papers," he said, cutting off her hurried explanations.

Heather was caught off guard. She had come prepared to do battle. She turned back to the lawyer, who had inched his way closer during the conversation, briefcase in hand. After a whispered conference, she turned back to Danny. "He says you have to read the papers," she told him. "You have to read them before you sign them."

"I don't care what they say," Danny responded mechanically. "If you want a divorce, I'll sign the papers right now, but I won't read them."

Heather turned back to the lawyer. "No, no," Gerry overheard him saying. "He has to *read* them first."

That was the first hint Gerry had of what was happening. In an instant, though, she put the whole story together—and she was furious. Heather and her mother had been staying in her house, eating her food, while all the time plotting this attack on her son. Last night they had gotten down on their knees with Gerry and her family and prayed, and this morning they had met with a lawyer before even seeing Danny.

She stood up on her toes and looked across the glass partition. Danny was sitting motionless, staring hollow-eyed into the middle distance. Look at him, she thought. Frail and weak and barely able to walk. How could she do this to him? Would he be able to handle it after all the pain and humiliation he'd been through? To have his family snatched away from him when family meant so much to him. Except for Gerry, they were his lifeline—his only connection to the past, to the Danny he was once and might be again someday.

She had a hollow feeling in her gut that her body said was nausea but her mind said was betrayal. It was incomprehensible that Heather could have come to the prison and seen Danny's pain face to face—and still do this to him. Why did it have to be now? Gerry said to herself. Now, when Danny needed her most? Why couldn't she have waited?

She looked at Danny again, and the nausea grew inside her. Oh, Danny, poor Danny, she thought. After everything else, how would he ever get through this?

A few hours later, Danny was taken in handcuffs to an interview room for a meeting with a staff psychiatrist. Once again, he seemed too weak to walk without assistance. He hardly seemed a threat. That must have been why no one was expecting what happened next. A few minutes into the meeting, Danny bolted out of his chair, ran to an adjoining bathroom, and locked the door behind him. The doctor summoned guards, but before they arrived, he heard the sound of breaking glass from inside the bathroom.

(9/13/89) *I just broke the mirror. I had on these heavy handcuffs. Even when I was talking to psychiatrists, they had me handcuffed. They didn't mess around with security in that place. I'm in the middle of a prison, inside of a locked-down ward with a room full of people, and I'm handcuffed. So I went into the bathroom. But I was too weak. I hadn't been eating for quite some time. I was trying to smash the glass. I lifted my arms up so that I could pry the mirror off the wall, and I smashed it on the toilet.*

I immediately began banging on the glass and they heard me. So they started banging on the door to try to get me to open it. I don't know what they thought I was up to. All I know is they wanted to get me out of there.

I held the mirror in my hands, with my wrists handcuffed in front of me. I had to smash it. Then somebody sprayed tear gas under the door. It blinded me. I couldn't even see what I was doing. It only took one slam to break the mirror into pieces. I did both wrists. I started bleeding a lot, but they got the door off in about three minutes. They got the hinges off somehow and dragged me out.

It had nothing to do with courage. That's another story. It involves something else. It really wasn't a suicide attempt. It was much more than that.

Part Four

61

Gerry first learned of her son's suicide attempt when she read about it in the paper the next day.

> COLUMBIA—A man accused of being a serial kidnapper and sexual assaulter tried to commit suicide Tuesday in a prison here shortly after learning that his wife had filed for a divorce, a prison spokesman said.

Once again, Gerry felt in her heart the familiar battle between anxiety and anger: anxiety for Danny, anger at the way they were treating him. Why was the media informed of his suicide attempt before his family? In fact, as Gerry read the obscene details—"Starrett had two cuts of about an inch on his left arm, and 1½ inches on his right arm ... the wounds required 11 stitches"—she still hadn't been called. Did they think his family wouldn't care? Did they even think about his family? When she called the prison, they said, "We can't tell you anything!" The papers and television and a million strangers out there were entitled to everything—right down to the number of stitches in Danny's arm—but not his mother?

She had seen it before, a hundred times in the months since Danny's arrest, in big ways and little ways, in official pronouncements and casual asides, in media specials and furtive glances: The accused doesn't have a family. The accused doesn't *deserve* a family. If the accused had a family, they would have to treat him like a human being.

The next day, Gerry and Richard descended on the prison and met with Warden Kenneth McKeller. Gerry made all the usual arguments about the treatment Danny was getting, about the insensitivity of the psychiatric care, the humiliation of the living conditions, the prejudice of the media coverage, the agony and anger of those who loved him. Given all that, said Gerry, it wasn't surprising that Danny had tried to take his own life. McKeller listened in benign boredom up to that point, but at the mention of the suicide attempt, blurted out, "That wasn't serious."

Gerry stopped in midsentence, wondering if she had really heard what she thought she heard.

"That so-called suicide attempt," said McKeller with contempt, "was nothing but a plea for sympathy. He wasn't really trying to kill himself. If he had been serious, he would have gone for the jugular vein."

Gerry spent the next few days making the usual round of plaintive-angry phone calls trying to make sure that Danny's wounds—both physical and emotional—were being treated. She talked to doctors and lawyers and prison officials, but mostly she talked to Danny. "Heather *does* love you," she told him, trying desperately to defuse the impact of the impending divorce. "She just isn't the right person for you. Family is important to you. Family plays a big role in your life. You were doing your part—working hard, bringing home a paycheck, providing a home for Heather and Allison. But Heather wasn't doing hers. She was going off to see her family at times that were important to you. She wasn't cleaning the house. She wanted to get a job. Home and family weren't as important to her as they are to you."

Then, just when Danny seemed back on the road to recovery, just when he started eating again and the color returned to his cheeks, the shattering news came from Georgia.

They wanted to kill her son.

62

The call for blood came from a Georgia prosecutor, Michael Eubanks, who had been in his job for only a year in a state where D.A.'s earned notches in their belts for death-penalty convictions. A former Peace Corps worker, Eubanks had been, by his own account, a "soft-headed, soft-hearted liberal" on the death penalty at one time. He could still remember reading in the paper about a local obstetrician who had performed mandatory sterilizations on women after their third pregnancy and thinking, "This is Nazi. We can't have this!" But all that had changed—whether from an attack of conscience or political ambition wasn't clear—when he left his father's dry-cleaning business and entered the public arena. Now he considered the doctor "an advanced thinker, ahead of his time."

The conversion had come early in his career, when he worked on the case of an Atlanta man who took revenge on a waitress who insulted him, beating her, burning her with cigarettes, cutting her with knives and razor blades, pouring salt in her wounds, strangling her to death, and then stuffing her body into a trunk. When the trunk proved too small, he broke her bones into pieces so she would fit.

Working on that case, Eubanks had seen the light. "It just struck me for the first time," he said later, "with vivid clarity that there are some people who are just outside humanity. And so this pleasant, liberal philosophy that had very little to do with the real world began to crumble under the weight of the fact that the world is filled with terrible people and that for some of them the only logical outcome is death."

Now he was calling, with all the conviction of the converted, for the death of Danny Starrett.

Starrett's behavior had "removed him from the realm of humanity," Eubanks declared to reporters. "This is not a human being. If he were a mad dog, rabid and running the streets attacking people, you couldn't find a single person outside some New York City animal-rights activist who would have a problem with shooting the dog down and getting rid of it. Or if he were a cockroach running across the kitchen floor, most people wouldn't think twice about stepping on him. Frankly, that's the way I look at people who do things like this."

He was undeterred by the fact that South Carolina courts had already sentenced Danny Starrett to three consecutive life terms without possibility of parole. Attorneys in his own office and even some of the police officers involved in Danny's capture argued that too much money had already been wasted on Danny Starrett. South Carolina had spent tens of thousands of dollars prosecuting him and would spend hundreds of thousands more warehousing him for the rest of his life. What was left for the state of Georgia to do? What would be the point of adding another life sentence or two when he already had three?

Even when a court in Charleston added another two life sentences without possibility of parole, Eubanks was undeterred. "Instead of housing this man or giving him a chance to murder a prison guard or to be paroled," he said defiantly, "why not just get rid of him? In addition, society has a very legitimate right, in my opinion, to seek revenge for unspeakable acts. When people like this are loose in the world and kill people in terrible ways, my notion of humanity is not offended by killing them."

Eubanks scoffed at those who accused him of political opportunism. To those who doubted he could get a death-penalty conviction after two South Carolina courts had already accepted pleas of guilty but mentally ill, Eubanks said it didn't matter. In Georgia, a mentally ill person could still be put to death. The law protected only the mentally retarded from the electric chair. Danny Starrett had murdered Jeannie McCrea in Georgia, and Georgia would demand its rightful revenge.

"We've got a neurotic, totally uncorrectable human being here," said Eubanks, "and it seems crazy, especially in a world that's already got at least fifty percent too many people, to keep this one around if we don't have to."

When Gerry Starrett read those words, she turned pale. Would she tell Danny? If she didn't, who would? The last of the South Carolina cases was almost through, and they didn't have an attorney in Georgia yet. Until now, they had relied on public defenders, hoping to save their money for the fight in Georgia, where the stakes would be highest. Now, their savings were virtually wiped out, the business was in ruins, and they still didn't have a lawyer in Georgia.

She and Richard called dozens of legal aid organizations, public-interest law firms, anti-capital-punishment groups, anyone with a reputation for defending death-penalty cases, first in the Southeast, then everywhere in the country. They sent out what seemed like hundreds of letters: "Can you help us? Can you tell us where to find help?" But the response, by phone or by letter, was always the same. They were sorry, but Danny didn't fit their client profile. He was too middle-class, too well educated, too well off. He could find the money to hire his own lawyer, even if he had to borrow it. He at least had the potential to raise money. Their clients didn't. He was also white, and, as one lawyer told Gerry, "There are more issues when you've got a black defendant."

By the time Gerry called Millard Farmer, an Atlanta criminal lawyer, she was desperate. If Farmer couldn't help them, there was only one place left to go: the public defender's office. After Danny's experience in South Carolina, Gerry didn't want that. On the long, straight road from Augusta to Atlanta to see Farmer, she tried to think no farther ahead than the next mile marker. Somebody had once suggested that her ordeal was like an alcoholic's: The only way to survive was to take it one day at a time. "Sometimes I can't even make that," she sighed. "Sometimes a day is far, far too long."

Later that same day, Farmer turned them down. But he did recommend another lawyer: a Vietnam vet named Augustus Siemon—known as "Bud."

63

Like Gerry Starrett, Bud Siemon was a warrior. For Gerry the battles had been against her family, her hometown, and her insecurities. For Siemon, a military brat with a dozen hometowns and a surfeit of self-confidence, the battles had always been against larger, unseen enemies. At Pepperdine College, he fought school officials who, even as Watts burned around them, insisted on curfews and dress codes and drinking rules so strict that students could be expelled for having a glass of wine with Thanksgiving dinner at home.

When he left Pepperdine after just six months and transferred to Michigan State, Siemon missed a semester—a lapse that left him exposed to a prowling draft board in the early years of the Vietnam War. Unlike a lot of young men, he took the draft notice in stride. He never had liked school very much. He never was very good at sitting still—whether in school or in church—and the prospect of solving problems in the real world instead of in the classroom excited him. But he also believed in finishing what he started, so he joined ROTC, completed his schoolwork, and graduated as a lieutenant in the U.S. Army.

There was no question about where he would go next. In 1970, almost every new lieutenant was going one place: Vietnam. Figuring he needed every advantage he could get, Siemon went first to Airborne school and then, after signing up for an extra year of duty, to Special Forces school. When he emerged, Bud Siemon was a member of the most elite fighting force in the army, the Green Berets.

So how did Pepperdine's rebel without a cause come to wear the green fatigues of his government's army? At a time when other rebellious spirits of his generation were demonstrating in the streets or fleeing to Canada to protest the war, why was he marching in the vanguard of the legions of the establishment? When did James Dean become John Wayne?

Siemon didn't see it that way. By his lights, he was still fighting the system—only from within. Unlike his father, a "hard-ass conservative," Siemon opposed the war. He considered it politically "dumb" and militarily "a serious mistake." He even wrote letters in support of friends' petitions for conscientious-objector status. But he resented even more the way the machinery of war had been rigged to favor the white children of the rich and middle class. "I don't think it's fair that the most educated people in the country are using their educations and the sophistication that they learn at universities to dodge the draft," he said. As a college-educated, white, middle-class kid, Siemon felt the best way he could fight the unfairness of the system was by going *in*.

So he went. He spent eleven months there, first as an infantry platoon leader, then as a reconnaissance platoon leader in the jungled mountains of northern South Vietnam. The rugged country was thick with V.C. on the move, and hardly a day passed that his patrol didn't set up an ambush or bump into one themselves. In all the firefights and monsoons and mini-epidemics of malaria, though, he lost only one man—and that was to friendly fire. He came close to death himself a couple of times: once when a rocket landed at his feet but didn't go off; again when the rain-soaked fuse on a booby trap took an extra few seconds to burn down, giving him just enough time to jump behind a rock before the bomb exploded. For learning poise under pressure and self-confidence, Siemon would often say, there was no better classroom than war—even if the disciplinary rules were a little harsh.

When he returned from Vietnam, Siemon enrolled in law school at Georgia Tech. Ever since childhood, he had had a vague ambition to be a lawyer. *Perry Mason* had been his favorite TV show, *Witness for the Prosecution* his favorite movie. Still, there were no lawyers in his family; he hadn't known any growing up; and the first real trial he saw from start to finish was the first one he did himself.

He had been in law school only a year when he decided to make his career in criminal law. This time the reason was clear. He had taken some time off school to work in the Georgia prison system as a legal aid counselor, interviewing and screening prisoners who asked to see a lawyer. As inmate after inmate told him their stories, the first thing Siemon noticed was how incompetent most of the lawyers were who represented them.

"It bothered me as a human being to see people being treated the way they were by the legal system," he said later, "and I found it offensive that there should be so much difference between the quality of representation people get with court-appointed lawyers as opposed to the quality of representation they get if they can afford to pay."

After a year of freelance work for indigent clients, Siemon moved to the public defender's office in nearby Waycross and inherited his first death-penalty case. A mentally retarded seventeen-year-old boy had gotten high on drugs, walked into a clothing store, and terrorized a couple of young college kids who were working over Christmas vacation. He wound up killing one of them and sodomizing the other. The police chased him from the crime scene to his home and arrested him in bed with the money and the gun. In other words, he was guilty. There was no question about that. The only question was about punishment. The prosecution asked for death. The boy got life. Bud considered that a victory.

Winning felt so good that he decided he had found his calling. He wanted to spend the rest of his life winning death-penalty cases. Over the next few years, on the rare occasions when he was asked why he was drawn to this odd, precarious niche in the great edifice of the law, he would talk about helping people in trouble, about the adrenaline high of playing the game for the highest stakes, and about the immorality of state-sponsored killing. But the real reason he liked winning death-penalty cases, he had to admit, was that *he wasn't supposed to.*

The system was rigged to make these cases certain losers. First, by discouraging good lawyers from taking indigent cases. Even on run-of-the-mill criminal cases, local judges invariably appointed either young, inexperienced lawyers trying to build a practice or old, over-the-hill lawyers looking for a little extra cash. No one else could afford to take them. When Siemon started off as a public defender, he was paid $10 an hour. Although the pay varied from court to court—a judge might pay several hundred dollars for a plea and several hundred more for a trial—it was always pathetic, and it didn't get any better if the stakes were life and death. His total pay for the first death-penalty case he defended: $800. In fact, as the stakes went up, the quality of representation typically went down. That was because the publicity that inevitably surrounded death-penalty cases put the most political pressure on judges and prosecutors to guarantee that the system produced the "right" result: that is, the result their constituents wanted.

"Judges follow election returns," Siemon was fond of saying. Judges were like any other professionals—particularly any other politicians. They wanted their area of the government to be perceived as functioning efficiently and in the public interest. And if the public was overwhelmingly in favor of capital punishment—as it was in Georgia— the public interest was in seeing those cases that hit the public spotlight wind up, not just as death penalty cases, but as *successful* death penalty cases. So the temptation was irresistible to appoint lawyers who wouldn't get in the way of the "right" result. Siemon had seen lawyers appointed to defend death-penalty cases who hadn't done a criminal case in years or lawyers fresh out of law school who had never tried *any* criminal case.

And because there was no money in defending death-penalty cases, there was no incentive for anyone to develop an expertise in it. So even if a judge wanted to appoint a competent lawyer, he would have a hard time finding one.

Add to this that the typical client in a death-penalty case was poor, uneducated, black, and accused of some especially shocking, senseless, reprehensible crime, and it was hardly surprising that most capital cases were nothing more than a lockstep to the gallows.

To break that lockstep was the sweetest joy in Bud Siemon's life.

Sure, he hated the money—or, more precisely, the lack of it. In his career, he had litigated sixteen death-penalty cases and been involved in another fifty or sixty, and from all those cases he had made less than $25,000. There was no money for an office, for a secretary, for a computer. And without them he had trouble supplementing his income doing more traditional legal tasks. He couldn't handle the paperwork. He hated it when people said they envied him because he didn't care about making money. He did care. He cared that he was always in debt. He cared that his son would have to pay for college someday without any help from his dad. He cared that he hadn't bought a new car since 1977.

Yet he knew the system was designed to make him feel that way, to push him into more lucrative legal work so it could get on with the rigged business of death. But the anger he felt at his plight was turned back on the system and fueled him for another battle. "In this field, you're constantly saying, 'I understand the game you're trying to play and, well, fuck you—I'm going to do it anyway,'" he would say. "'I refuse to surrender.'"

He never had surrendered—and never lost. Of all the clients he had ever represented at trial, either as lead counsel or co-counsel, none had been executed. He had learned his lesson well in Vietnam: It doesn't matter how good you are or how much your men love you or how much they hate you. In a firefight, all that matters is who's breathing when it's over.

64

A week after the meeting with Millard Farmer, Gerry Starrett opened her front door in Evans and saw a handsome young man with red hair, wearing a rumpled suit and tie. "I'm Bud Siemon," he said to her astonishment.

Because he knew the Starretts had been through so many legal battles and so many lawyers already, Siemon skipped the usual niceties. "First off, let me tell you that I am not a miracle worker," he said. "I've read about your son's case in the newspaper. I don't know all the details, but I know that he has pled guilty to the South Carolina offenses and I know this isn't a whodunit. He is guilty as charged and is currently serving five life sentences. Am I right so far?"

He was, although it made Gerry uncomfortable to have a stranger give voice to her most secret thoughts. Only because Millard Farmer had given her Siemon's credentials and track record did she refrain from interrupting him with a defense of her son.

"But you should know," Siemon continued, "that this is typical of death-penalty cases. Only rarely when somebody gets arrested for a crime like this is there a question about guilt. What usually happens is that the defendant gets appointed a lousy lawyer, the lousy lawyer's got no resources to try the case, and therefore the district attorney has no reason to negotiate. It's a good bet, maybe a sure bet, that he'll win and get whatever he wants from the jury.

"That's where I come in. My job is to create reasons for the district attorney to negotiate. And the way I do that is by making his life as difficult as possible. I create conflict with him and conflict with the judge. I try to create conflict in the system. I try to keep the system from smoothly grinding Danny down." Gerry found Siemon's slightly subversive smile hugely reassuring.

"Of course, that can be a long, long process. I know you hear 'death penalty,' and you think that if Danny goes to trial in July, he'll be executed in August. Fortunately, it doesn't work that way. Think of it not as a battle but as a series of battles—as a war. And it's my job to make each battle as protracted and costly as I possibly can."

*　　*　　*

Siemon wasted no time in joining the battle.

He fought them on the extradition. If Danny had been a normal prisoner, he could have been routinely extradited from South Carolina to stand trial for murder in Georgia and then returned to South Carolina to complete his sentence. Any sentence handed down in Georgia would be served after the South Carolina sentence was completed.

But Danny Starrett was not a normal prisoner. If he was sentenced to death in Georgia, would they return him to South Carolina to finish his sentence there, as the rules of extradition required? If they did, he would never be put to death because his sentence—five life terms— would never be completed. Or would they keep him in Georgia and put him to death, in which case he would never get to finish his South Carolina sentence? And what would happen if he received less than a death sentence in Georgia? Would he be returned to South Carolina, destined never to serve any time in a Georgia prison? And if that was the case, why bother to prosecute him in Georgia at all?

But Siemon believed he knew the answers to all those questions. Simply put, Georgia wanted Danny Starrett extradited because they wanted to put him to death. And South Carolina was only too willing to go along if Georgia could do what their courts couldn't. For officials in both states, a death sentence was a foregone conclusion. In fact, the governors of South Carolina and Georgia quickly signed a special executive agreement that provided for exactly that: Daniel Starrett would be extradited to Georgia to stand trial for the murder. If he was sentenced to death, Georgia didn't have to bother returning him.

Siemon protested what he labeled a travesty of justice as various South Carolina officials made a show of reviewing the propriety of the extradition agreement. "We know how this is going to turn out," he sneered to reporters after a five-minute hearing on the issue, a hearing at which Danny had appeared with shackles on his wrists and ankles and closed his eyes as the charges were read. "This was a mere formality, a sham."

But it was a losing battle. Within days, Danny was standing in a Georgia courtroom, eyes closed again, trying not to listen as a prosecutor formally announced that state's intention "to have Mr. Starrett electrocuted for the Columbia County killing of a fifteen-year-old Irmo, South Carolina, girl, Jean Taylor McCrea."

He fought them with motions. For example, a hefty, sixty-four-pager charging the Georgia judicial and prosecutorial selection process violated the Fourteenth Amendment; another motion requested money to hire an investigator and forensic psychologist; a motion was filed for a community survey to assess the effect of the ongoing media blitz on his client's right to a fair trial; a motion requested travel money for defense lawyers, investigators, and witnesses; a motion sought daily transcripts of trial proceedings—at public expense, of course—and on and on. When the judge started denying the motions, Gerry expressed her concern. "Pre-trial motions have multiple purposes," Siemon assured her, "and in most instances the relief that we actually seek in the motion is the least of those purposes."

Gerry also wanted to know why, in this blizzard of motions, there wasn't one to move the trial. After all the adverse publicity, surely Danny stood a better chance of getting a fair trial somewhere else.

Siemon was noncommittal. He certainly agreed with Gerry that in heavily publicized cases, jurors often feel like they don't have a free hand in deciding the case. They feel their community will judge them on how they judge the defendant. But, Siemon explained, "if we ask for a change, there's always a chance that the judge will send us someplace worse."

In fact, Siemon had already looked at the census figures for Columbia County and concluded that it probably wasn't a very good place to try Danny's case. But he didn't want to rush into filing for a change of venue, not just because the judge might send them even deeper into the pinewoods of rural Georgia, but because he knew that a poisoned publicity well could work to his advantage. By picking a jury in a hostile community, he had a better chance of working an error in the jury selection. "Things happen, people say things, jurors get together and talk," he told Gerry, "or the local newspaper prints an inflammatory argument right in the middle of jury selection." In a case that would be as difficult to win as Danny's, it could be the deciding factor.

He fought them in the press. Danny was sick, Siemon emphasized in every interview, and the state of Georgia had no business prosecuting a sick man. "I hope civilization has not deteriorated to the point where we execute people found to be mentally ill," he told a group of reporters, reminding them that Danny had already been judged mentally ill by two South Carolina courts. "This isn't a case where a lawyer is standing up to try to tell a jury his client is mentally ill," he said. "That's not a question. He's been *found* to be mentally ill."

He fought them with politics. In a politically conservative community like Augusta, Siemon knew, one charge would hurt the prosecution more than any other. "The capital murder trial of Richard Daniel Starrett is likely to be the most expensive in Columbia County's history," cautioned the Augusta paper in an article that Bud Siemon could have written and almost certainly planted, "and county commissioners and court officials are unsure of how the county will pay for it." According to the article, potential costs, estimated at $100,000 to $200,000, "had already stirred debate over the propriety of such a trial for a man already serving five life terms in South Carolina."

On the record, Siemon dismissed the county's estimates as optimistic. "The actual costs will be much higher than local projections," he warned. County officials "don't realize how complicated all this will be," he explained. "You're looking at a quarter to a half million dollars to try to put this guy in the electric chair." Why, he wondered, did the Georgia prosecutor feel the need to make such a "major commitment in terms of resources, time, and money," given the statements by South Carolina prison officials that Danny Starrett would never be released?

When questioned about the cost, county officials reluctantly admitted that they were "unsure how the county will find the extra funds. We'll try to find it within the budget," they said. "The only other alternative is to raise taxes, and that's not on the agenda."

He fought them in the courtroom. At the first prearraignment hearing, it was clear that Siemon's public-relations campaign was already paying off. Eubanks's assistant, Richard Thomas, argued that Danny Starrett should not be considered mentally ill in Georgia, despite two guilty-but-mentally-ill pleas in South Carolina, because "the question of his mental competence has never been submitted to a *Georgia* jury." Judge Franklin Pierce bristled. "And just why do you think they're going to find anything different in this state?" queried Pierce, whose many years on the bench had left him too skeptical and too close to retirement to care about the political crosswinds swirling around the case.

"We don't agree with that finding, Your Honor," said Thomas lamely. After further questioning from Pierce on the sensibility of trying a man who was already condemned to a life behind bars, Thomas could do little more than insist repeatedly that Danny Starrett "deserved" the death penalty. "Under the circumstances presented as we know them," he concluded grandly, if vaguely, "we think the punishment needs to fit the crime."

From her seat in the front row of the gallery, Gerry looked over at her son. He sat straight in his chair, as she had taught him, but his head was down. She couldn't tell if his eyes were open or closed. He never moved, not even to shuffle his feet or rearrange the clasped fingers of his hands. He might as well not have been there at all. At one point Pierce looked at him and asked, "Mr. Starrett, are you satisfied with your representation in this courtroom today?"

Danny seemed startled when he realized the judge was talking to him. He opened his mouth to speak, but before he could, Bud Siemon jumped up. "By answering that question, Your Honor, we don't mean to make any concessions as to whether or not my client is competent— legally competent or mentally competent."

Pierce nodded impatiently. Then, in a tiny voice that Gerry could barely hear from just a few feet away, Danny answered. "Yes, sir."

He fought them with delay. After the same hearing, Siemon requested and Pierce ordered a mental evaluation for Danny at Central State Hospital, a high-security mental facility in Milledgeville, halfway between Augusta and Atlanta. When the prosecutors pressed for a schedule for the upcoming arraignment and other hearings, Pierce dismissed their haste. "Everything is on hold until we have a report on this man's mental state," he said. "And there's no way to predict how long that will take."

It was perhaps Siemon's greatest victory. A mental evaluation would take several months, maybe more—months in which he could look for more sand to throw in the engine of official death. After the hearing, Gerry asked, "What happens when the evaluation is done?" But Siemon knew she was really asking: "What happens when you run out of sand?"

65

From the beginning, Siemon had told his client (for Gerry was his client every bit as much as her son) that all these battles—the motions, the delays, the politics, the publicity—were directed to one end only: a plea bargain. But Gerry refused to believe it.

"If only Danny's story could be told to a jury," Gerry said. "If only we could just tell people, if only you could explain to a jury what he was really like, the jury would never give him a death sentence."

"Yes they would," Siemon said, for the hundredth time. I believe absolutely that if your son goes to trial, he will get a death sentence."

Gerry thought for a minute. "Is it his manner," she wondered, "the fact that he seems so rational?"

"Insanity defenses are extremely difficult to win," Siemon instructed. "That's what the statistics say. That's what my experience says. I have to make my judgments on the basis of experience, Mrs. Starrett, not love."

Siemon told her about a case in rural Georgia where a girl had climbed out of the bedroom window of her father's house one night and run off with her boyfriend. The father came looking for them with a shotgun. He found the boy's car parked in the local lovers' lane. He yanked open the car door, and there was his daughter down on the floor in the front seat, giving the boy a blow job. So he blew the boy's head off.

Gerry cringed—partly from the gruesomeness of it, but partly from its eerie familiarity. In the months since Danny's arrest, she had often imagined other tragic scenarios that might have taken her Danny away from her. What if he had died in a car crash? What if he had been killed by some crazed gunman? How much worse would that have been in some ways? And how much better in others?

Siemon continued his story over Gerry's displaced thoughts. "Now, the father comes into court and claims temporary insanity. And the jurors think, 'Well, hell. I would have done the same thing.' "

Gerry saw the end of the story coming. "They acquitted him?"

"They acquitted him," Siemon confirmed. "But that's not insanity. That's just being mad as hell. Insanity is what your son's got, Mrs. Starrett. But a juror is not going to look at what he did and say, 'I would have done the same thing.' Lawyers like me can talk all they want to about *intent* and *competence* and the rest, but what it really comes down to is whether they *forgive* him."

Gerry thought about that for a moment. "You don't think a jury would forgive Danny," she finally said, "even when he's clearly insane?" It was the first time Siemon had heard her use the word *insane*. Before, it was always *ill*, or *sick*, or *not well*, or *not himself*. "Don't you think a jury will recognize that?" she asked, half pleading.

"Mrs. Starrett," Siemon sighed, "a jury will look at the number of crimes, the number of victims, their ages, and the fact that he did the same thing over and over again."

"But he's *sick*," Gerry cried.

"He may be," Siemon said, "but it's not as though he's frothing at the mouth or eating flies. Believe me, Mrs. Starrett, it will be impossible to convince a jury that somebody as intelligent and meticulous as your son is crazy, no matter how crazy he may be."

"Danny is basically a good boy—"

"*It doesn't matter,*" Siemon flared, grabbing her full attention with his deeply creased brow. "The only thing that really matters is keeping him alive."

For the first time, Gerry seemed to hear him.

"Knowing that," he pressed, "would you still like to see a trial rather than a plea?"

Gerry cast her eyes down in thought. "Yes," she finally said. "I guess I would. I would like to see Danny be found not guilty by reason of insanity."

Siemon had lost his patience. "Is that just because you would rather have him perceived as a mentally ill person than a morally evil person, Mrs. Starrett? Is this all about appearances? Are you willing to risk your son's life over appearances?"

Gerry masked her rage and stalked away.

A few days later, a headline in a paper drew her attention to the kind of article that she had vowed she would never read again: DAHMER JURY REJECTS INSANITY DEFENSE. Despite herself, Gerry read the descriptions of Jeffrey Dahmer's crimes: how he had meticulously hunted and killed his victims, then either ate them or preserved them for later consumption. And yet the jury found him sane—at least sane enough to put to death. She wondered for the first time if it was possible for sane people to do insane things. And she was reminded of what Siemon had told her: "What it really comes down to is whether they *forgive* him."

She immediately called Siemon and told him a plea bargain was all right with her.

66

The prospects for a plea bargain looked much brighter when the mental evaluation came back from Central State Hospital. After three months of regular, lengthy interviews, Dr. Robert J. Storms, the hospital's senior psychologist, found Danny Starrett "marginally competent" but not competent enough to enter a plea.

Eubanks was apoplectic. He dismissed Storms's report as "more of the same psychological mumbo jumbo and pandering to criminals who commit violent acts and then want to have them excused by modern-day witchcraft. I don't accept any of that for a moment. My opinion," he fumed, "is that this is a ruse and subterfuge to avoid prosecution, just another chapter in the drama of a defendant who wants to avoid being punished for his acts."

Measured by prosecutorial distress, the evaluation was a thundering victory—but only a temporary one. When questioned by Judge Pierce at a hearing, Dr. Storms conceded that his patient's prognosis was "uncertain." "He certainly has the potential to be restored to his competency status," he said, meaning that the issue of competency was by no means closed. Hearing that, Pierce ordered Danny back to Central State for an additional ninety-day period of treatment during which Storms and others would attempt to "get him competent"—at least competent enough to stand trial.

For the next three months, while Danny submitted to yet another round of interviews and evaluations, Bud Siemon and Mike Eubanks sparred in court papers. Eubanks, fearing that Judge Pierce would go soft when the report came in, demanded that the issue of Danny's competency be settled at a special hearing before a jury. "I want that issue out of the way," he told reporters. "Quite frankly, I think it's a bogus issue." Siemon, who also had recognized Pierce's sympathy to his arguments, responded by agreeing, in principle, to a competency hearing, predicting confidently that such a hearing would "bear out Dr. Storms's opinion." But he wanted it to be a "bench trial"—that is, a hearing without a jury, in front of a judge, presumably Pierce.

Seeing himself about to be outflanked, Eubanks accused Judge Pierce of personal bias and demanded that he disqualify himself from the Starrett case. It was a risky move designed to stifle both Pierce and the mounting chorus of criticism in the media about the cost and wrong-headedness of trying a man already condemned to many lifetimes in prison.

Siemon fired the final round in the exchange by filing for a change of venue—moving the trial out of the Augusta area. Danny Starrett could never get a fair trial in Columbia County, he declared. The reason? District Attorney Michael Eubanks. "The district attorney and his office have chosen to throw gasoline on the flames of hostile publicity," Siemon told reporters. Partly as a result of that official incitement, Danny Starrett had "received more media coverage and attention than any prior case in the history of Columbia County." As an example of media hostility, he cited an editorial in the *Augusta Chronicle* that "openly called for Mr. Starrett's execution and featured a picture of the state's electric chair."

But Eubanks was unmoved. No maze of motions or minefield of public relations could deter him. He wanted a trial; he wanted a conviction; he wanted a death sentence. And he wouldn't talk to Bud Siemon or Judge Pierce or anybody else about a plea bargain. Even after Pierce hinted broadly that he would welcome a plea bargain as a way of avoiding what he saw as an expensive and unnecessary trial, Eubanks was a stone wall. The problem, by Siemon's calculation, was partly just Eubanks's obdurate personality and partly the politics of death in a deeply conservative state. But, as in most capital cases, the problem was mostly public relations.

Every day, more articles appeared fanning the public's fervor for a public execution. Members of the victims' families were quoted in the papers, questioning everything from Georgia justice to Judge Pierce's manhood. "I don't think there's any question our family wants him tried," a spokesman for Jeannie McCrea's family told reporters. "I'm willing for a judge and jury to make a decision, but not for a judge to sit back in a chair and make that kind of decision." The McCrea family was reported to be frustrated over Pierce's "apparent attempts to avoid a trial." They demanded a public forum for "an airing of exactly what happened" and rejected any talk of a plea agreement. "It's not fair to anybody," said the spokesman, "especially not to Jeannie. She didn't do anything wrong. That kid did nothing except answer the door one time too many."

The chief obstacle to a plea bargain was no longer a matter of law; it was a matter of public relations. To overcome it, Siemon turned to one of his clients, an experienced image consultant and media adviser, Gerry Starrett.

Not long after the editorial appeared calling for Danny Starrett's execution, readers of the *Augusta Chronicle* opened their paper to a story with a very different angle on the city's most publicized murder case. "No matter what Geraldine Starrett is doing," it began, "her eldest son is always on her mind."

"I'm working on two levels all the time," she said. "I have something else I'm doing, but it's always there. His face is always there. I wake up in the middle of the night, and that's what I'm thinking about. I wake up in the morning, and that's what I'm thinking about."

The public learned for the first time that Richard Daniel Starrett, whose mug shot they had seen dozens of times on the front page, was known as just plain Danny to his family. And far from being a troubled black sheep, this Starrett was "the one who did things to bring the family together—planning family dinners, organizing outings," the one who "brought Christmas presents for people in area shelters, read voraciously, and had a knack for telling jokes."

Gerry described her son several times as "sick" and wondered touchingly about her own responsibility for his sickness. "People say you're not responsible," she confessed, "but there's no way we can understand how he was in so much turmoil for so long and we could not know it." She wondered if she should have known, could have known, or could have done something to prevent it. "I think I did everything a parent was supposed to do. I don't know what more I could have done." Such questions "tormented" her, she admitted, yet she was "at peace" with her parenting.

What she was not at peace with was the way the media had been treating her son and her family. Their world had been turned "upside down," she said, "forever changed." The son and brother they loved was being portrayed as "a monster, an evil person." "I feel sick," said Gerry. "Sick is what I feel." And very angry. Angry because she passionately believed Danny was mentally ill—sick with an illness just like any other physical illness. Angry because the public was ignoring the fact that Danny had already been found mentally ill by two South Carolina courts. Angry because prosecutors wanted not only to deny him proper medical help but also to put him to *death*. Yes, she did feel like a victim sometimes, she said—if you define victim as "something out of your control that happens to you and causes you pain. That's not a plea for sympathy. That's just a fact."

The best she could hope for was that somewhere, somehow, a doctor could penetrate Danny's psyche and learn the cause of his actions, and that maybe what was learned from Danny's case "could be used to prevent something like this from ever happening again. In that way," Gerry concluded, "maybe something positive can come out of this chaos and pain."

What had she learned?

"That what I thought was real, now I don't know. If someone you love so much is hurting so much, is so sick, and you don't see it, you don't know what to believe anymore. You have to learn even the simplest things all over. There's nothing to rely upon. I don't know what I'm seeing anymore. I don't know what's truth anymore."

Was she afraid?

"I'm afraid of not handling this well," she said. "That's my greatest fear."

When word of the interview reached Mike Eubanks, he blasted back, archly complimenting Gerry Starrett on a "great public-relations job," although not a surprising one "when you look at Mrs. Starrett's business, The ImageMaker. It's like something out of a Dickens novel," Eubanks told an interviewer. "You couldn't invent a detail like that."

When asked if he faulted the Starretts for their defense of Danny, he balked. "I don't fault them one bit for doing everything they can," he said. "Well, let me back off. I do fault them. If I had a child who was a rapist, kidnapper, murderer, I would be afraid he might be going down the same path as Ted Bundy and want him stopped."

But wasn't Gerry Starrett just doing what a mother was supposed to do: defend her son? "Does a family *always* have to stand by one of their own?" asked Eubanks. "Why do they? Why does the motherhood relationship require you to do everything to protect someone who has done terrible things that you yourself can't possibly condone? I think that it allows families to justify doing almost anything and taking almost any position, no matter how irrational, in the defense of someone who's not defensible.

"I think this kind of campaign happens only when the criminal

comes from an upper-middle-class family. And I think its primary purpose is simply to remove some of the stigma. Instead of having a psychopathic, murdering, low-life son of a bitch, which Danny Starrett is,
in my opinion, they have a sick boy who needs to be treated. He didn't
really do these things, the *sickness* did them, and the sickness can
somehow be cured—through surgery or therapy for whatever, and then
the good Danny will be restored and the evil Richard will be gone."

And no, the suffering of Gerry Starrett did not change his mind
about a plea bargain. Danny Starrett would be tried and convicted and
put to death.

67

Dr. Robert Storms—chief forensic psychologist at Central State Hospital—was a rumpled, overweight, professorial man who had, by most accounts, the keenest eye in the entire Georgia department of corrections.
No one could spot a schizophrenic or a psychotic or a multiple personality like Bob Storms. Perhaps his greatest talent, though, was spotting
"fakers"—accused criminals feigning insanity to escape long prison
terms or, more often, death sentences. He could spot fakers even when
it was an insane person doing the faking. "No one plays crazy like a
crazy person," Storms was fond of saying.

Unfortunately, not all the people he encountered in his job as a forensic psychologist were "on the couch." (Actually, most of his interviewing
was done across a table on hard chairs in little rooms with linoleum on the
floors and bars on the windows.) All too many of them were practicing law
in courthouses such as the Columbia County Courthouse, a marvelous
redbrick Victorian structure in Appling, Georgia. Storms had been to the
building often to help the lawyers distinguish between the crazy criminal
and the merely criminal; between those who went to prison and those who
went to the "hospital." It was a Catch-22 sort of job, and no one was more
aware of its peculiar nature than Bob Storms.

Or enjoyed it more. Storms took a sly pleasure in explaining his most bizarre cases to friends over lunch. A favorite one concerned an inmate who had taken a woman on a date, had sex with her, hacked her body to bits with a chain saw, then went to sleep with the bloody body parts beside him in bed. Later, in prison, he requested conjugal visits with a woman he had met through a prison dating service—a woman who knew everything about his past. Here was the question, Storms would say with a twinkle in his eye: Who was crazier? The chain-saw lover or the woman who wanted to have sex with him?

Storms was summoned to the courthouse by Bud Siemon for a conference on the Danny Starrett case. In Judge Pierce's chamber—actually just a big, unused room with a table, several chairs, and a few out-of-date lawbooks—the principals in the case assembled to discuss the question that had been burning a hole on the front pages of every newspaper for weeks: How would Danny Starrett plead?

The real problem, Storms knew, was that Eubanks and a lot of people like him didn't consider injuries to the psyche injuries at all. If they didn't see a bleeding wound or a bandage or a scar, they refused to believe there was an injury. To them, child abuse, addiction, psychoses, and the rest were all just excuses, not wounds.

Storms had encountered Eubanks many times before, and in other cases like Danny Starrett's, cases where the issues in dispute were unseen wounds and the very real harm they can cause. From the first, the two men had not gotten along. In one of their first courtroom confrontations, the Augusta police had arrested a young man—a kid actually—for murder. Soon after the arrest, the police produced a complete and very eloquent confession. When asked by the defense attorney to examine the accused, Storms could see immediately that the boy was retarded. In court, Eubanks argued that he·was nevertheless competent to confess. "He's not even competent to *talk,*" Storms corrected him.

Another time, at a sentencing hearing, Eubanks was passing around the pictures of the murder victim—a typical prosecution ploy. When he finally passed the pictures to Storms for comment, Storms took one look and said, "Listen, this is just not the most heinous crime. I've seen far worse."

"Oh, yeah?" Eubanks challenged, obviously flustered. "Do you want to tell us about them?"

To Storms, Eubanks's challenge was what a straight line is to a comic. With a scowl of gravity, he turned to the judge. "Your Honor," he warned, "this is pretty graphic stuff." Then he told about a man he had worked with in prison who had smothered his wife, dismembered her, cut off her arms, cut off her legs, and then tried to put the body back together.

Eubanks stalked off.

Despite their professional feud, Storms had tried to warn Eubanks against pressing the Starrett case. Even before the first hearing in front of Judge Pierce, he had told the D.A. informally, "I am going to write a letter to the judge, and it's basically going to say that Starrett is crazy." Eubanks's reaction was typical Eubanks, Storms thought. He said he wouldn't drop the case "because I'm getting more and more faith in the jury system to dismiss what experts like you say."

Why was Eubanks pursuing the Starrett case so aggressively? Storms wondered. Was it pure political ambition? Eubanks was widely known to covet an elective judgeship. While it was true that death-penalty cases had a special cachet among Georgia D.A.'s—they kept an informal count of who had the most men on death row—this wasn't really a death-penalty case. Storms had discussed the case with five or six prominent D.A.'s in other jurisdictions, outlined the facts, especially the five life sentences, and all of them agreed that Eubanks was wrong to push for the electric chair. "It's in South Carolina," they said. "Why not leave it alone?"

Why not, indeed? Storms wondered as he sat in one of the hard, uncomfortable chairs in Pierce's makeshift chambers, listening to Eubanks explain one more time why Danny Starrett was competent to stand trial. "Richard Daniel Starrett was at the beginning stage of a Bundy progression," he intoned. "Had Starrett not been caught, there is absolutely no question that he would have continued to kidnap and rape women." How could he be so sure? "Because that kind of personality needs an escalation of thrills and titillation. The risk factor has got to be higher, the drama has got to get greater. I think he was off and running."

"Georgia has a law against executing the mentally retarded, Your Honor." Bud Siemon rose to his feet. "As a matter of fact, I worked on the case that helped change the law, the case of Jerome Bowden." Storms knew about the Bowden case. Mentally, Bowden was barely functional, but he was proud. Just a few days before he was scheduled for execution, a psychiatrist gave him an IQ test and poor old Jerome thought the idea was to do well on it. So he tried as hard as he could on the test, and that got him killed. The media picked up on the sorry spectacle of Jerome, pleased to the end that he had done so well on the test, beaming with pride as they led him off to the chair, and the Georgia legislature immediately passed a law that prohibited executing a mentally retarded person. Too late for poor, proud Jerome.

But not for Danny Starrett, Siemon argued.

"Nobody is suggesting that Richard Daniel Starrett is mentally retarded," Eubanks snapped, then adding with a chuckle, "not even Dr. Storms over here—whose IQ is almost as high as Mr. Starrett's. The defense contends that he is merely mentally ill. And under Georgia law, a mentally ill person *can* be executed."

Strange as it sounded, Storms knew Eubanks was right, at least technically. In Georgia, as in most states, mentally ill people could be put to death. No less an authority than the U.S. Supreme Court had given its okay to that.

"It is true, Your Honor," said Siemon, "that no court has decided if the Georgia law applies to the mentally ill as well as the mentally retarded. But if the state of Georgia isn't going to execute a mentally retarded person like Jerome Bowden, why should it execute a schizophrenic, or a psychotic, or a mentally ill person like Danny Starrett?" Like the Starrett family, Siemon had taken to calling his client "Danny." It humanized him. Eubanks stuck defiantly to "Richard Daniel Starrett."

Siemon pointedly reminded Pierce that over the previous decade there had been a series of defendants, all of them seriously mentally ill, who received death sentences at trial only to have those sentences reversed on appeal. "Judges, even appeals judges," Siemon purred, "are human. They read the facts of the case and realize just how sick these people are, and they look for ways to reverse their convictions."

Siemon listed the cases by name, from memory. "I've been involved in all these cases," he concluded, "and what's happened in every case is that we've gotten reversals because judges don't want to execute a crazy person."

It was vintage Bud Siemon, thought Storms: an argument based on people, not legal principles. Siemon would have made a stellar psychologist. Hell, he *was* a psychologist.

Next, it was Storms's turn. He had been in this chair, or one like it, hundreds of times. But whether looking out on a packed courtroom, or a jury, or just a judge and a few lawyers, he always had the same queasy feeling. He was a brain surgeon explaining a delicate procedure to a shop class. Using one crude tool (psychology) to guide an even cruder tool (the law) to fix an organism as delicate and subtle as the human psyche was an activity doomed to failure—and likely to kill the patient.

"Mr. Starrett fits the profile for paraphilia," Storms began, recapping the contents of the evaluation he had prepared for Judge Pierce months before. "Paraphilia is a disorder that involves recurrent intense sexual urges and sexually arousing fantasies that generally involve nonhuman objects, the suffering or humiliation of oneself or one's partner, or children or other nonconsenting people." And although Mr. Starrett knew the difference between right and wrong at the time of the crimes, his actions were "significantly influenced" by his thought disorder. The disorder, in turn, was influenced by heavy drinking, "which further diminished his impulse control—"

"I'm sorry to interrupt you, doctor," said Pierce, who had been mostly silent up to this point, "but what I'm interested in here is the plea. What, if anything, is Starrett going to plead? My question to you is simply this: Is he, in your opinion, competent to formulate and enter a plea?"

"Danny is unique," Storms began. "Most of the people who are incompetent are incompetent because they are either too retarded or too out of touch with reality. I mean, they really don't know where they are and what they are doing. But Danny isn't like that. Danny's incompetence comes from his hallucinations, or his delusions, or whatever you want to call them."

Eubanks sprang to his feet. "Your Honor," he said, "the defendant is just trying to avoid responsibility for what he has done." That was so much like Eubanks, Storms thought. Put your eye on the target, bulldoze straight for it, and never look up. " 'Paraphilia,' " Eubanks scoffed. "That's a joke. That makes nearly every male in the United States mentally ill. I think we all have some hang-up. Whether we like women's legs or get off on silk or something, we are all paraphiliacs." Siemon and Storms exchanged glances.

Eubanks continued, "What all this boils down to is that they are saying that Richard Daniel Starrett was mentally ill and shouldn't be held accountable for his acts because he got sexually aroused by kidnapping women and tying them up. If we buy that, there are a whole bunch of folks out there that are going to be given a license to do what they want to and, hey, they're just mentally ill."

Storms waited until Eubanks sat down before responding. "He was not faking, Your Honor. As far as I can see, he is clearly psychotic." Storms allowed himself a brief but very professional flash of anger. "And I would remind Your Honor that the doctors in South Carolina also found him mentally ill."

"So what is the bottom line?" Pierce wanted to know.

Storms held up his hand and listed his conclusions, one to a finger. "He *is* mentally ill. I *am* sure about it. He is *not* faking. He is *not* competent."

"Will he ever be competent?" asked Pierce.

"At this point, I don't think so."

Eubanks demanded to know why, a few months before, Storms had described Danny as "marginally competent" and suggested that he could be made competent enough to stand trial.

"That was before all these delays," Storms replied. "Now he is neither of those, nor is he close to either of those."

"You mean he became less and less competent as time passed because of the delays?" Siemon clarified. They were, of course, his delays.

"In my opinion," said Storms, "he has come apart psychotically, come apart mentally, since I wrote my original letter to Your Honor. When I first saw him, his mental condition was already very fragile."

Eubanks had heard more than he could stand. "You shrinks are all alike," he exploded. As he jumped up, his chair made a shrill, screeching sound on the floor. "You're too involved in this case. You're overinvested. You don't know what you're doing. It's just like the Tankersley case."

Jamie Tankersley had been high on booze and drugs when someone came at him with a gun. Tankersley shot the man with the gun, then two companions in less than five seconds. Eubanks, as prosecutor, had claimed that all three killings were premeditated, but Storms, as forensic psychologist, had said that five seconds wasn't enough time for premeditation—that the second and third shootings were reflex actions.

Again, Storms waited until Eubanks flopped back down in his chair before responding. "Yeah, well, who won that case, Mike?" Tankersley had, in fact, been found not guilty on the first murder charge, guilty on the other two, but the issue of premeditation was decided in Storms's favor.

The use of the familiar sent a crimson wave of indignation over Eubanks's face. The conference had not been going well for him. Now it threatened to turn into a rout.

"As I recall," Storms continued, taunting, "you didn't get *any* death penalties. Mike, get used to it. He's crazy. I told you he was crazy months ago. I'm telling you he's crazy now. He's *crazy.*"

Pierce reached instinctively for a gavel but, finding none, banged his palm several times on the arm of his chair to get the combatants' attention.

"Mr. Eubanks," said Pierce fiercely, "you seem to think that doctors are all voodoo practitioners or witch doctors, whether they're in South Carolina or Georgia. Well, I don't think so. This doctor here thinks that Starrett is incompetent, and I want to hear what he has to say."

Siemon concluded with what he thought was his most potent argument to the practical-minded Pierce, the argument that he had already planted in the media and hoped Pierce had heard. "Your Honor, a year ago this defendant was sitting in a prison cell in South Carolina. He was getting the treatment he needed for his mental illness, he was not a threat to anybody, he was paying his debt to society. He would never have left that prison, not for the rest of his life, if it hadn't been for the district attorney here and his determination to pursue a conviction he can't possibly win and, even if he did win, would never survive on appeal.

"Your Honor, I can only speculate on the district attorney's reasons for pursuing the death penalty against my client, but I do know that his efforts have already cost the taxpayers of Columbia County a lot of money, and if he takes this case to trial, the bill will only get bigger. And the appeals will be costly. And all the time the state of Georgia will be paying to incarcerate and treat Danny Starrett."

Siemon's tone turned soft and comradely. "Now, Your Honor, we both know that Columbia County is not a wealthy county. We both know that the state of Georgia has better things to do with its tax dollars than taking the burden of Danny Starrett off the taxpayers of South Carolina. Is there really any good reason for the county or the state to incur the expense that it's going to take to try to put Danny Starrett to death?"

Eubanks jumped up and started to speak. "Your Honor, I can prove beyond a reasonable doubt—" But Pierce cut him off in midsentence. "Mr. Eubanks, I am tired of you going around trying all these death penalties, wasting all this taxpayers' money, and then losing." Clearly, Pierce had read the papers. "Someone has got to stop you, and that someone is me."

"Your Honor, where do we draw the line?" Eubanks sputtered. "When is justice too expensive? Once you start asking questions like that, they have won. The thing is over. It's very simple."

"I'll tell you what's simple, Mr. Eubanks," Pierce roared. "What's simple is that we are here to do one thing and that is to enter a plea. I'm telling you the time has come to send this case back to South Carolina. Do I make myself clear, Mr. Eubanks?"

68

Mike Eubanks didn't so much agree to a plea bargain as he washed his hands of the whole case. "If Starrett wants to plead guilty and Pierce wants to sentence him to life," said Eubanks, "I won't do anything to stop it, but I certainly won't do anything to help it."

Siemon didn't care. A plea was a plea.

A few days later, he was on the road to Milledgeville to fit the final piece into this yearlong puzzle: Danny's agreement.

It had been more than two years, and many nights in fleabag motels, since Siemon's first trip to see Danny Starrett. He had been at CCI in Columbia then, in the death-row cell block, and the hellish conditions were all that Danny could talk about. The guards had brought him into a little office there in the bowels of that dyspeptic place, behind five sets of locked gates, and they had him in chains, which they refused to remove.

Siemon had been surprised at how small he was, more like a teenage boy than a man, especially standing next to the six foot one inch ex-Green Beret. It didn't take long to establish a rapport, though. Siemon could relate to Danny far more easily than to his typical client, an underprivileged black who never had a white friend in his life until this one walked into his cell and offered to save his life.

In contrast, Danny was articulate and responsive. But the more Siemon talked to him, the more he sensed there was "something off." He seemed to remove himself in a way Siemon had never seen before— and he had seen some strange people in his line of work.

Still, Danny seemed to follow as Siemon described the dilemma he faced. He told him it was a terrible case, and the chances of winning it with a jury were almost nil. The only two things he had in his favor, said Siemon, were his color and his family. If they didn't save him from the electric chair, nothing would. It was very straight talk, and Danny appeared to take it in.

Finally, Siemon explained that his game plan, in virtually every death-penalty case, was not just to take a plea but to *cause* one: take the initiative and try to force the prosecution to offer a plea. Normally, Siemon told prospective clients that he wouldn't take their cases if they demanded a not-guilty plea or if they refused to accept a plea bargain, but he didn't feel the need in this case. After all, Danny had already pled guilty to all the South Carolina charges.

At the time, Danny seemed to understand the plan, although as soon as Siemon had finished his spiel, Danny wanted to talk about politics and the importance of the family and the Republican party. It was certainly one of the most unusual jailhouse interviews Siemon had ever conducted, but, then, they were all unusual. In his business, there was no such thing as a garden-variety case. And when all the conversation was done, he left thinking, "When the time comes, he'll make the right decision."

Now the time had come.

When they brought Danny into the visitors' room at the Binion Building at Central State Hospital, he looked like a different man from the hollow-eyed waif of more than two years before.

"Congratulations," Siemon said as he reached out to shake Danny's hand. "We won."

Danny smiled skeptically as he took Siemon's big, creased hand in his thin, pale one.

"We got the plea," Siemon said triumphantly. "Now you write me if there's ever anything I can do for you in the future."

"I can't take it," said Danny softly.

Siemon was sure he had misheard.

"I can't take it," Danny repeated.

"What do you mean you can't take it, Danny?" Siemon stammered. "You remember way back in Columbia . . . you said that you . . . you gave me the impression that you would take a plea."

"Well, I never really told you I would," Danny corrected. "Besides, I didn't think you would ever get them to offer one."

"I know I went over this with you," Siemon said. He was used to getting resistance from clients whose lives he was trying to save, but this? He reminded himself that the most important thing was to get the job done, and it wouldn't help to scream and shout—which is what he felt like doing. It would just take a little more time talking and explaining and cajoling.

"Why can't you take the plea, Danny?" asked Siemon, carefully modulating his voice to conceal his anger.

"Because I didn't do it," said Danny. "HE did it."

Part Five

69

Every day in every way I'm getting better and better and better.

What the mind can conceive—and believe—it can achieve.

Happiness does not depend on who you are, what you are, or where you are, but solely on what you think.

Where there is a will, there is a way.

Make it happen.

For a dream comes through much activity, and a fool's voice is known by his many words.

(2/12/90) As far back as I can remember, even as a child, I thought that there was something different about me. Not different good, different wrong. It felt as though there was something there that had to be controlled, but I could never put my finger on it. It was like there was a wall somewhere inside, and not only did no one else get past it, but I couldn't get past it either. And it was always there.

It wasn't until I left home and went to Georgia Tech that things started happening. I started picking up somebody else's thoughts—some other thinking processes. At first, I could hardly make them out. I could hear somebody saying something, but I couldn't make out the words, except that they were sexual kinds of statements. I could not stop them. I could not control them. They came of their own accord, even when my mind was totally engaged in other things. They simply were not my thoughts. More and more, I began to view them as belonging to another person.

Eventually, I became convinced that what I was dealing

with was not some abnormal process going on in my mind but a completely separate mind, a completely separate consciousness. It was completely independent of me and it wasn't just me losing control of my life; it was something else taking over control of my body. My body was wanting to go places and do things I wasn't really trying to make it do. I perceived a real fracture. I could really feel the presence of something else moving my body.

The best way to describe it is with a metaphor. It's as if I'm sitting at the front of a bus. I'm driving, and I've got a clear, bright view of everything in front of me. Then, all of a sudden, I feel as though I'm being pulled out of the driver's seat and pushed back to the rear of the bus. All of a sudden, the view becomes telescopic. I'm losing focus. I'm being pulled farther and farther back. I feel myself losing control of my body. And I feel a presence. I feel HIM.

When the transition is complete, I feel as if I'm sitting in the back of the bus looking over HIS shoulder. There is someone else in front of me, driving the bus, controlling the body we share.

I sit here watching the body move. The head turns, and wherever the head turns I can see, but I'm not turning the head. When the head turns, I can see the girl walking on the sidewalk or sitting in the car in the next lane. If the girl turns off the freeway, HE pulls in behind her and starts following her. Why, I don't know. HE follows and follows and follows her.

Eventually, HE starts to pull back and fade away. And then I take back control.

HIS thoughts seem to focus on one obsessive track: girls and sex. Themes of violence unfailingly trigger HIM. Consequently, I tried to avoid such things, but I was fighting a losing battle. It was everywhere—in books, in movies and on TV, in the news. Even the sight of an attractive girl alone could trigger HIM.

In the beginning, a constantly shifting equilibrium seemed to develop between us. Depending on where we were, who we were with, or what we were doing, one of us would dominate more often than the other. As a general rule, HE left me alone when other people were around, especially family and friends. But when watching movies filled with sex and violence, HE ran wild.

Other things which invariably triggered HIM were detective magazines. They offered HIM a perfect combination of sex and violence. Whenever I went to the convenience store, I tried to make sure I didn't walk down the aisle with the magazine rack, because if I did, there was no stopping HIM.

There I am, standing in the store, holding onto this milk and Coke and whatever else, wanting to walk on by, but I can feel HIM coming. My body stops and HE pushes past me. HE buys the magazine. I don't want the magazine, I don't want anything to do with the magazine, but HE buys the magazine.

I never read any of that stuff. I wasn't at all like HIM, I didn't want to have anything in common with HIM. And the whole process frustrated me intensely because HE was spending my money.

I tried desperately to stop HIM, but I couldn't. It was beyond my control. I felt as though I was secretly drowning and no one could help me, not even Heather. I dared not tell her. What would she do if she found out? Would she stay married to me if she thought I was some kind of nut? Often I thought of seeking professional help, but I was embarrassed and afraid. I would imagine myself committed to a hospital where people were given shock treatments and wandered aimlessly around with blank drug-induced stares on their faces.

Even when HE wasn't there, I knew HE wasn't far away. Like someone with a secret drug or alcohol dependency, I simply tried to control it as best I could and keep it hidden from the world.

For a while, there was something like an equilibrium be-

tween me and HIM. And for a while, things were stable. We each had our areas of control. HE would make his collections of books and magazines, drive around randomly, and follow girls, and that's all HE did. It was like we each occupied our own sphere, and there were limits to how far each one could go in any one direction.

Like, if I wanted HIM to leave the gun at home, HE wouldn't, and I couldn't make HIM. But I could take the bullets out of the gun and put them in my pocket, and HE couldn't stop me from doing that. That worked out nicely for a while, but then HE got stronger, more demanding. And at the same time I seemed to be getting weaker. I was losing control. I felt more and more helpless. Then HE began to get out of hand. And the equilibrium went crazy.

HE began doing things HE had never done before. HE started going to houses under the pretext of looking at advertised merchandise. HE would go in, and talk to them, and look at whatever was for sale, and then leave. It seemed to give HIM an immense feeling of control. It was almost as if HE were seeking the very sense of control that I was losing. Each time HE went to a house, I felt sick, as though I was going to throw up. But HE was always calm and cool.

Then one time, HE pulled up to a house and a girl answered the door. HE went in, looked at the appliance or furniture or whatever, and then asked to use the phone. HE took the phone off the hook and then, without any warning, reached out and grabbed her by the arm. I tried to jerk it back, but HE wouldn't let me. I went into a complete state of shock. I completely blacked out. The next thing I remember is coming down the stairs and feeling sick.

Eventually, HE overwhelmed me. I desperately tried to withdraw as far away as I could. I didn't want to see what HE was doing or hear what HE was saying. HE made me hate myself. I felt so horribly ashamed. All my life I had been quite idealistic. I always believed good would triumph over evil and

*that the good guys would win in the end. And I thought that
I was one of those good guys. I wanted to help people, not
hurt them.*

*Yet here I was, caught up in an unimaginable nightmare
over which I had little control. I didn't know where to go or
who to turn to. I felt hopeless. I felt desperate. I fought HIM in
the only way I could. I left fingerprints wherever possible,
even though HE tried to wipe them clean behind me. I always
hoped HE had missed some. And when HE planned to put false
tags on my car, I managed to stop HIM. I kept praying someone would see the number and call the police. But they never
did. I'd say to HIM, "I'll turn myself in and that will be the end
of my life. Even just one time will be enough to put me away
for twenty years. My life will be over. My dreams dead—no
career, no future." But HE would try to tell me that it really
couldn't be that bad for the girl. You know, HE was only with
her for a couple of minutes. And HE would say HE didn't want
to get caught. So HE wouldn't let me drive to a police station
and just turn myself in.*

*I tried to allow HIM as little opportunity as possible. I fre-
quently worked long hours and spent the remainder of my
free time with my family and helping in my mother's business. I knew that as long as I was around people I loved or
people I knew, then I was usually safe from HIM. I knew
that whenever I was left alone with HIM, bad things were
bound to happen.*

*But HE saw what I was doing. One time when Heather
and Allison were in California, I made plane reservations to
join them. I was going to surprise them. But as I drove home
from work one afternoon, I saw an attractive girl pull up next
to me. She looked over at me and smiled. I felt instant panic.
I was alone in my car. A moment later, I wasn't alone anymore. HE was there. HE followed her all the way to her house.
Then HE returned to my empty house, sat down, picked up the
phone, and canceled my plane reservation.*

I have come to think of this body no longer as completely mine, no longer as belonging to me. I see this body as shared. HE's speaking through the same tongue, same lips, same vocal cords as I am. In fact, sometimes when this is going on, I wonder if it is HE that is inside of me or me that is inside of HIM.

Then HE found Jeannie, and Jeannie and I found each other, and life changed forever.

(3/16/90) I told Bill Galardi and David Caldwell about HIM, but apparently the truth wasn't bad enough for them. My lawyer brought me some of the reports that Bill and David wrote up after our interviews and I only had to read a short way through them before I got very upset. They identified me and HIM as the same person throughout! I couldn't believe it. Their reaction was, "Oh, come on, we weren't born yesterday. Don't try to pull this psycho bullshit on us."

The police think it's a lie, the doctors say it's a delusion, and some people think it's a rationalization—that I can't cope with the guilt. Dr. Harold Morgan thinks that I developed this second being to dump all these evil acts on because I am trying to cope with the reality that I actually did these things myself. That HE is a guilt-coping mechanism. If that is the case, it's doing a very poor job of taking away my guilt.

When I told Dr. Storms that I initially interpreted HIS thoughts as voices, he said that hearing voices was a common result of stress. He said it was just my own thoughts, but I'm certain it wasn't. Anyway, that was his diagnosis. Of course, I tried to argue with him, and he tried to be polite, but he sees people all the time. He nods his head and looks at his watch. He's heard it all. He's seen it all.

70

Dr. Robert Storms had never seen anybody quite like Danny Starrett before. He didn't really fit the classical profile of a serial anything. Right before he started his evaluation, Storms had been reading a lot of the literature on sex killers and Danny didn't betray any of the usual signs: He wasn't a loner or the product of a troubled childhood. In fact, he appeared to be quite the "all-American, Boy Scout type."

And what was all this talk of HIM?

When Storms first heard Danny's rambling description of HIS role in the crimes, he thought of multiple personality disorder, a dissociative disorder in which one part of a person's consciousness is basically disassociated from the other, waking part. A person with MPD typically manifests more than one personality, and these other personalities may or may not be conscious of each other. Two Hollywood movies, *Sybil* and *The Three Faces of Eve,* had popularized MPD and, at the same time, made it the most glamorous—and most overused—diagnosis in the canon of modern madness.

The other problem was that an MPD diagnosis typically involved intense childhood abuse of some kind, and even after Storms went through the family history in detail, he could find nothing to indicate that Danny had been abused.

One of Danny's previous doctors had labeled him an "extremely narcissistic obsessive-compulsive personality," a mouthful that meant simply that he wanted to control everything and that the desire to control everything was a selfish one. The same doctor thought that Danny's obsessive-compulsive disorder would become more prevalent and more problematic as time passed and would, eventually, blossom into a full-fledged thought disorder. Storms had seen this happen often: People who were very obsessive and compulsive—who had to have things a certain way—began to panic and lose control if things weren't just so, and then became even more obsessive.

Another doctor thought Danny might be schizophrenic. After all, schizophrenia was a thought disorder characterized by delusions and hallucinations. That would explain HIM. Pursuing that theory first,

Storms gave Danny several doses of an antipsychotic drug, Navane, often used to treat schizophrenics. To Storms's surprise, Danny flew into a rage so severe that he had to be put in seclusion. Storms concluded that the drug had "stripped away Danny's defenses and exposed some core anger and core shame." But anger and shame over what?

The more Storms listened to Danny's rambling monologues on HIM, however, the more he became convinced that he understood HIS effect, even if he did not yet understand HIS cause.

Danny, when he thought he was being Danny, operated entirely on the level of acceptable clichés, an art he had learned from his father. It was as if he had no personality of his own but was merely a vehicle for the expression of socially acceptable norms—from familyhood to politics to sexual appetites. Meanwhile, all of the emotional baggage that was not acceptable, but that lay at the core of his psychological self, was loaded onto HIM. Because Danny Starrett had never integrated the elements of his real identity as it was developing into his socially acceptable identity, he had never become a resolved human being.

What made this interesting to Storms, extraordinarily interesting, was that the same could be said for people in general, for all those people who mouthed clichés in lieu of expressing genuine feelings, and therefore remained forever unresolved, stuck in a personality limbo.

But that was getting ahead of himself. Before he could fully understand and treat Danny Starrett, who appeared to be highly resistant to any kind of psychological therapy, Storms needed to listen more.

71

(4/4/90) *My relationship with women has always been one of romance and flowers and love notes. In other words, fairly normal. My fantasies were always idealistic, chivalrous. I was the knight in shining armor. I wanted girls to like me, to love me. Those were my fantasies. I liked to impress girls. I wanted them to like me for who I was. I liked intimacy, companionship, communication, sharing, and caring.*

My sexual development was fairly boring. The earliest incident I can remember is playing doctor, which is very normal. Then there was the incident where I spied on a girl. I did that once or twice and never did it again. I felt terribly ashamed of that. If I had to identify one place where I began to feel the loss of control, that would be it.

When I was a boy, I drew monster pictures, and I was obsessed with monster faces for years and years. Looking back, I wonder if that was my subconscious expressing HIS existence. When I was seven, I also drew pictures of underground factories where girls were processed into dog food. That was so completely out of keeping with my character, my fantasy life, and the rest of my childhood that it must be evidence of HIS existence, evidence that by age seven HE existed in such a way that an idea like that would occur to HIM and HE could pass it through me.

Then there was the incident where I found the cache of bondage magazines. I think HE was in an embryonic state back then, although capable in some subliminal way of sensing and being affected by external events. Although those magazines excited me as a boy, because of the pictures of semi-nude women, the presence of chains and ropes didn't excite me at all. They made absolutely no sense to me. If that incident had affected me personally, I would have been caught up in that kind of material as a teenager. But I wasn't.

In fact, as a teenager, I had a healthy attitude towards sex. I liked girls. I liked girls to like me. I liked missionary-position sex. I am a traditional, boring kind of person. I had some sexual experiences before HE came on the scene. They were the normal, teens-go-out-and-get-drunk experiences, like having sex in the back of a car. That's the kind of sex I would have. If I liked a girl, I would like her to like me, and I'd want to go out and have sex with her. After HE came on the scene, it made sex very difficult.

When I had sex with Heather, HE would come out and get more aggressive with her, and I would have to try to act as normal as possible so Heather wouldn't find out what kind of person HE and I were.

HE was always there telling me that Heather didn't love me anymore anyway. Every time she came in the room, HE went on and on about it. "Of course she doesn't love you," HE would say. "She's going to leave you and take the baby with her!" HE would laugh endlessly at me, calling me a fool and an idiot. "Just look at your marriage. Heather doesn't do a thing you tell her. You want her to work less hours, to spend more time at home with the baby, and she couldn't care less." It got so bad that I found it almost impossible to be in the same room as Heather or Allison because the minute they came in, HE did too, with his endless carping and complaining and name-calling. I knew that I still loved Heather, but I wondered if maybe HE was right about her. Maybe she really didn't love me anymore.

(4/11/90) In most of the early assaults, HE went into somebody's residence, and HE was in and out in fifteen minutes. But then HE brought a girl home. I had become psychically numb to the other incidents, but when HE first brought a girl to the house, I went completely berserk. I didn't want that. I didn't want him bringing HIS stuff into my life. I didn't want HIM bringing that into my home. But HE was in control, and I had to withdraw—go as far back on the bus as I could—and not be involved in what was happening.

When we got to the house in Martinez with Chrissy, HE took her to a closet, chained her ankles together, and forced her inside. I got back in control long enough to tell her I didn't want to hurt anyone and ask her if she wanted something to eat or drink.

Then HE *took over again. "Well, I want to have sex,"* HE *said.*

When they were finished, I reemerged. Chrissy was very upset, and I tried to console her. "I'm trying to stop HIM*," I said. "I really feel terrible about this, but* HE *just doesn't care who* HE *hurts."*

She told me that she was a virgin.

"I won't let HIM *hurt you," I tried to reassure her.*

When she started complaining about a stomach flu she'd picked up from her mother, I tried to reason with HIM*, begging* HIM *to let her go. "I don't care about her stomach flu,"* HE *said.*

I went and got her an Alka-Seltzer, but she said it wouldn't help. All the time, HE *kept laughing at me, telling me how weak and ridiculous I was.* HE *obviously hated me.*

I suggested that maybe a shower would make her feel better, and while she was in the bathroom, I begged HIM *to leave her alone. "She's sick," I said. But* HE *refused.*

Before long, she began to ask when she was going to get to go home. "She's not having a good time. Please take her home," I pleaded. "She's sick."

"Nope," HE *said. "I don't want to take her back. I want to keep her around a little longer."*

I was getting more and more scared about some real harm coming to her, so I resorted to booze—the one thing that seemed to block out HIS *voice. I lay down on the carpet and stared at the ceiling, trying desperately to block* HIM *out of my thoughts so I could think up a way to let Chrissy go. "I've got to stop* HIM*!" I told myself.*

First, when HE *wasn't looking, I unlocked the front door. Then I tried to stop thinking about what I had done so* HE *wouldn't hear my thoughts. Then I pretended to be asleep. That way, I could just let Chrissy walk out of the house and, when* HE *ordered me to stop her, pretend not to hear* HIM*.*

I closed my eyes and pretended, hoping desperately that Chrissy would take it upon herself to flee.

Which she did.

When HE *realized what I had done,* HE *was furious.* HE *jumped up and went out to search for Chrissy but couldn't find her. I had never felt such hate emanating from* HIM. *After a while looking around the neighborhood, I went back in the house without having caught sight of her. Of course, I knew that it was only a matter of time before the police arrived, and there was no way they could arrest* HIM *without arresting me, too.*

The only solution seemed obvious. I got out my gun, fully intending to use it on both of us. I couldn't kill HIM *without killing both of us. But still it was the only solution. "Your life is over," I told* HIM. *"You've destroyed my life and I'm going to kill you."*

I thought maybe I should call the police first—they were going to find out soon enough, anyway. But HE *said that was a ridiculous idea. "You always were stupid and weak,"* HE *said.*

HE *made me drive around for a while, looking for Chrissy. But I didn't find her, so I drove back by the house and the police were already there. Maybe* HE *was right. Maybe it was a ridiculous idea, and I was stupid and weak. I had actually aspired to living a normal life with a normal job and a normal wife and a normal child.*

I felt waves of hatred coming from HIM. *"Do you realize what you've done?"* HE *screamed. "You've made it impossible for me to have sex again!"*

I felt a burst of gratification. Stopping HIM *was, after all, the whole idea. But then the implications of everything began to overwhelm me.* HIS *life was over, but so was mine. I had wanted to get away while getting* HIM *caught. That was a crazy idea. Now I had gotten both of us caught, and we would both have to pay the price. I would never be able to look my family in the face again—my daughter, my wife, my* mother. *All of those months and years of keeping them in the dark, of protecting them, was all for nothing. Chrissy would tell the police and the police would tell them. None of them would ever really be able to understand about* HIM, *to understand that* HE *was guilty of these terrible acts, to sympathize with my efforts to stop* HIM. *Again and again suicide seemed to be the only way out. My life was over.* HE *had destroyed everything.*

I wanted to stop and give myself up to the police, but HE *absolutely refused.*

"I want to see my wife and my baby one more time," I told HIM. *This time* HE *didn't seem to have an objection, so I headed west. Without credit cards or cash, I had no choice but to steal the gas. As I drove off, feelings of guilt clutched at my stomach. Maybe* HE *had done terrible things, evil things.* HE *had even stolen things before, a few magazines and the like. But I had never so much as shoplifted a baseball card. I had never knowingly broken a law in my life. I belonged to the Republican party, after all, partly because it was the party of law and order. And here I was, reduced to stealing gas like some two-bit hoodlum.*

When it was clear that the police weren't right on my tail, I stopped the car by the side of the road and prayed. Prayed that God would finally take HIM *away for good, now that* HE *had destroyed my life. I prayed that God would just let me make it to California to see my wife and baby one more time.*

I can't begin to describe the self-loathing, the self-hatred. I am a good person, and the day that I stop believing in that is the day that HE *will swallow me up.*

72

Bob Storms sat in the conference room at the Binion Building, fumbling with the VCR. He had spent fourteen years working with some of the most complicated mechanisms on the planet, but video technology remained a mystery to him. He pushed all the buttons he knew, then sat back and waited for the grainy images of Danny Starrett and Chrissy Blake to appear.

Storms didn't care what the prosecutors said. He was *glad* Danny had destroyed the other videotapes, the dozens of videos he had made of the other girls he assaulted. If he hadn't dumped them all in a trash bin during his flight to Texas, Storms would have had to watch them all—every dismal, pathetic hour of them.

It was an incredible stroke of luck, clinically speaking, to have a tape of a crime being committed. Storms's job, after all, was to assess criminal behavior; yet so much of his work was done at one remove (the patient's story), or two removes (the police version of the patient's story) from that behavior. This time he would get to observe the behavior first-hand. Danny's strange story about another consciousness only made the tape more curious and singular. This was actually a videotape of HIM.

What he saw when the tape came to life was only this: a mouth and a penis. He waited and waited. Five minutes went by: and still a mouth and a penis. He thought about the descriptions of the crimes he had seen: Chrissy Blake's statement and those of other girls. Where was the gun? If it was there, it was off camera. It was, basically, an interminable blow job. There is very little to say about it, Storms thought, except that it went on and on and on.

Fifty minutes into the tape, the scene changed. The tape showed two figures, a male and a female, sitting on a modern, nondescript sofa in a modern, nondescript, dimly lighted living room. The girl is young and pretty, with dark hair and a porcelain complexion. The boy is Danny. They're listening to heavy-metal music, only she doesn't seem to be listening. She looks terrified, angry, depressed, sullen. He looks uncomfortable—as if on a first date that isn't going well. Their eyes never meet.

Finally, over the music, he speaks to her. "What kind of pizza do you want?"

Now *that,* Storms thought, is interesting. The sex act itself was dismally boring, but Danny's ability to disassociate was one for the textbooks. Storms couldn't have asked for a clearer sign that there was something not right about this man. He was *so casual.* He acted as though it was an awkward date, nothing more. What kind of music did she like? What did she want on her pizza? Meanwhile, this girl is sitting there absolutely traumatized and angry and scared. Every time he moves on the sofa, even just to offer her something, she flinches. She keeps her head down with her eyes riveted to the floor the whole time. But to him it's just this normal, everyday sort of date. There is nothing in his voice or manner to suggest that he has just kidnapped and raped this girl.

The next time Storms saw Danny, he told him he had seen the tape.

"You shouldn't have watched that," Danny flared. Then he sat back in his chair and folded his arms. It didn't take a trained psychologist to see that this was a sensitive subject. "You know, HE's very diabolical," Danny warned. "But HE's not a raving animal. HE's a cold, dispassionate, rational animal." Danny said HE had wolf eyes. In fact, he had drawn a picture of HIM with wild animal eyes, and he showed the picture to Storms.

Storms had come to accept Danny's straight face and subdued, earnest manner. HE really did exist in Danny's mind. Danny really was hearing HIS voice. But Storms knew that even simple stress could make people hear voices. If Danny was under enough pressure in his life, and he began thinking unacceptable thoughts, he could psychologically externalize those thoughts into a voice. For Danny, Storms decided, HE was just a massive defense mechanism.

Storms wanted to know if HE had ever come out during sex with Heather, Danny's wife. In his interviewing, he had heard that Heather did not like to perform fellatio—and had made that fact clear to Danny. In fact, she had complained to Gerry that her reluctance was causing "marital difficulties." Basically, Danny wanted her to and she wouldn't. Was it true? Storms wanted to know.

"I'd rather not talk about that," said Danny.

Suddenly, Storms felt a longing for a regular, everyday eating-disorder case.

73

(9/12/90) Dr. Storms never came down and talked to me about what he thinks about HIM, what his diagnosis was, until I read his report to the judge. He said I was delusional. That was on the front page of the newspaper. The judge released the report to the media, so it ended up on the front page, which really made me feel wonderful. That was the final straw.

I decided that I was fed up. After listening to Storms and four or five other doctors come up with four or five different explanations, all of which were dead wrong, only then did I realize that if anyone was going to figure HIM out, it was going to be me. Since I had nothing else to look forward to but death row or the prison yard, I had nothing to lose anymore. I was no longer afraid of HIM. I had spent the majority of the previous ten years running from HIM, denying HIM, concerned not with trying to understand or explain HIM, but with just the precise opposite: ignoring, minimizing, rationalizing. Now I decided I would try to understand HIM from a scientific basis.

I realized that Storms and the other doctors were groping around in the dark, in this infant science called psychiatry. They were children playing with the universe. The human mind is so complex. I realized I had a better perspective on myself than anyone else. I'd had a longer time to observe HIM than anyone else.

All science begins with observation. It is my observation that HE manifests all the qualities of a distinct personality. HE exhibits emotional responses (although HE doesn't seem to have the capability to experience higher emotions and things of that nature). HE is capable of drawing on memories (where else could HE come up with some of HIS ideas except from the books and magazines HE's read). HE has a distinct personality, and I have seen HIM doing things in a logical pattern (picking up a rental car and going from point A to point B). In short, HE manifests all those qualities of consciousness that I do: personality, beliefs, motivations, memories, thinking, planning. Every characteristic I can think of that my consciousness possesses, HIS possesses. Hallucinations and Freudian psychological processes don't tell you coherent, rational things. They don't try to manipulate you intellectually, as well as emotionally, the way HE does me.

So my basic premise is this: HE exists. HE is real. HE is a fully functioning consciousness. Now the question that I am confronted with is how could one central nervous system have two consciousnesses? It seems like such a preposterous idea. I have certainly never read of anything so ridiculous, so outrageous. My scientific mind insists that if it is going to accept this fact, I have to be able to demonstrate some plausible, physical process that could give rise to such a thing. What physical processes had to occur in this brain to allow these two separate consciousnesses to develop? That's what I need to understand.

The key moment came when I read a book called Left Brain, Right Brain *by Robert Ornstein. I had heard about things like split-personality and dissociative states before, but I was flabbergasted when I read this book. It thrilled me. It was all about HIM.*

The book describes how the brain is divided into two hemispheres, and each hemisphere has its own particular functions. Those functions vary, depending on which hemisphere is dominant. If one hemisphere is injured, the brain can, by itself, shift some of the functions of that hemisphere to the other hemisphere. But in some cases, the shifting doesn't happen completely. Sometimes, if there's a massive injury, all of the functions can shift to the uninjured side. But sometimes it's possible that some of the functions shift and some remain. In studies of patients whose hemispheres have been disconnected, what are called "split-brain" pa-

tients, they found what appeared to be dual thought processes. As in the case of the man who buttoned his shirt with one hand and unbuttoned it with the other.

I asked myself: What is required in a bicameral mind for two completely separate consciousnesses to exist side by side? I believe most psychoneurolinguists would agree that human consciousness is dependent upon complex language-mediating processes in the brain. Without those, we would not be able to do the sophisticated abstract thinking that makes us distinctly human. So, if there were two independent operating consciousnesses in one central nervous system, it seemed to me that there had to be two independent language-processing neuro-networks. And the simplest, most logical, most elegant way to find two neuro-networks separated would be between the two hemispheres. Scientists always make the simplest assumption first.

According to the split-brain studies, then, for two separate language centers to arise, there had to be some physical separation of the two hemispheres. In the case of the split-brain patients, it was the cutting of the connector between the two hemispheres, the corpus callosum. But I had already had an MRI scan, and it showed no abnormalities in the corpus colosum. So if my corpus callosum was completely intact and completely functioning, then why did these dual processes develop? Why didn't they integrate? Why didn't they communicate across the corpus callosum and integrate HIS and my personalities—the emotions, the feelings, the thoughts, the memories? Why didn't we become one seamless whole, one complete consciousness?

I concluded that the head injuries I sustained as a child—falling off the sliding board and out of the car—had impeded the ability of my two hemispheres to communicate and therefore integrate. When I went into the hospital after the second head injury, they thought I had a tumor and they did find some evidence of abnormal electrical activity. That is indicative that something was going on way back then. Those injuries left my left side weaker, which indicates soft-tissue damage in the right hemisphere.

I postulated that because of these injuries in the right hemisphere, my brain lateralized speech capabilities to both hemispheres. Lateralized speech capabilities would also explain my childhood stuttering. It was simply the result of competition between two different speech centers to control the speech process. Both the stuttering and the dyslexia indicate that there was some kind of abnormal lateralization process going on in my brain that was necessary for two speech centers to develop.

Next, I asked myself, even if there were separate speech centers, didn't they have the same genetic heritage, and weren't they exposed to the same life experiences, the same culture? Why wouldn't they have evolved in parallel? Why wouldn't HE and I respond emotionally in the same way? Why wouldn't we have the same memories? Why wouldn't we have the same personality? How could HE and I be so different?

Given that consciousness is a manifestation of physical processes, and that there are two different consciousnesses, there must be different physical processes going on. Assuming that the two consciousnesses are localized with one in each hemisphere, then at some level these two hemispheres must be different. There must be some structural differences at the neuro level. There must be some biochemical differences such that, when these eyes and these ears and these sensory organs are taking in information from this body, the two consciousnesses, HE and I, are interpreting or experiencing that information differently. And that is giving rise to different memories, different attitudes, different beliefs, different emotional profiles, different personalities. Is that actually the case? I don't know, but it's very plausible. The mechanisms necessary to cause it are there. So that's basically the theory . . .

*   *   *

(9/21/90) Some people accuse me of being overanalytical. I present my theory to Dr. Storms, and he just lets it roll off and continues on. Dr. Storms never directly refutes anything that I say. He's too good a psychologist for that. I'm sure that he is used to talking to people that have all kinds of delusional theories.

I'm sure that he would argue that the delusion is my belief that HE exists at all. He says, "Sure, you can come up with all kinds of plausible rationalistic explanations. A paranoid schizophrenic can create all kinds of plausible explanations for why that person turned in behind him on the same street. But his belief that someone is following him is in fact itself a delusion." That's what he would say.

But I told him that I wasn't just creating this theory out of nothing. At each point, I came up with a link in the chain. I saw that there was at least some circumstantial evidence, historical evidence in my life, medical evidence, personal-experience evidence that was important. So it wasn't as if I was pulling things out of nowhere and building them, linking them together to reach the foregone conclusion. Anyone could see that I wasn't building a house of cards.

The only thing Dr. Storms did ask me is what the consequences would be if my theories turned out to be true.

I told him that then everyone would have to say, "Okay, Mr. Starrett is crazy. He's not some evil man that likes to go around hurting people."

74

Bob Storms wasn't sure what to make of Danny's theories. He was convinced that Danny was far more emotionally and psychologically disturbed than he was willing to admit—to himself or to his family—

and that he was bright enough to play all sorts of games to avoid that admission. "He has his story down," Storms would say, "as well as his graphs and his patter." At one point, Storms asked Danny to give a lecture to some medical students, and Danny dazzled them. He said, "My name is Danny Starrett," and, boom, just launched right into dual consciousnesses, bilateralism, and HIM. He had been over it so many times in his head, in his cell, he had it down cold. And to hear him talk (except that he never mentioned the murder), no one would ever think there was anything wrong with Danny Starrett, not *this* Danny Starrett.

But there had been other times, in more private moments, when Storms had been able to pull from Danny things that seemed real. When he didn't feel that he was going to be ostracized or criticized or that somebody was going to say, "That's crazy." Those were the times, Storms thought, when he really did seem crazy.

Some of Danny's other doctors had listened politely to his explanations of HIM and then basically ignored them. Storms wasn't sure what he thought. Did Danny's behavior have an organic cause—*organicity* as it is called in the trade? If so, Danny could almost certainly avoid the death penalty. But organicity usually had to be something specific and detectable, like a brain tumor. Storms, who had once worked as a forensic psychologist in the Washington State reformatory, remembered an inmate who had a hydroma growing in his brain—only nobody knew it at the time. The poor man was in such terrible, constant pain that he would go on these horrific "tears"—uncontrollable binges of violence: kidnapping, assaulting, raping. In prison, the pain got so intense that he repeatedly slammed his head against his cell wall to make it go away, slammed it so hard that the cell bars rattled. In the process, he rearranged the shape of his skull to relieve the pressure. Eventually, they found the tumor, drained it, and put in a shunt to prevent pressure from building up again. After that, he was a radically different person.

That was organicity. But Danny Starrett's case was nothing like that. He had some unusual spikes on an EEG that might be evidence of seizure activity, but what did that prove? At times, however, listening to Danny ramble on endlessly about HIM and dual consciousnesses and the rest, Storms thought perhaps his delusional disorder did have an organic origin, even if not of the kind or magnitude Danny had so baroquely imagined.

Still, he wasn't ready to dismiss those imaginings out of hand. With some trepidation—was he taking his patient's delusion too seriously?—he asked a colleague who had also worked on Danny's case, Joel Green, to run Danny's theories past a real expert on brain function and consciousness, Julian Jaynes. Jaynes was the author of *The Origin of Consciousness in the Breakdown of the Bicameral Mind,* an astonishingly original and widely acclaimed book as well as a huge bestseller that had helped revolutionize the theory of consciousness even as it remade popular conceptions of how the mind works.

Jaynes, however, was reluctant to offer an opinion based solely on Green's telephone description of HIM. "It sounds like a very complicated case," Jaynes demurred. "I don't know whether there is any clarity when there is neurological damage this way. As for this idea of another person, it could be the neglect syndrome."

The neglect syndrome?

"In cases of an injury to the parietal lobe in the right hemisphere," Jaynes explained, "people sometimes go through this extraordinary thing that lasts for a couple of weeks, lying in bed in the hospital and asking the nurses to get *this other person* out of their bed. It's as if the left side is another person completely. Their left hemisphere doesn't recognize the left side of their body. They put on clothes only on the right side. The same sort of polarization may be mixed up with your case."

Jaynes recommended that Green call Martin Orne, a forensic psychiatrist and an expert in consciousness, hypnosis, and memory errors. Orne had been involved in some of the biggest criminal psychiatric cases of the previous twenty years, including Patti Hearst and the Hillside Strangler. Green called Orne and laid out the case in a nutshell: highly educated engineer with a wife and child arrested for multiple rapes and one murder. Family, friends, everybody, stunned, amazed, disbelieving—

"Let me guess," Orne interrupted. "He's giving you lots of reasons why his problem isn't psychological but physiological. I would take everything he says with a grain of salt."

"He's been reading in the lay literature, and he's come up with this theory of two consciousnesses in the same brain." Green explained HIM.

Orne was distinctly unimpressed. "They *all* have a HIM." Whether it was a creature from outer space, some malevolent movie star, or, in Danny's case, a second consciousness, someone else was always in charge when the criminal was committing his crime. "If your guy's been reading in the popular literature," said Orne when Green was finished, "I suspect he's thinking multiple-personality disorder."

"That's what we thought," Green agreed.

"It reminds me a little bit of the Bianci case," said Orne, speaking of the Hillside Strangler, "where Bianci conned four psychiatrists into believing he was really an MPD." Green knew that Orne wasn't one of the four. In fact, it was Orne who had succeeded in documenting that Bianci was faking.

"Do I read you right? You think that all this stuff about another personality is likely made up," Green asked, "delusional?"

"Well, I've got to tell you, if I were in prison for the rest of my life with nothing to do but figure out reasons I shouldn't be there, that's what I would do. Wouldn't you? Let's face it, that's his sole job in life. The fact that he's a bright person makes it even more likely."

Orne talked about another case he was involved in, the Carson case, in which a young man had shot both his parents in the head and then claimed to be an MPD. "Everybody was buying it," Orne recalled. "They thought he was crazy. So I examined him, but he wouldn't talk to me because he knew I had done the Hillside Strangler case. He would just sit there, mute. And then he would go back to the ward. What he didn't know was that I had arranged to have a listening device planted in the ward. And lo and behold, as soon as he got back, he was talking up a storm. There is no illness I know of where you can't talk. These people are much better at inventing unknown illnesses than at having them."

Orne suggested that Green put himself in the shoes of the patient. "You may or may not want to commit the crime again, but you certainly want sex again. And if the crime involves sex, well, then, you probably can't wait to commit the crime again. So I always assume that the patient's major effort, whatever he thinks about or talks about, is all related to how he can get out to get women and do whatever he likes to do to them again. That's what he lives for."

Green suggested that, at thirty-two, Starrett probably still had "a lot of testosterone flowing through his veins."

"And if he's well fed and housed and has all the necessities," said Orne, "what's the one thing that's missing? Sex."

"So you think someone can have a fetish of this kind, a brutal sadistic fetish, and still be essentially sane?"

"Of course. And I'll bet his wife didn't know. I'll bet that he was a nice husband and a gentle father. Right?"

"Exactly right." Green was impressed.

"Well, you know, look, maybe he believes it," said Orne, backing away just a little. "But I'll bet he doesn't. My guess is that the whole thing is largely a charade."

Orne thought of one last question. "Is he hurting?"

"He doesn't show it," said Green, "but, yes, I think he's hurting a lot."

"Well, that's too bad," said Orne. "Of course, if you set him free he might stop hurting very quickly, but he would be committing these crimes again. Just don't ever forget that—and don't ever turn your back on him."

The very next time he spoke to Danny, though, and listened to another hour of philosophy mixed with brain physiology, Storms dismissed Orne's advice. Although he agreed that many criminals who pretend to be crazy are, in fact, sane and running a con, he also believed that some actually are crazy.

And Danny was one of those.

75

(3/7/91) *He began, as he always did, by looking things up in* The Carolina Trader. *He called and got directions to the girl's home. Jeannie McCrea answered the door. "I'm here to see the bedroom furniture," he said. She let us in. I couldn't believe how they always let us in.*

Jeannie led us upstairs.

I instantly took a liking to her, and started begging him to leave her alone. But he wouldn't budge. Instead, he pulled out a gun. Then he tied her hands and decided to take her back to my house in Martinez. That idea made me sick to my stomach. I pleaded with him, "Please don't take her back to the house," but his decision was final.

When we got to the Martinez house, he took Jeannie to the closet in the third bedroom and locked her in, tying a chain through the hole in the bottom of the door and padlocking it around her ankle. I was feeling more and more guilt-stricken over what we were doing.

I was also growing more and more worried that, sooner or later, and probably sooner, he was going to want Jeannie to give him a blow job. I kept pleading with him to leave Jeannie alone. I was liking her more and more, and, to my amazement, she seemed to like me, too.

I decided to tell Jeannie about him. I explained that I wasn't responsible for kidnapping her. That it was all his fault. To my surprise, she seemed to accept this as her fate. She even seemed to accept me at my word when I told her that I was pleading with him to leave her alone and not to mistreat her.

Then the moment came that I had been dreading. He wasn't willing to wait any longer. So I turned to Jeannie and said he wanted to have sex with her. "I don't want him to," I said, by way of apology.

I could feel myself falling in love with Jeannie, and I felt that she was doing the same with me. I asked her if she would like to stay with me until she went to New York on a school trip.

HE didn't like any of this romantic talk one bit. "I don't like your liking her," HE said.

"I don't care," I told HIM.

We had sex several more times, and Jeannie seemed to like it.

It wasn't until a few days later that it occurred to me that HE hadn't shown HIMSELF for days. For whatever reason, HE was leaving Jeannie and me pretty much alone. Then one day I said I wanted to take a shower, and Jeannie said she wanted to join me.

(3/26/91) How many lives have I devastated? How many people has HIS insane obsessions brought pain and suffering? Why could I not find a way to stop HIM long before HE consumed and overwhelmed me?

I don't think I'm going to make it. Jeannie, where are you? I am lost, Jeannie. So lost. At night I dream my dreams, and when they are good I find my beloved Jeannie. But then morning dawns and these comforting visions of the night fill my mind, and I realize I am still in Hell, a Hell far more terrible than any the hand of man could hope to construct, a Hell of the human mind, without walls but inescapable.

I am alone. Where is Jeannie?

(3/29/91) I went back to the bathroom and looked at Jeannie's unconscious form. HE was everywhere, saying, "She's dead, she's dead." I said she was just asleep, but HE kept saying, "She's dead, you idiot! You need to get rid of the body. Put her in a bag. Get rid of her."

"No, she's not dead," I said. "She's just sleeping." That's when I started drinking, trying to blot out everything—what

had happened, HIM, everything. A little while later, HE told me to take Jeannie's body out to the car and put it in the backseat. HE was doing the driving, and I didn't have any idea where we were going.

When we got an hour or so away from Augusta, somewhere in South Carolina, HE started saying, "Let's dump her by the side of the road." I didn't want to do that. I thought about how much Jeannie liked the water and decided to look for a stream somewhere. I was crying. I convinced HIM to let me drive down a dirt road and eventually I found a stream.

"Let me do it," HE said.

"Don't you touch her!" I screamed. Then I pulled her body out of the car and dragged it to a suitable spot by the creek. I sat down next to her. I had brought a gun along and I wanted desperately to have the courage to use it on myself, so that I could stay there forever with Jeannie, but HE wouldn't have any of it. "You're not going to kill us," HE said.

Then I heard some cars coming down the road. "We've got to go now!" HE ordered.

"No," I said, "I want to stay here with Jeannie."

"You idiot!" HE said. "Someone is going to come and find us!"

But every day for several days afterwards, I drove back to the spot near the creek where Jeannie's body lay, wanting to bring her back home with me. And every time HE would put his foot down. "Absolutely not!" HE would say. "You really are crazy!"

(4/1/91) I don't think I'm going to make it through. But what's one more failure? I failed to stop HIM and innocent victims suffered. I failed to hide the gun somewhere else before we went in to take a shower and now by a horrible accident my Jeannie is gone. My sweet Jeannie, whom I love more than my own life.

I prayed to God and Jesus to let Jeannie come home and

take my soul in her place, even if it means I must go to Hell. Sometimes I think I'm already there."

(4/7/91) *The Sunday Jeannie and I spent at Jekyll Island on New Year's was overcast like today. But we hardly noticed. The whole world seemed to be shining for us both. I'll never forget that trip. We had the time of our lives. Jeannie absolutely loved the convertible. We drove with the top down the whole way there.*

No one could ever understand what happened between Jeannie and me. I suppose they think I'm a completely deluded fool. They simply cannot accept the fact that something very real and very beautiful occurred. One sad and lonely young woman and one desperate, lonely man brought together by fate. The sadness, the loneliness, and the desperation of a troubled mind all faded away, overwhelmed by an unstoppable new power, the power of love.

It seemed the more our love grew, the more control I got back from HIM. HE *couldn't understand what was happening. I could tell* HE *was afraid. With Jeannie's love, I felt I could finally defeat* HIM.

Jeannie, where are you? You're out there somewhere. You're out there. It only remains for me to find you. And I will! I promise you, Jeannie.

> *A love cut short by tragedy.*
> *What then must I do?*
> *If you cannot return to me,*
> *Then I shall come to you.*

(4/13/91) *Happy Birthday, Jeannie! Where are you? Are you home now? I can hardly stand it. Please call or come see me, or somehow send word.*

(4/15/91) *It's a miserable, cold, rainy day outside. But I'm as happy as can be. I wonder what Jeannie's doing today. I imagine she's spending it with her family, or perhaps she went out with some friends. I can't wait to see her!*

(4/21/91) *If I hoped to bring Jeannie back to this world, I knew what I must do. I was prepared. I loved her, even more than my own life.*

Eventually, I got my chance.

I was taken down to the cell-block office. A supervisor came in and handed me some papers. They were divorce papers from Heather. No sooner had he left than Dr. Morgan came in to continue my evaluation. Just like one of Pavlov's dogs I began to withdraw in a conditioned response as soon as I heard the sound of clanking keys approach my cell. I had come to learn that this sound meant I would soon be taken out somewhere, and that always meant pain. Lawyers and investigators and psychiatrists all wanting to drag me through my private hell of memories again and again. As my mind drifted over these thoughts I tried to concentrate on what Dr. Morgan was saying, but I found it almost impossible. My mind reeled in chaos. There was a roaring sound in my ears and my heart was pounding. I kept seeing Jeannie's face whenever I closed my eyes.

Dr. Morgan wondered what was wrong with me. He glanced at the papers I held in my hand and asked what they were. I said they were divorce papers from my wife. He assumed the divorce papers to be the source of my distress. How could he have known? How could he have possibly guessed what was raging through my mind at that moment? Dr. Morgan asked me if I intended to contest it. I said no. He then inquired about my daughter, Allison. I thought of her smiling face. I saw Jeannie's smiling face. I felt completely numb. I stood up, asked them to excuse me, and walked out of the room.

It was time.

As I crossed the outer waiting room and entered the rest room, I noticed a guard sitting there waiting to return me to my cell. I locked the bathroom door behind me. I went to the mirror, raised my hands over my head, and brought them down as hard as I could, striking the glass with the edge of the handcuffs. It made a loud bang but refused to break. I tried again, but still no success. I realized that after fasting for so long I had little strength left. I reached up and forced my fingers behind the top edge of the mirror, then pulled out and down, letting my weight do most of the work. It came off easily. I turned the mirror over and slammed it against the edge of the toilet, shattering it into dozens of pieces. I sat down on the floor.

At that moment someone managed to spray tear gas under the door. It caught me right in the eyes, stinging terribly. I could barely see. Between the cuffs and my burning eyes, I had to struggle to pull up my sleeves and expose my forearms. I blindly reached out and picked up a piece of glass and began to cut across the skin. I could feel it cutting deeply. The noise outside was getting louder. They were working on the door with some kind of tool. They would have to force the door open. I needed at least a few minutes. I had to find an artery quickly.

I whispered Jeannie's name each time I cut, to give me strength. I was afraid to die but was prepared. It was the only way I could bring her home to her family now. If we cannot be here together, then I will go there so that she may return.

Yet now I must wait a little while longer to accomplish this. They did not allow me to escape this earthly hell so easily. Within a matter of minutes after I locked myself in the rest room, they got the door off and dragged me out. At that moment I hated everyone in that room more than I have ever hated anything in my entire life. I wanted to tear them apart with my bare teeth and hands. How dare they try to stop me from saving Jeannie?

But with determination and patience I shall eventually find the means to outwit them.

*　　*　　*

(4/22/91) *They carried me down to the infirmary, where the doctor stopped the bleeding and stitched my arms up. Then I was wheeled down to an observation cell. My clothes were taken and I was given a plastic hospital gown to wear. I was placed on a wide metal table with a suicide blanket lying on it. My hands and feet were bound tightly to the four corners. A bright overhead light burned into my unblinking eyes. Several people came and tried to talk to me, but they were a million miles away. I could barely hear or see them.*

After a couple of hours tied to the metal table, I was released and placed in belly chains. About an hour later they removed these also. I tried to rest lying on the metal surface but it was impossible so I sat up and leaned against the wall. The overhead light remained on through the night. But still, darkness seemed everywhere. Occasionally a nurse came in and took my temperature and blood pressure. She would then urge me to get some sleep. I was sure it had to be a cruel joke on her part. I was once again under twenty-four-hour watch. Every fifteen minutes the guard would scribble down in his log whatever I happened to be doing at that time, which was invariably staring at the wall.

(4/23/91) *I was returned to my cell. It had been completely stripped. All my personal things were gone. Even my pillow, blanket, and mattress had been removed. I was left with only a metal surface on which to sleep and a suicide blanket. As the guards who brought me to my cell turned to leave, one of them said, "If you try to kill yourself again, man, call me first. I got to see this shit!"*

It was cold last night. The metal bed was impossible to sleep on. It was difficult to keep warm in the thin hospital gown, and the inflexible suicide blanket made an almost useless cover. Once again I spent most of the night sitting up staring at the wall. I watched the roaches swarm out under cover of darkness and scurry around the cell. I tried to keep my mind blank but thoughts of Jeannie slipped ever quietly to the surface. Her beautiful smiling face seemed to shimmer in the air before me. I reached out, but then she was gone.

(5/17/91) Wherever I turn, I see her face. Whenever I listen, I hear her voice. Not fate, not death, not stone-carved destiny, shall prevail against me in my search. I shall find my love, my sweet Jean McCrea.

> *How is good o'er come by evil?*
> *By what monstrous upheaval*
> *Has my mind been torn away*
> *These hands another to obey.*
> *God, I beg you come reclaim me.*
> *Do not allow man to defame me.*
> *Hold outstretched your gentle hand.*
> *Help me flee this mortal land.*
> *Take me to the one I love.*
> *Let us embrace the world above*
> *And wander there one endless day.*
> *My love and I, my Jean McCrea.*

(7/1/91) It's an absolutely brilliant Saturday morning outside, a wonderful day for the beach. If Jeannie's not there already, I'm sure she'll be headed that way over the Fourth of July weekend. She is there and I am here. I wonder if she's thinking of me now. I wonder if she's remembering what we had and dreaming of what we might have had. I wonder if she still cares.

I've been trying to get up the courage to call her. But I'm afraid. I'm sure she's read about everything in the papers by now. What does she think of me? Is everything we had gone? I couldn't survive it. I must find out. Should I call, or write first?

(7/10/91) I wonder if Jeannie's back from the beach now? Should I try to call? But what if her mom or dad answers? I don't think they would be very happy to find out she'd been with me instead of with friends over the holidays. She would surely catch it if they ever found out.

(8/16/91) Jeannie should have received my letter by now. She must have read it. What is she thinking? Is she remembering? I remember one night when she taught me how to play solitaire. We had MTV on while we played. Jeannie was sipping on her peach wine coolers and snacking on Pringles potato chips, in the silver can. It had to be the Pringles in the silver can! No other kind would do for her. I ordered a Domino's Pizza, a pepperoni one. No other kind will do for me. We ended up getting into a pepperoni-throwing food fight. What a mess we made.

The times we had, Jeannie. As you read my letter, remember these times. I remember them. Please, Jeannie, give me just one chance. I must see you. I must speak to you.

(8/18/91) I was hoping to get a letter from Jeannie today but none came. I tried to call again—no answer. I'm still unsure as to whether or not I'm dialing the right number.

(8/19/91) She must have read my letter by now. I should receive one from her by Monday at the latest, that is, if she doesn't hate me now.

(8/21/91) No letter yet.

(8/24/91) No letter.

(8/25/91) She must have it by now. I tried to call again. A girl answered but I could tell from the sound of her voice that it wasn't Jeannie.

(9/4/91) It's been almost three weeks since my letter was mailed. Why hasn't she written me back? Was my letter lost? Was her letter lost? Did her parents open my letter and then not give it to her? I put a false name and return address on the envelope.

(9/13/91) No letter today. I wonder if Jeannie saw the news or read about me in the newspapers. The court date has been set for this Friday. Jeannie must have refused to testify. Maybe she still cares for me in spite of what she's found out from the papers.

Jeannie, please don't hate me because of what you read in the papers. You know the real me. You know who I am. You know what we had together and what we felt for each other. Don't let it die.

I've been thinking about it for a long time now, and I think I've finally figured out why Jeannie hasn't written me and why everyone keeps saying bad things about her. I think she probably got into another fight with her stepfather and just ran away again. She was having problems with him before.

How am I going to reach her? How will I find her while I'm trapped in this hell? Maybe she'll come back home by Thanksgiving. Maybe I can call her then. Please come home, Jeannie. I must see you. You have to let me explain everything.

(12/7/91) HE'S right. I am a fool. A pathetic, self-deluded fool. Jeannie's not at the beach. Jeannie's not with friends. Jeannie's not coming home for Thanksgiving. Jeannie's gone and I'm alone, alone in hell with HIM. On Monday, I got back the first part of my journal. Mom had been keeping it for me. Last night I finally forced myself to read it. It said Jeannie's gone.

For many years now, in fact my entire life as far back as I can remember, I have lied to myself, hid from myself, from truth, from what I am. And I have become very, very good at it over time. Finally it became a part of me. I can no more stop it than I could stop my heart from beating. During my drive towards California that fateful night, I convinced myself that I had defeated HIM forever and that HE was gone. But I knew deep down inside that I had only defeated HIM for the moment.

And then I convinced myself that Jeannie was still here, that she was just a phone call or letter away. But she's not. It frightens me. What else am I firmly convinced of today that tomorrow I shall find out is just another self-deluding lie?

Goodnight, my sweet Jeannie. My heart and my soul are with you, wherever you are. And they always will be.

Jeannie Starrett and Daniel Starrett.

Jean Taylor Starrett

Jeannie T. Starrett

Jeannie Starrett

RDS & JTS

(12/21/91) Today was the day three years ago when HE found Jeannie. And then Jeannie and I found each other. Was it fate? Was it our destiny? I feel as though I were being turned inside out. I feel HIM moving deep within me. I can feel it right now. I love you, Jeannie. I hate YOU. She was mine, she was never YOURS.

(12/24/91) It's Christmas Eve. Three years ago Jeannie and I were in the living room playing a board game. When I went to make another drink, I heard Jeannie call from the living room for me to bring more chips. She called me, "Hey, you!" Then she asked in a slightly exasperated voice if I was ever going to tell her my name.

I hesitated. There was no reason not to tell her, no reason to worry about HIM anymore. HIS control over me was slipping further every day. For the first time in many years I felt hopeful about the future. I saw a light at the end of a long, dark tunnel, a terrifying and lonely tunnel which I had traveled for so long. And it was Jeannie who was holding that light, guiding me to freedom.

As I walked out into the living room I could feel HIM moving. I could hear HIM screaming for me to stop. But HE was a million miles away. It was only a whisper. I ignored HIM. And then I told her my name. She said she was going to call me Richie. That gave her the giggles. But from that time on she frequently called me Danny Boy.

I'll never forget that night. I felt like someone who had just had a heavy weight removed from his shoulders.

(4/13/92) Today is Jeannie's birthday. I tried to call her, but a man answered and so I hung up. She never answers the phone. She's probably out celebrating with friends.

They showed Jeannie's picture on TV. They said I killed her. But they are wrong. They must be. Why would I wish to harm someone I loved, someone who loved me?

At one point, I thought Jeannie was gone. But I have come to realize that those were false memories that HE planted in my mind to make me believe that she was gone, to weaken me so that HE can destroy me.

Jeannie gone? That's ridiculous and outrageous. I realized that wasn't true a long time ago. I believed it but now I know that it's not true and I don't believe it anymore. Even though I wrote about it in my journal. And I talked about it with the police. I know it can't be true. Because it's preposterous that I would do anything to harm her, and it's preposterous that I would allow HIM to do anything to harm her. I have the memories, but I believe that HE's planted them in my consciousness.

It just doesn't make any sense. The right version is that Jeannie is not gone. I took her home. But I'm not stupid. They wouldn't be pressing a capital murder case against me if they didn't think somebody had died, and they must have somebody's body. I'm not stupid.

(6/6/92) I don't know why she hasn't tried to reach me. Maybe she did try to reach me. She doesn't know anything about HIM, she doesn't know anything about what HE had done before, and I'm sure she has read about all that in the newspapers. I'm sure she despises me.

Sometimes I think HE's the real person inside the body and I'm just an illusion, the mask HE shows to the outside world.

> *I took the masks off one by one*
>   *Until I came to me.*
> *But that one fell off just as well,*
>   *And there alone was HE.*
>   *RDS*

76

Bob Storms decided the only way to get the answers he needed was to hypnotize Danny Starrett. He had been trying for months to coax from Danny the details of Jeannie McCrea's death. He listened for endless hours as Danny talked about brain physiology and ethics and politics and philosophy and HIM but never once talked about Jeannie McCrea. He not only refused to admit that he had killed her—he denied that she was dead. Once or twice, Storms had ventured near the subject by asking about "the body"—the one in the creek bed where Danny led the police—but Danny would quickly correct him: "I led them to *a* body."

It wasn't Jeannie McCrea's body?

No, he would say. "Jeannie's not dead."

But how did he know there was a body in the creek bed?

And then he would shut up. No matter how Storms broached the subject, no matter how carefully he plotted his approach, no matter how positive and open the conversation up to that point, he always hit the same wall. Sometimes it was a wall of silence, sometimes a wall of frenetic, disjointed denial, sometimes a wall of evasive non sequiturs; but always a wall. Danny could be stunningly lucid on every other topic. Sitting in the interview room in his tight jeans and polo shirt, with his preppy haircut, controlled gestures, and quick smile, he looked like the picture of yuppie sanity. But mention the name Jeannie McCrea, and he would disintegrate into a fierce cloud of denial and delusion.

Storms was reminded of another patient he had evaluated recently: James Brady, a.k.a. the Perimeter Mall shooter. Brady, a part-time bill collector, had strolled into the big mall on the outskirts of Atlanta and gunned down five shoppers the day after he was released from a mental hospital. When the police arrested him, he still had his discharge papers on him. Brady's delusion, Storms discovered, was that his neighbors in California were operating a machine that monitored his thoughts twenty-four hours a day. And the only way he could break the machine's grip on his brain was to "go out and shed white blood."

Like Danny Starrett, Brady seemed normal enough: very bright, personable, articulate, conversant. That was why the hospital let him out. He *seemed* okay. But if you mentioned "the machine," he went off. From normal and pleasant to straight-out psychopathic in a matter of seconds. Danny was the same way. He was fine—as long as you didn't mention Jeannie McCrea.

Now Storms would try hypnosis to break through his defenses, to find out what really happened that night in the bathroom of the Starrett house in Martinez. Was it really an accident, as Danny claimed? Did the gun just happen to be in the bathroom drawer? Loaded? Did Jeannie really reach for it? If so, why? Or did Danny intentionally shoot her? These were questions that, after more than a year of investigation, remained unanswered because the answers lay where no subpoena could reach: inside Danny Starrett's head.

Storms knew that he was approaching the session with a bias. He just could not believe Danny Starrett was a killer. Psychotic and delusional, yes, but not homicidal. Of all the crimes he had committed—those that were known, anyway—only one had resulted in death. He hadn't even hurt the others, except psychically. He tied them up and scared them—God knows, he scared them to death and scarred them for life—but all he ever forced them to do was suck.

There was no question that he hated women. Rape, after all, whatever the specifics, is the ultimate act of rage against women. But even there, Danny was not a classic rapist. He didn't beat the women he kidnapped, he didn't whip them, he didn't mutilate them. Storms had once evaluated a man who used to put a shotgun up women's vaginas and pull the trigger. During their interview, he had asked the man why he did it. "Because I like it," he said.

That was a classic rapist.

No, whatever Mike Eubanks said about a Bundy progression, Storms was willing to stake his professional reputation on the fact that Danny Starrett was not a killer.

Then what did happen in the shower?

Storms had worked with everybody—police, prosecutors, defense lawyers, and other doctors—trying to reconstruct the events of that night and still was not convinced that anybody really knew the answer to that question. They *believed* that Jeannie was there voluntarily. She had been kidnapped, no doubt about that, but by the time she was killed, she and Danny had been to Hilton Head and Jekyll Island together. Witnesses from waiters to salesclerks had confirmed Danny's bizarre stories of playful dinners and carefree shopping sprees. Jeannie had missed multiple opportunities to run or scream or slip away. Hard though it was to believe, she *wanted* to be there.

Danny claimed he fell in love with Jeannie, but what seemed to Storms more likely was that she had developed some kind of Patti Hearst-like, Helsinki-syndrome, teenage crush on him. He was her walk on the wild side. He was good-looking, older (28), but not old, and, after he put away the gun, mysterious without being scary. He was, in the words of one of his doctors, "the hottest thing that had ever happened to her." It also appeared that Jeannie McCrea had been an unusually rebellious and adventurous fifteen-year-old with more than the usual share of adolescent problems at home, who saw Danny Starrett as the most exciting adventure of her young life.

Up to that point, everybody seemed to agree. Up to the moment when Danny and Jeannie went to take a shower in the master bedroom because the shower there was big enough for two, all the facts seemed to tell the same story. But what happened next? Did Jeannie discover the picture of Danny's wife and baby in the master bedroom, where she had never been allowed, and throw an adolescent tantrum? ("You're *married?*") Did she discover Heather's cosmetics in the master bath and accuse Danny of having another woman, despite his denials? Or did he find her eagerness, her pliancy so threatening that he had to get rid of her, whether or not he planned to kill her?

Storms considered the last of these the most likely. When suddenly his victim was beginning to have a good time, Danny didn't know what to do. He was no longer dominant. The other victims had fought and screamed and cried—exactly as they were supposed to—providing him all the resistance his fantasy demanded, acting exactly like the girls in all those pictures in all those magazines: screaming in pain and anguish and humiliation. Now, suddenly, instead of having a kidnap victim tied up screaming, he has a kid with a schoolgirl crush who, instead of begging him to stop, is demanding more from him. More and more and more.

Then she discovers he has a wife and has been lying to her. She flies into an adolescent rage. Suddenly, the whole thing explodes. The fantasy is a bust; she's too compliant. His marriage is threatened—Jeannie wants to get together again during the next school holiday, but Heather will be back by then. Jeannie is screaming. And Danny, who can't handle any kind of emotion, suddenly sees the hole he has dug for himself. He knows he has to get rid of Jeannie somehow. But she knows his name. She's seen pictures of his wife and child. And now she's screaming at him, ripping away at his fragile pretensions of romance. He's drunk. She's drunk. Maybe there's a scuffle. Jeannie is fearless by now. One of them picks up the gun . . .

The one thing Danny had told Storms about Jeannie, over and over, was that he loved her. How could he have killed her? Storms suspected that was a way of justifying killing her. ("But I did love her!") He probably did feel something for the girl, Storms thought. He might even have developed a crush of his own. After all, she was the first one who actually *liked* it. She flirted with him and flattered him and, on top of everything else, presumably liked to do what Heather refused to do. Given all the other problems in his marriage, Jeannie must have seemed like the girl of his dreams, for a while at least.

Storms had gone over every detail and every theory and had his questions ready when Danny came into the room for their session.

"Jeannie's not dead."

"Danny, you took them to her body."

"I took them to *a* body. That was not Jeannie."

"Well, who was it?"

"It was . . . I don't know who it was, but it wasn't Jeannie."

"Where is Jeannie?"

"Jeannie is stuck in the space-time continuum," Danny explained calmly, "stuck in another part of the space-time continuum. But I will get her. If I just read enough, learn enough, I will be able to manipulate time and rescue her. God manipulates time. There must be a mechanism. If I can live long enough to read and learn what God knows about time, I will be able to go back and rescue Jeannie out of the continuum where she's stuck."

Later, Storms talked to Gerry Starrett about Danny's delusional thinking. He explained how Danny's reading in science magazines and the popular press had gotten mixed up in his delusional system and produced "some pretty wild theories"—although he didn't describe them. The psychodynamic aspect of all this, of course, he told Gerry, was "just flat-out denial." Danny was telling himself, "I'm not the kind of person who can go out and do these things."

"Maybe there's a tumor," said Gerry.

"It would have been found in an MRI," Storms explained. "He's had an MRI. He's had multiple EEGs. He's had multiple neurological examinations. This is not something new here. He has had—"

"I know," she cut him off, "but what if it's one of those rare stories where they missed something?"

Storms struggled with his impatience. "Gerry, I know it would be nice to be able to pin it on something concrete, something specific that could be cut out. But we're not going to find it."

"What about the headaches?"

"Those are tension headaches," said Storms. "Contrary to what Danny says, they're not due to a cyst. They're not due to a tumor. They're not due to any kind of a growth in his head. They are tension headaches that he brings on himself. It's easy to understand why somebody who sees a girl and wants to kidnap her and rape her would feel a certain amount of tension."

"And the stuttering?" Gerry tried.

Storms folded his arms. "Anxiety, just social anxiety."

"But—"

"Gerry," Storms snapped, "what your son is doing is sitting in that cell and telling himself lies. He's telling himself that he's in control and that he's in power. But there is a part of Danny Starrett, a deeper part of him, that knows that he is not in control. There is a part of Danny Starrett, a part he's guarding fiercely, that knows he killed this girl and that he can never, ever forgive himself."

Gerry looked both chastised and frustrated. "I'm just trying to help my son," she said softly.

Then she had a new thought, a new cause for anxiety. "You're not going to tell him any of this, are you?" she asked, her eyes filling with fear. "You know, if you pull this crutch out from under him, what else are you going to give him? You're not giving him medication, you're not giving him psychoanalysis. You know, if he didn't have all these theories, if you took all this away from him and didn't put anything in its place, what would he have left?"

Storms put his hand on Gerry's shoulder. "His family."

77

(4/11/93) *I think my family really was an incredibly loving, normal, middle-American family. There was no serious dysfunction. Everyone has got some problems, of course. Nobody's perfect. My father was always worried about money. My mother and father had occasional spats. But I also remember my father giving my mother a hug, pinching her on the behind, giving her a playful smack, engaging in playful mischief with each other in front of us kids. Like I say, a normal family.*

When people talk about Ozzie and Harriet families, you think of families like ours: a good, solid, middle-American type of family that shared problems, but had more than its share of love. My mother always wanted to go to church more often, my father had more of an atheist-humanist outlook on life. My father went to play golf on Sunday.

(4/13/93) *There's a guy in here who killed his grandparents. He's an intelligent fellow. He's been institutionalized off and on, and has been diagnosed as having an "antisocial personality disorder" and he does. He has a very explosive temper. A lot of bitterness and anger. He killed his mother's mother and father, apparently in some kind of drug-induced psychosis. He just freaked out. He was living with them at the time. His parents put him in a psychiatric institution down in Florida, but he just had a very traumatic reunion with his mother about four months ago. She hadn't spoken a word to him in the ten years he has been here.*

He killed his grandparents ten years ago, when he was eighteen. His mother said she never wanted to see him again. She said she didn't love him. I just can't comprehend having my mother say that to me.

He told me about the reunion with his mother. They finally reconciled everything, and she started coming to see

*him occasionally. Apparently it was a very emotional scene.
The emotions that must have been going through his head—
I can't even comprehend. Anyhow, he says he wants to be a
nice fellow, but he has got so much anger, so much hate inside of him, he is still a very dangerous person.*

78

From the moment he met Danny's family, Bob Storms knew something
was wrong. Gerry and her two daughters, Helen and Gail, all assertive,
uninhibited women, sat forward on the very edges of their chairs, as if
only pausing briefly between life's bouts. They spoke emphatically, in-
structively, about their brother Danny. They couldn't say often enough
or emphatically enough how wonderful he was. "He should run for president," one of them insisted. The men of the family—Richard and his
son Robert—sat to the side, lean and mute, while the Starrett women
mounted a full, frontal assault on the injustice, the outrage, the incom-
prehensibility of Danny's fate.

Over time, Storms came to know each player in this ensemble better. Robert, the computer whiz: Mr. Eagle Scout; so sweet, so nice, so
much like Danny. Gail, the exceedingly competent hospital administrator. Helen, the determined ballerina turned Air Force cadet. Then there
was Sally, Robert's wife, the only woman in the family unrelated to
Danny by blood, and, perhaps for that reason, more like the Starrett
men than the Starrett women: nice, brittle, afraid to make a mistake, so
much like Danny.

Richard Starrett was a psychological black hole, Storms concluded,
"way out in the stratosphere." Something had happened to him in
childhood. Something unhealthy. He had grown up in the cowboy culture of a Mormon household in Wyoming, and Storms often wondered
what had happened in that house to produce such an angry adult. Gerry
had told him once that Richard's father ran his family with an iron

hand. His wife wasn't *permitted* to disagree with him—and never did. If she heard on the radio it was going to rain that day, but the father told her it wouldn't, she left her umbrella behind and never mentioned the radio forecast. Getting soaked was acceptable; disagreeing was not.

So why did this son of the Wild West marry an articulate, ambitious, flirtatious, steel-willed woman like Gerry Starrett, a woman who seemed, on first impression, the perfect Southern belle, all deference to her man, but in reality ran not only her family but also the family business? And why did his son, in turn, marry a woman who seemed like a "California beach-bunny cosmetologist," but as the years of motherhood wore on, yearned for a career of her own?

In an effort to find out, Storms had recommended several times, in a friendly way, that Richard see a therapist. "I want no part of that," he would say, to no one's surprise. Storms called it "the pathology of the typical American male": Never voice your feelings, never let them know you're hurting. He had seen it often enough—on both sides of the prison bars. "It's all western, Wyoming, tough-guy, massive-denial bullshit," said Storms, "and it would be funny if it weren't such a tragedy." Later, when he heard that Richard played poker with friends every week and had never once discussed Danny's problems, he wasn't surprised at all.

Storms was a firm believer that every family had its secrets. Where they differed was in how they handled those secrets.

His own father had been an alcoholic . . . in the 1950s . . . in the midwest. He was a "functional alcoholic," but an alcoholic nonetheless, and a lot of people in town knew it because he was also a prominent lawyer. The Storms family lived on a nice block where all the houses were big and all the husbands were depressed alcoholics. But nobody talked about it. It was the fifties, after all, and everyone was supposed to clamp down on the demons inside—whether inside the house or inside the head.

In the Starrett family, nobody talked about Richard's rage against women or what kind of husband it rendered him. Storms wasn't surprised to find that the Starretts' marriage was not the ideal union Danny insisted it was. Exactly when it had gone bad was open to question, but Storms suspected that it had been flawed from the start. Gerry had told Storms that for years she "tried to maintain for the kids' sake the idea that she had a real marriage."

Nobody talked about ten-year-old Danny's drawings of underground factories where women were chopped up and processed into dog food, either. If he had a kid who was making those drawings, Storms thought, he wouldn't need spinal taps and neurological exams to know something was wrong. Of course, nobody in the Starrett family talked about it. Gerry insisted that Danny was merely hyperactive, but Storms knew better. He knew that "any family that has a kid who goes manic and then retreats into his room for days on end, and they think that's normal, that's fucked up."

In fact, the closer Storms looked, the clearer it became that nothing about the Starrett family was normal. And nothing was more abnormal, more "fucked up," than the insistence, the droning insistence, that everything was normal. Every time he mentioned "family problems," Danny or Gerry would launch into a litany of warmth and unity: how much time the family spent together even after the kids were married and had lives of their own; how often they talked on the phone; how closely they were involved in one another's lives and called on each other for support in times of crisis; how even the spouses were caught up in the family spirit; and on and on. To Storms, it all seemed strangely defensive, like the behavior of an abused child, protecting the abuser from the outside world to uphold the family's honor.

"We all come from dysfunctional families in one way or another," Storms often said. "We don't even know what normal is." Yet every member of the Starrett family had conspired to maintain the fiction of normalcy. Gerry and Richard had lived emotionally estranged for much of Danny's childhood yet covered it up with pretending: pretending they had the perfect marriage, pretending they had the perfect family. Growing up with denial like that, Danny didn't need to be abused.

Was there abuse? Everyone in the family denied it vehemently—Danny especially—but Storms couldn't shake the thought. Life, of course, was rarely as neatly messy as a *Donahue* show. Just because no one could show any bruises or tearfully recall any beatings didn't mean there hadn't been abuse. Storms knew real abuse would have made everything easier. In a straight-out abuse case, a patient at least has something concrete to hang his problems on. He can say, "This definitely happened to me and it screwed up my life." He can start to transfer the blame off himself and onto his parents.

But in a case like Danny's, the parents couldn't be blamed for anything really terrible. Storms was always reminded of the line in *The Exorcist,* where the old priest wonders if evil isn't so much Satan and demons as it is just the little lies we tell each other and the small unkindnesses we do to each other every day unawares. The blame for *those* often stays put and slowly crushes the child while the parents remain forever perfect.

Storms had asked Danny once about his parents. "They're just about perfect," was the first thing he said. For Danny, everything about Danny had to be perfect. From his childhood pencils to his prison cell, from his parents' marriage to his love for Jeannie, he could not have anything out of place. The first time he came to Storms's disorderly office in the Binion Building, which was as much a reflection of Storms's mind as Danny's immaculate cell was a reflection of his, he couldn't keep still, he was so upset. (Thereafter, Storms messed it up before his every visit.) Having to live this massive lie of perfection, Storms believed—perfect son, perfect parents, perfect family—was more of a burden than any beating or molestation could ever be. So Danny ended up with all the rage and the hatred but without any of the means to express those feelings, because perfect sons didn't have those feelings.

Denial explained why the whole family, especially Gerry, was still feeding Danny's delusions. Storms had told her again and again that to continue to give support to Danny's two-consciousness theory was only to dig him deeper. The last time he had told her that, at a recent lunch, she had simply gotten up, excused herself, and left the table. Denial explained why Danny and his father, for all their hours of conversation, never talked to each other. They would patter endlessly about politics, philosophy, the Japanese trade imbalance or the existence of free will— always in the same self-important, meaning-of-life way—and never *once* mention the crisis that was consuming their family.

Denial. Denial. Denial. All roads led back to denial. Denial explained the family's bizarre reaction to the news of Danny's arrest. Storms had talked to them many times, both formally and informally, and was always astonished by how little they remembered of those first crucial days. And not just the excruciating, humiliating details. Whole months of Gerry's life, months of vivid fear and anguish, had simply disappeared: like the problems in her marriage, denied out of existence. Her entire lifetime, she had been denying whatever threatened her most. Now it was Danny's turn.

79

(5/1/93) *Bud Siemon and I talked for almost three hours. He said it was my last chance to accept the guilty plea offer. He said if I refused and went to trial, I had a good chance of getting the death penalty. He said it would destroy my family and that they would have to move away from Augusta. He said all the victims from South Carolina would have to come down and testify, and it would hurt them and their families too. He said it would ruin my chances of getting serious help from any doctors if I was on death row because they wouldn't want to get involved in the legalities.*

If I accept the plea, if I do what Bud wants, then I die. If I don't accept it, everyone else gets hurt, and I die anyway. I have no escape. So, I can't do it. I guess if someone offers you the choice of dying today and dying tomorrow, which are you going to pick? Tomorrow. If I don't accept the plea bargain and am sentenced to death, at least I have a few more years to fight or do something positive in my life.

It's a leap of faith for everyone outside of my brain, but HE is every bit as real to me as the threat of the electric chair. The threat that comes from HIM is no more of a leap of faith for me than the threat of the electric chair. They are both real phenomena, not psychological. They are not imaginary, not hallucinations.

I can understand what they're feeling. But can they understand what's going through my mind when someone you love is standing there behind you, there is a cliff right in front of you that they can't see, and they're saying, "Go ahead and step forward, step forward, step forward"? They are trying to push you off a cliff, and the fact that they love you isn't going to make that fall any less fatal.

Epilogue

80

Gerry Starrett turned her white Mercury Grand Marquis onto 25 South, set the cruise control to sixty-five, and searched the radio dial until she found her favorite easy-listening music station. She was alone in the car, although she didn't realize it until she reached 121 South, a stretch of road so deserted, so desolate, so devoid of human presence, that locals called it the Woodpecker Trail. This was, in fact, one of the first times she had been alone, really alone, in more than two years.

It was also the first time in those two years that she had allowed herself to think long and hard about death.

Once again, the story had begun with a phone call. Only it wasn't the police this time. It was a cousin in Appling County telling her that her Aunt Tarpee, her father's sweet, good-hearted, devoutly religious sister, had died. The news was hardly unexpected. Aunt Tarpee, after all, was ninety-three years old. What was unexpected was the story that came with the news. Like so many of Gerry's relatives, Aunt Tarpee had lived her entire life within a five-mile radius of her house in Appling County, growing old on the same tobacco farms where Gerry had grown up. Then one day a few months ago, just after her birthday, she decided she was ready to go. She was tired, she was ninety-three, and she just wanted to die.

So she called all of her children to come home to see her one last time. And when they had all arrived—most lived in the area—she sat them all down around her bed, looked each one in the eye, and asked them one by one, "Are you living according to God's word?"

They all knew what she meant. So did Gerry. She wanted to make sure that she would see them all in the next world.

"Yes, I am living according to God's word," each child, some in their seventies, answered in turn.

At which, Aunt Tarpee sighed with relief and said, "Now I feel all right about it." And then she died. Right there, with all her children around her, she closed her eyes and died.

Recalling the story brought tears to Gerry's eyes. That was the way she wanted to go.

Now she was on her way to Aunt Tarpee's funeral, she and hundreds of other relatives from across the Southeast, all on their way home to Appling County. Despite her grim mission, though, Gerry felt strangely buoyant, almost elated. She hadn't felt this unburdened, this *alive,* since the police called looking for Danny. It had been more than two years of agonizing uncertainty. Two years of closing her eyes at night and seeing his face. Two years of waking up in the middle of the night and thinking about him. Does he have anyone to talk to? Does he still laugh? People used to love to hear him laugh. Two years of waking up in the morning and thinking about him some more.

Until recently, those thoughts and a thousand like them would have kept her at home, even during Aunt Tarpee's funeral. Until recently, she couldn't go out to buy groceries without hesitating: What would happen if they called while she was out? Would she come back to find he'd slipped away forever? Especially since the suicide attempt, she had felt like every minute away from the lifeline of a telephone was a little abandonment, a little death.

Now she was alone, on the road to Appling County, without a phone and without fear, feeling freer than she had in her whole life.

It was hard for Gerry to believe that only a few months had passed since she and her family were locked in a death struggle with Danny over the plea bargain. Bud Siemon had worked out a deal that seemed to satisfy everyone. If the prosecution dropped its demand for the death penalty, Siemon would agree to trim his case to the bone: get rid of all the shrinks except Storms, call no witnesses, conduct no investigation, waive a jury, and let a judge decide the case. To satisfy Danny's demand that the victims not testify, the prosecution would have to drop all counts except the murder charge. That way, the state's only witnesses would be the medical examiner and the cop who had taken Danny's confession and accompanied him to the body. The whole case—plea, trial, sentencing—could be done in one day.

Prospects for the deal looked even better when Mike Eubanks announced he would run for an open judgeship. He eventually lost the election, but not before being replaced on the Starrett case by a less obdurate, more tractable prosecutor.

Siemon took the new deal to Danny. In addition to all the usual arguments—it was a no-win case, jurors wouldn't be able to understand Danny's complex psychological arguments, the prosecutors would show grisly photos and put Jeannie's mother on the stand in tears—Siemon tried a new one. "The plea means nothing," he said. "It's just a way to get out of this legal nightmare. It's got nothing to do with any reality. What happened, happened. Whatever you did, you did. Whatever you didn't do, none of that is changed by what happens in court. It's an artificial process that the state puts people through to resolve criminal indictments. Think of it like graduating from high school. You can graduate from high school and be no smarter or dumber than you were two weeks before you graduated from high school."

Danny bit his lower lip in frustration. "You don't understand," he told Siemon. "HIS reality is as real to HIM as my reality is to me, and I can't understand HIS reality, so there is really no sense in my trying to tell HIM what to do because I don't understand."

Neither did Siemon. "Given the absolutely clear demonstrable certainty of the electric chair up against the effectiveness of HIM in killing you when HE gets the chance—and HE has never succeeded before—there doesn't seem to be any doubt about which one you should choose if you want to live."

"That's because you aren't aware of the magnitude of HIS capabilities," said Danny. "Still, I think it's deeply in your mind that HE is only some nebulous thing. But HE is real."

"Be reasonable," Siemon begged.

Danny was utterly calm, surreally calm. "You know, people can accuse me of a lot of things, but they cannot accuse me of being irrational and illogical."

In desperation, Siemon turned to Gerry. At a family meeting in her immaculate living room, he laid out the case against Danny. At previous meetings like this one, he had hedged around the truth. When someone asked, "What are Danny's chances?" he would say, "Well, I can't really quantify a percentage, but eighty-twenty, ninety-ten would be ball park"—that is, a ten percent chance of getting a life sentence and a ninety percent of getting death. But this time his conclusion was unflinching: "If Danny goes to trial," he told them, "he *will* get a death sentence."

The only way out, said Siemon, the *only* way, was to convince Danny to take the deal.

Now it was the family's turn.

One by one, or sometimes in pairs, Gerry sent them to Milledgeville to talk to Danny. First the siblings, Helen, Gail, and Robert, some with spouses, some without. They urged him to be reasonable and cooperate so he could seek better medical help and maybe a chance to prove his theories. When reason didn't work, they tried love. "It should make a difference to you," they said, "that we are on your side."

The only unexpected visitor was Danny's grandmother, Arline Williams, who drove three and a half hours from Appling County to beg her grandson to choose life. At one point, she leaned against a table and lowered her slender, seventy-year-old body to one knee.

In stark contrast, Richard also came, by himself, for a man-to-man talk. He laid out all the options along with the arguments for and against each one. It was a very rational presentation and was followed by a lengthy discussion of the nature of reality. Inexplicably, Danny later described the meeting as "an extremely painful experience."

No matter who came, though, Danny told them all essentially the same thing: "If I do what you're asking me to do, I will cease to exist. HE will kill me. I know it. HE has tried to kill me before and HE would try again. You just don't understand. You would have to be inside my head and live there for a while to understand." He then repeated what had become almost a mantra: "If you have a choice of dying today or dying tomorrow, if you want to live, you are going to take tomorrow—so that's what I've done, I've taken tomorrow instead of today."

No one knew what to think. Of all the things Danny Starrett had done, nothing seemed crazier than refusing to take a plea that would save him from the virtual certainty of the electric chair. What was an additional life sentence or two in Georgia when he was already serving five life sentences in South Carolina? He would be exchanging lifetimes he would never see for the chance to live out the only one he would see. It was something for nothing. But no matter how many times it was explained to him, Danny refused to accept it.

Did he *want* to be killed? His doctors were split. Some thought he was just playing a game because he wanted to stay in the Binion Building. If he accepted the plea, he would be sent back to CCI, where he wouldn't receive the same doting attention; he would be just another troubled prisoner in a crumbling warehouse. Cynics suspected it was all an elaborate con, Danny's very rational way of convincing the people of Georgia he really was crazy and therefore shouldn't be put to death. Bob Storms wondered aloud if Danny had been "bullshitting" his doctors all along.

Everyone wondered if Danny was trying to commit suicide—again. Bud Siemon confessed to a reporter, "It wouldn't surprise me one bit at any point in time to get a call that Danny has killed himself. When somebody is as crazy as he is, I don't think you could ever rule that out." But every time Bud or Gerry or anyone else raised the subject with Danny, he heatedly denied any intent to end his life, although he conceded that death was "a very attractive thought on many dark nights." He told Siemon, "I'm not trying to kill myself, and I'm not trying to get the state of Georgia to do what I can't do myself. On the contrary. I am fiercely struggling to keep my head above water."

Why did he want to live?

"I have things I need to do," he would say mysteriously, "some very real goals that require functioning, mind and body, and therefore I can't let HIM kill me, I can't let the state kill me. I have to survive, somehow, some way." When Storms pressed him for what things he needed to do, Danny grew evasive—the same way he grew evasive at the mention of Jeannie McCrea. But from their previous conversations Storms understood that Danny's "very real goals" were to learn as much as God about "the mechanism of time" and retrieve Jeannie from the space-time continuum.

Finally, Gerry came. She was so used to thinking of every visit as possibly her last with Danny, she had a hard time convincing herself that this one really was special. She came without Richard, which was special, although she took care to coordinate their arguments in advance. Danny thought they split their visits in order to make their case twice. He didn't suspect there were deeper reasons.

She begged him to accept the plea because it was "the best thing to do, the right thing to do." She made all the same arguments everybody else had made about finding doctors who could help him.

"You don't really understand intensely enough just what kind of threat HE poses to me," said Danny.

Gerry screwed up her courage for a last assault. "I know that sometimes I've been too protective of you, Danny. Sometimes I don't tell you everything I'm thinking. But I want you to know that I am fully aware of just how enormous a force HE is in your life. I respect that and support you in that. But you should also respect us. We're your family, and we're concerned about you, and all of us think you should make a different choice than the one you're making. You should have some respect and consideration for what's going on in our heads, the same way you want respect and consideration for what's going on in yours."

Danny held his head in his hands and slowly shook it back and forth. "You don't understand, Mom," he repeated over and over. "I feel like I'm driving on a mountainside on a sunny day with all of you sitting in the car, but I'm the only one not wearing a seat belt, and a Mack truck is approaching."

Gerry looked at her son. His hair was badly cut and seemed thinner than just a few weeks before. His face was pale and bony, his cheeks sunken, his eyes tired, bloodshot, and hollow. His clothes hung mournfully on his thin limbs. In past visits, she would have dwelt on all that. Whatever she came to say that day, no matter how well rehearsed, would disappear from her head, leaving only the sight of her dying boy and the overwhelming pain in her heart.

In the past, she would have struggled through the pain, fought the tears, mouthed some brave words, and gone home to weep. But this day, for some reason, she looked at Danny's bent figure, his head propped wearily on an elbow, and saw not just Danny but the room around him, too. It was a nurse's office, filled with the paraphernalia of personality—exactly the kind of stuff that Gerry had forbidden on the immaculate countertops of The ImageMaker: little plastic figures, a model airplane, wooden flowers and plastic butterflies—magnetic ones affixed to a filing cabinet; a calendar with men in swimsuits; a yellow diamond sign, "Hugs not Drugs," with an American flag stuck in it; a crude child's drawing of a nurse pasted on the wall beneath a more elaborate poster reading: "She is America's most cherished citizen, a woman in white with God in her hands. She's a nurse."

And there was another poster showing Santa Claus, his sleigh and all the reindeer in full flight, racing through a moonlit night full of stars high above a snow-topped little town with yellow firelight in every window. The thought of Christmas—of Christmases past and Christmases future—hit Gerry harder than any physical blow. Danny would never know Christmas again. Whether or not he accepted the plea bargain, whether or not Bud Siemon won the trial, whether or not the state of Georgia put him to death, Danny would never see another Christmas. Sure, Gerry and the others could visit him and bring him gifts, but Danny would never sit around the tree again, never wrap presents at her side again, never string the house with lights again, never hug her on Christmas morning again.

Danny wasn't free to do any of those things—or anything else. For the rest of his life—what . . . 30, 40, 50 years?—he had only one option remaining: whether or not to accept this plea bargain. After that choice was made, his life would no longer be his. Every choice would be made for him, every day, for the rest of his life. It was a prison of inevitability, a prison of expectations, and it was far worse than any prison of walls.

But was her life so different? Gerry wondered. Wasn't she in a prison of her own—not a prison of walls, but a prison, like Danny's, of expectations? Richard expected this, her family expected that, friends expected something else, the public something else. Even Danny had built walls of expectations around her, walls as impregnable and confining and tormenting as anything he had endured. But whereas Danny had no control over his imprisoned life, she did. And whereas Danny couldn't leave his prison, she could leave anytime she chose.

That day, Gerry went home and, instead of crying, called a lawyer. She wanted a divorce.

She had been trying for a decade or more to get Richard to "let go, just let go" of whatever it was that was tying him up inside. But he never would. For some reason, he never could escape his own prison, and so Gerry had spent years in lockup with him. Now that she had decided to set herself free, she felt only sadness for Richard, who, like Danny, would never know freedom.

When she told Richard, he immediately assumed it was all about Danny. "Because of what has happened to Danny," she fired back, *"life* has become more important to me. But this is about me, not about Danny."

"This won't save him," Richard said bitterly.

"If I can't save him," said Gerry, "at least I can save myself."

The next time she visited Danny, she came alone. She sat down across from him, steeled herself against the heartbreaking sight of him, and began her pitch. "If you don't want to do it for yourself, do it for us, do it for the family. The family is falling apart. If you go to trial and get a death sentence, we couldn't endure it. *I* couldn't endure it."

Danny didn't take the hint. Instead, he launched into his usual defense. "I'm trapped, Mom. If I do what you and Dad and Bud are asking me to do, I will cease to exist—"

She held up her hand to stop him in midsentence.

And then she told him.

For the first time in Gerry's memory, Danny was speechless. When he finally spoke, it was to ask in a plaintive voice the obvious and most painful question: "Is it because of me that this happened?"

"If it is, son," said Gerry, "I'm grateful to you." Then she told him a story that had been on her mind for some time, but she had always been afraid to tell him. She had been giving an interview when a reporter asked, "How has all of this affected you personally? How has it changed your life?" Gerry responded instantly, without thinking what she was saying, "It's made me free."

The reporter looked at her with a deeply puzzled expression. "What do you mean by that?"

Gerry thought for a moment. "I really don't know what I mean," she said.

Well, now she knew. Now, finally, after her last visit with Danny, she understood what she had meant that day. "I have done everything right," she explained. "I have worked forty hours a day, making sure that everything about this family was perfect, and all of a sudden, none of it makes any difference. And so all that effort, I now realize, just doesn't matter. And, in a way, understanding that has set me free."

The next day, Danny informed Bud Siemon that he would take the plea.

In the Richmond County Courthouse in Augusta, with all his family filling the front rows of the courtroom, Danny Starrett was tried for murder before a judge—in one day. Gerry sat perfectly still in a blue print dress, while in the seat beside her, Richard squirmed in anger and torment. Bud Siemon had planned the whole event to avoid any blowup by Danny that might shatter this fragile arrangement of justice. The prosecutor did his part by never mentioning Jeannie McCrea's name, although he angered the Starretts by never once looking in their direction. "Our family has knelt down and prayed for God to give help to the victims and their families," Richard complained afterwards. "Why can't they do the same for us?"

When it was over, the judge sentenced Richard Daniel Starrett to five life sentences, to run consecutively. With the sentences in South Carolina, that made ten lives all together.

After that day, Gerry never worried about Danny again—at least not in the same way. She still had waking nightmares about what might happen if he ran into "some male three times his size who was raised on the streets and didn't share Danny's concept of reasoned discourse." But at least the real nightmares were gone, the ones that had come in the middle of the night to roil her sleep, the ones in which a child wandered into the path of an onrushing car or teetered on the edge of a great cliff while she watched helplessly from a distance, unable to run to save him or call out a warning.

By the time Gerry arrived in Appling County, the Big Creek Primitive Baptist Church was already filled with more than seven hundred relatives. Gerry stood in the bursting chapel, surrounded by family, and realized that every single person there knew about Danny. The family grapevine had carried every ugly nuance to the far corners of the country.

Only a few months before, the fact that her "secret" permeated the room would have mortified Gerry. The indignity and embarrassment of it would have driven her silently out the door during the last prayer, so she could slip into her white Marquis and be gone before the weight of their collective disapproval crushed her. That is, if she had bothered to come at all. But she was free of that now.

This was a different Gerry Starrett. She prayed the old prayers and listened to the Bible readings just as she used to in her parents' house around the dinner table. But she knew that there was no place in these people's religion for her. Theirs was a religion of punishment, not compassion, after all, and getting divorced was something good folks didn't do.

But she was free of that now.

After the service, she was prepared for the knowing, damning glances and, even worse, the hypocritical smiles and sanctimony. But she wasn't prepared for the indifference. Out of more than seven hundred relatives, all of whom knew of her family's agony, all of whom had known and some of whom had loved Danny, how many came up to her and asked about him? How many offered their condolences or even the consolation of simple questions like "How are you doing?" or "How is Danny?" Only one. Not even the relatives who had promised to come to the final hearing and never showed up.

But she was free of that now.

First, she had wondered if living a socially appropriate life made any difference, then if organized religion made any difference. Now she wondered how much extended family really meant in the end. Danny wasn't the only one who surrounded himself with spheres of delusion.

In the weeks since the hearing, she had gone to each of her children—there was no doubt in her mind how much *they* meant—and asked if there was anything about their childhoods, anything about their family, anything at all, that they wanted to know. There would be no more secrets.

She was free of that now.

On the way home in the car, she could find only country music stations on the radio. The bittersweet twang reminded her of the only country lyrics she had ever committed to memory:

You got to sing like you don't need the money
Love like you'll never get hurt
You got to dance like nobody's watchin'
It's gotta come from the heart if you want it to work.